CITY COLLEGE NORWICH

LIBRARY SERVICES

D0994605

WITHDRAWN
FROM
STOCK

188 201

Impact maths 3 G

NORWICH CITY COLLEGE LIBRARY

Stock No   188201

Class   510

Cat   Proc.   3WL

About this book

Impact maths provides a complete course to help you achieve your best in your Key Stage 3 Mathematics course. This book will help you understand and remember mathematical ideas, solve mathematical problems with and without the help of a calculator and develop your mental maths skills.

Exercises you should try without the help of a calculator are marked with this symbol:

Finding your way around

To help you find your way around when you are studying use the:

- **edge marks** shown on the front pages – these help you get to the right unit quickly

- **contents list** and **index** – these list all the key ideas covered in the book and help you turn straight to them.

- **links** in the margin – these show when an idea elsewhere in the book may be useful:

There is more about division on page 61.

Remembering key ideas

We have provided clear explanations of the key ideas you need throughout the book with **worked examples** showing you how to answer questions. **Key points** you need to remember look like this:

- **The distance around the edge of a shape is its perimeter.**

and are listed in a **summary** at the end of each unit.

Investigations and information technology

Two units focus on particular skills you need for your course:

- **Using and applying mathematics** (unit 17) – shows you some ways of investigating mathematical problems.

- **Calculators and computers** (unit 18) – shows you some ways of using calculators and computers and will help with mental maths practice.

10
11
12
13
14
15
16
17
18

Heinemann Educational Publishers
Halley Court, Jordan Hill, Oxford, OX2 8EJ
a division of Reed Educational & Professional Publishing Ltd
Heinemann is a registered trademark of Reed Educational & Professional Publishing Ltd

OXFORD MELBOURNE AUCKLAND
JOHANNESBURG BLANTYRE GABORONE
IBADAN PORTSMOUTH NH (USA) CHICAGO

© Heinemann Educational Publishers

Copyright notice
All rights reserved. No part of this publication may be reproduced, stored in a retrieval system, or transmitted in any form or by any means, electronic, mechanical, photocopying, recording, or otherwise without either the prior written permission of the Publishers or a licence permitting restricted copying in the United Kingdom issued by the Copyright Licensing Agency Ltd, 90 Tottenham Court Road, London W1P 0LP.

First published 2001

ISBN 0 435 01831 0

05 04 03 02 01
10 9 8 7 6 5 4 3 2 1

Designed and typeset by Tech-Set Ltd, Gateshead, Tyne and Wear
Illustrated by Barry Atkinson, Barking Dog and Tech-Set
Picture research by Jennifer Johnson
Cover design by Miller, Craig and Cocking
Printed and bound by Edelvives, Spain

Acknowledgements

The authors and publishers would like to thank the following for permission to use photographs:

P1: Robert Harding/K. Gillham; P3: Robert Harding/Gina Corrigan; P15: Bruce Coleman Collection/Kim Taylor; P43: Aviation Images; P78: Empics/Matthew Ashton; P90: EPL/Richard Smith; P113: Tate Picture Library; P129: NASA; P130: photodisc; P183: Bruce Coleman Collection/Hans Reinhard; P238: Corbis; P246: Bruce Coleman Collection/Pacific Stock; P247: Ford; P288 (left): Robert Harding Picture Library/David Poole; P288 (right): Robert Harding Picture Library/Robert Francis; P304: photodisc.

Cover Photo by Tony Stone Images.

Publishing team

Editorial	Design	Author team	
Sue Bennett	Phil Richards	David Benjamin	Gina Marquess
Susanna Geoghegan	Colette Jacquelin	Sue Bright	Christine Medlow
Maggie Rumble	Mags Robertson	Tony Clough	Graham Newman
Harry Smith		Gareth Cole	Sheila Nolan
Nick Sample	**Production**	Diana DeBrida	Keith Pledger
Gwen Allingham	David Lawrence	Ray Fraser	Ian Roper
Des Brady	Jason Wyatt	Peter Jolly	Mike Smith
Sue Glover		David Kent	John Sylvester
Margaret Shepherd			
Ian Crane			

Tel:01865 888058 email:info.he@heinemann.co.uk

3G Contents

11 Decimals

12 Percentages

13 Probability

17 Using and applying mathematics

18 Calculators and computers

1 Number

1.1 Place value

You can write any number using the digits 0, 1, 2, 3, 4, 5, 6, 7, 8, 9.
The value of each digit depends on its place in the number.

725 886 200 people speak Mandarin Chinese

■ **A place value diagram can help you read large numbers.**

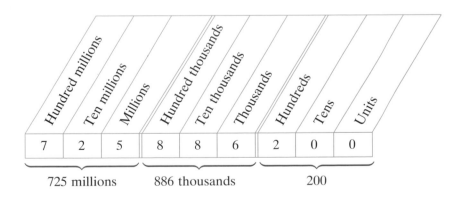

You say:
Seven hundred and twenty five million, eight hundred and eighty six thousand, two hundred.

Example 1

What do the digits 2, 3, 4 and 5 stand for in 540 932 869?

Think of the number 540 932 869 in terms of a place value diagram:

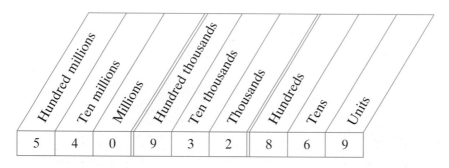

2 means 2 thousands = 2000
3 means 3 ten thousands = 30 000
4 means 4 ten millions = 40 000 000
5 means 5 hundred millions = 500 000 000

Example 2

How many millions are there in 836 448 925?

There are 836 millions in 836 448 925.

Hint: The gaps in the number show where the millions and thousands are:

836 448 925

|
| thousands
millions

Exercise 1A

1   What does the 8 stand for in each number?
   (a) 85 634 952   (b) 802 341 554   (c) 8 903 612
   (d) 48 563 795   (e) 285 032 041   (f) 764 843 529
   (g) 57 548 322   (h) 458 231 456   (i) 386 397 675

2   How many millions are there in each number?
   (a) 365 773 498   (b) 3 722 483   (c) 87 098 354
   (d) 201 574 909   (e) 40 693 276   (f) 780 408 993
   (g) 5 093 774   (h) 834 003 473   (i) 45 830 920

3 Write these numbers using digits:

   (a) Twenty eight million, five hundred and sixty two thousand, one hundred and twelve.

   (b) Seven hundred and fifty two million, nine hundred and thirty three thousand, five hundred and two.

   (c) Six million, sixty four thousand, eight hundred and ten.

   (d) Thirteen million, seven thousand and fourteen.

4 These pupils have been finding out about different countries.

My country has a population of five million, one hundred and eighty eight thousand.

Mine has twenty eight million, five hundred and thirteen thousand people.

There are one hundred and forty nine million, eight hundred and ninety nine thousand people in the country I've chosen.

The country I've chosen has more than two hundred million people living in it.

Auija   Sian   Kylie   Ghaniyy

   (a) Match each pupil to a country in the table.

   (b) Which country is left?
   Write its population in words.

   (c) Bangladesh has a population of one hundred and seventeen million, three hundred and seventy two thousand. Write this number in figures.

Country	Population
Algeria	28 513 000
Russia	149 899 000
Denmark	5 188 000
USA	262 693 000
Italy	57 333 000

1.2 Ordering numbers less than a thousand

Ian has been studying the heights of some of the world's tallest buildings.

Building	Height in metres
Empire State Building	381
Oriental Pearl TV Tower	468
Amoco Building	346
Moscow TV tower	528
Bren Tower	465

He wants to put them in order of size, starting with the smallest.

First he sorts them using the **hundreds** digits:

381	468	346	528	465
381	346	468	465	528

381 and 346 each have 3 hundreds.
He sorts them using the **tens** digits:

381	346	468	465	528
346	381	468	465	528

468 and 465 each have 4 hundreds and 6 tens.
He sorts them using the **units** digits:

346	381	468	465	528

The order is 346, 381, 465, 468, 528.

346	381	465	468	528

■ **To order numbers less than a thousand:**
- **sort them by the hundreds digits**
- **then sort them by the tens digits**
- **then sort them by the units digits.**

Exercise 1B

1   Put each set of numbers in order of size, starting with the smallest.

(a) 422, 267, 413, 278, 211

(b) 765, 317, 306, 747, 738

(c) 294, 827, 258, 847, 831

(d) 598, 549, 374, 596, 346

(e) 368, 737, 579, 572, 728

(f) 659, 596, 592, 687, 654

2   This table shows the height in feet of some of the world's highest dams.
Write them in order of size, smallest first.

Dam	Height in feet
Inguri	892
Mica	794
Nurek	984
Chivor	778
Chicoasen	869

3   The road signs show the distances in miles of different cities from Penzance.

| Edinburgh 564 | Newcastle 484 | Glasgow 562 | York 409 | Hull 415 |

Write the cities in order of distance from Penzance, smallest first.

1.3 Ordering numbers bigger than a thousand

Graham is researching some of the world's largest deserts.
He wants to arrange them in order of size starting with the
smallest.

First he puts them into two groups, those with thousands
only and those with millions.

Thousands only   **Millions**

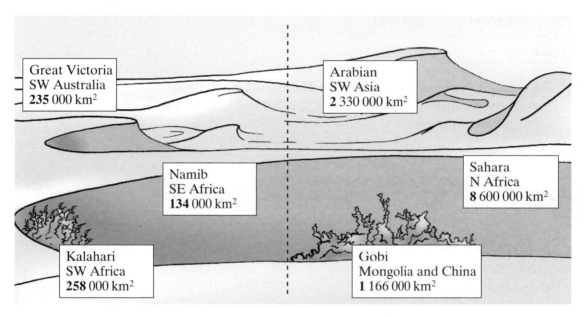

Great Victoria
SW Australia
235 000 km^2

Arabian
SW Asia
2 330 000 km^2

Namib
SE Africa
134 000 km^2

Sahara
N Africa
8 600 000 km^2

Kalahari
SW Africa
258 000 km^2

Gobi
Mongolia and China
1 166 000 km^2

He puts the **Thousands only** group in order by looking at
the number of thousands: 134, 235, 258.

Namib SE Africa **134** 000 km^2	Great Victoria SW Australia **235** 000 km^2	Kalahari SW Africa **258** 000 km^2

Then he puts the **Millions** group in order by looking at the
number of millions: 1, 2, 8.

Gobi Mongolia and China **1** 166 000 km^2	Arabian SW Asia **2** 330 000 km^2	Sahara N Africa **8** 600 000 km^2

Now he can he write his information in a table, in order of size.

Desert	Area in km^2
Sahara	8 600 000
Arabian	2 330 000
Gobi	1 166 000
Kalahari	258 000
Great Victoria	235 000
Namib	134 000

■ **To order numbers larger than a thousand, sort them into a thousands only group and a millions group. Put each group in order.**

Exercise 1C

1 Write the populations of these European cities in a table in order of size.

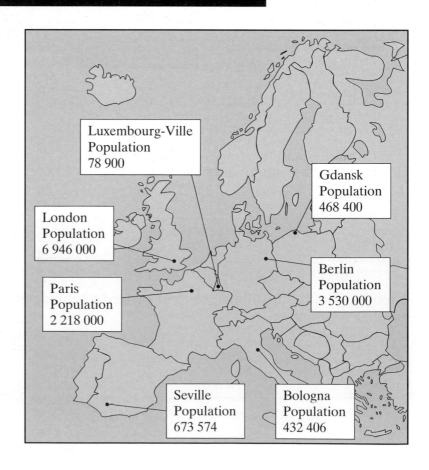

Luxembourg-Ville
Population
78 900

Gdansk
Population
468 400

London
Population
6 946 000

Berlin
Population
3 530 000

Paris
Population
2 218 000

Seville
Population
673 574

Bologna
Population
432 406

2 Write the areas of these countries in a table in order of size, with the smallest at the top.

Canada
9 971 500 km²

Brazil
8 511 965 km²

Japan
381 945 km²

Pakistan
803 943 km²

India
3 166 829 km²

Nigeria
923 768 km²

3 This table shows the circulation of daily newspapers in 1994.
Write the information in the table in order of size.
Put the newspaper with the largest circulation at the top.

The circulation of a newspaper is the number of copies sold in one day.

Newspaper	Circulation
Daily Express	1 545 389
Daily Mail	1 746 894
Daily Mirror	2 735 309
The Daily Telegraph	1 035 487
The Guardian	405 124
Independent	328 863
The Sun	3 645 834

4 This table shows the number of people who speak English in different countries.
Write the information in order of size.
Put the country with the largest number of English speakers at the top.

Country	English speakers
Australia	17 073 000
Canada	26 620 000
Tonga	96 300
United Kingdom	57 384 000
Fiji	740 000
United States	251 394 000
St Lucia	151 000

1.4 Adding and subtracting multiples of 10, 100, 1000

The multiples of 10 are 10, 20, 30, ...
They are the answers in the 10 times multiplication table.

Example 3

Work out $40 + 30$

Think of $4 + 3 = 7$

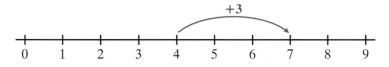

Now make all the numbers ten times bigger:

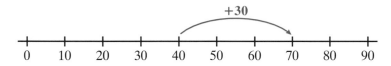

So $40 + 30 = 70$

To find $400 + 300$ just make the numbers 100 times bigger:

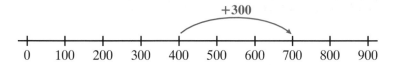

So $400 + 300 = 700$

In the same way $4000 + 3000 = 7000$

You need to take care when adding or subtracting a mixture of multiples.

Example 4

Work out $400 + 30$

Think of $40 + 3 = 43$

400 is a multiple of 100.
30 is a multiple of 10.

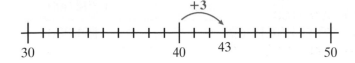

Now make all the numbers 10 times bigger

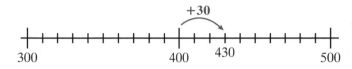

So $400 + 30 = 430$.

Example 5

Calculate:

(a) $800 - 300$
(b) $13\,000 - 7000$
(c) $8000 - 300$

(a) $8 - 3 = 5$
so $800 - 300 = 500$
(b) $13 - 7 = 6$
so $13\,000 - 7000 = 6000$
(c) $80 - 3 = 77$
so $8000 - 300 = 7700$

Exercise 1D

1 Calculate:

(a) $20 + 60$ **(b)** $50 + 40$
(c) $300 + 500$ **(d)** $700 + 200$
(e) $3000 + 5000$ **(f)** $40 + 30 + 20$
(g) $200 + 300 + 200$ **(h)** $60 + 50$

2 Work out:

(a) $90 - 30$ **(b)** $8000 - 5000$
(c) $700 - 300$ **(d)** $60 + 30 - 40$
(e) $800 - 300 - 200$ **(f)** $300 + 500 - 400$
(g) $30 + 20 + 20 + 10$ **(h)** $50 + 40 - 70$

3 Calculate:

(a) $300 + 20$ **(b)** $300 - 20$
(c) $600 - 40$ **(d)** $500 + 60$
(e) $4000 + 600$ **(f)** $7000 - 300$
(g) $5000 + 400 - 60$ **(h)** $200 + 700 - 30$

4 You need four squares of paper with numbers and letters written on them, like this.
Use Activity Sheet 1 or copy these:

90 40	30 20	30 20	40 30
A	**B**	**C**	**D**
40 30	60 80	10 50	60 70

30 20	30 20
B	**C**
60 **80**	**10** 50
90 **40**	**40** 30
A	**D**
40 30	60 70

BC
AD gives

$80 + 10 + 40 + 40$
$= 170$

Arrange your squares to make a larger square so that the total of the four middle numbers is:

(a) 100   **(b)** 150   **(c)** 200   **(d)** 250

(e) Can you make any other totals with the four squares?

5 Find a route through the maze that gives a total of:

(a) 100   **(b)** 150   **(c)** 200

Start →

+100	+200	−70	−30
+300	−90	+40	−50
−20	−60	−80	−70

→ Finish

1.5 Rounding numbers

Rounding to the nearest 10

Sarah, Kim and Rajesh are selling tickets for their school disco.

I've sold about 20 tickets

I've sold about 30 tickets

I've sold about 30 tickets

Sarah

Kim

Rajesh

Altogether they have sold about $20 + 30 + 30 = 80$ tickets.
They each rounded their number to the nearest 10.

■ **To round to the nearest 10 look at the digit in the units column:**
- **If it is less than 5 round down.**
- **If it is 5 or more round up.**

"Approximate to the nearest 10" and "Write correct to the nearest 10" both mean the same as "round to the nearest 10".

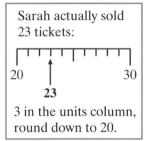

Sarah actually sold 23 tickets:

3 in the units column, round down to 20.

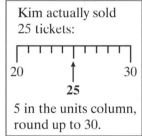

Kim actually sold 25 tickets:

5 in the units column, round up to 30.

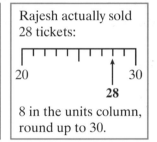

Rajesh actually sold 28 tickets:

8 in the units column, round up to 30.

You can use rounding to find approximate answers.

Example 6

Round each number to the nearest 10,
then add to get an approximate answer for

$68 + 53$

68 rounds to 70
53 rounds to 50
so $68 + 53$ is about $70 + 50 = 120$

Example 7

Anya sold 30 tickets for the school disco, rounded to the nearest 10.
How many tickets could Anya have actually sold?

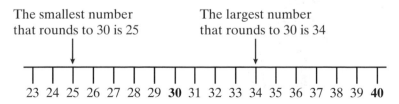

The smallest number that rounds to 30 is 25

The largest number that rounds to 30 is 34

So Anya could have sold from 25 to 34 tickets.

Exercise 1E

1 Round these numbers to the nearest 10:
(a) 39 **(b)** 82 **(c)** 48 **(d)** 75
(e) 64 **(f)** 91 **(g)** 86 **(h)** 31
(i) 35 **(j)** 47 **(k)** 17 **(l)** 97

2 Approximate these numbers to the nearest 10:
(a) 428 **(b)** 582 **(c)** 793 **(d)** 895
(e) 346 **(f)** 599 **(g)** 801 **(h)** 476
(i) 347 **(j)** 864 **(k)** 608 **(l)** 735

3 Write these numbers correct to the nearest 10:
(a) 3476 **(b)** 4723 **(c)** 8463
(d) 3737 **(e)** 45 938 **(f)** 47 239
(g) 245 893 **(h)** 3435 **(i)** 24 245
(j) 34 996 **(k)** 42 995 **(l)** 39 998

4 Round each number to the nearest 10, then add or
subtract to get an approximate answer.
(a) $34 + 48$ **(b)** $57 + 38$ **(c)** $79 + 54$
(d) $64 - 38$ **(e)** $87 - 34$ **(f)** $94 - 35$
(g) $83 + 59$ **(h)** $163 - 24$ **(i)** $147 - 86$
(j) $46 + 32 - 56$ **(k)** $85 - 46 + 28$ **(l)** $278 - 37 - 25$

5 Sarah, Kim and Rajesh sell some more tickets.
They each round the number of tickets they sell to the
nearest ten.
How many tickets could each have actually sold?

6 This table shows the height in feet of different types of tree.

Each number has been rounded to the nearest 10.

(a) What height could each tree actually be?

(b) An alder tree grows to a height of 65 feet. How would you write this in the table?

(c) A birch tree grows to a height of 33 feet. How would you write this in the table?

Tree	Height in feet
Ash	60
Elm	90
Oak	80
Pine	120

Rounding to the nearest 100 and 1000

Daniel, Jodie and Liam have been delivering leaflets for charity.

Altogether they have delivered about

$400 + 400 + 500 = 1300$ leaflets

They each rounded the number of leaflets they delivered to the nearest 100.

■ **To round to the nearest 100 look at the digit in the tens column:**

- **If it is less than 5 round down.**
- **If it is 5 or more round up.**

"Approximate to the nearest 100" and "Write correct to the nearest 100" both mean the same as "round to the nearest 100".

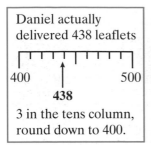

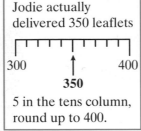

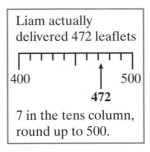

Daniel actually delivered 438 leaflets	Jodie actually delivered 350 leaflets	Liam actually delivered 472 leaflets
400 ↑ 500 **438**	300 ↑ 400 **350**	400 ↑ 500 **472**
3 in the tens column, round down to 400.	5 in the tens column, round up to 400.	7 in the tens column, round up to 500.

You can also round to the nearest thousand.

■ **To round to the nearest 1000 look at the digit in the hundreds column:**

- **If it is less than 5 round down.**
- **If it is 5 or more round up.**

"Approximate to the nearest 1000" and "Write correct to the nearest 1000" both mean the same as "round to the nearest 1000".

Example 8

Find an approximate answer to $873 + 418 + 450$

Round each number to the nearest 100 then add.

$$
\begin{array}{rr}
873 \text{ rounds to} & 900 \\
418 \text{ rounds to} & 400 \\
450 \text{ rounds to} & +\ 500 \\
\hline
& 1800
\end{array}
$$

so $873 + 418 + 450$ is about 1800

Example 9

Find an approximate answer to $5834 + 6502 - 4398$

Round each number to the nearest 1000, then add and subtract to get an approximate answer.

$$
\begin{array}{rr}
5834 \text{ rounds to} & 6000 \\
6502 \text{ rounds to} & +\ 7000 \\
\hline
& 13\,000
\end{array}
\qquad
\begin{array}{rr}
 & 13\,000 \\
4398 \text{ rounds to} & -\ 4000 \\
\hline
& 9000
\end{array}
$$

so $5834 + 6502 - 4398$ is about 9000.

Example 10

There are 3700 different species of cockroach
in the world, rounded to the nearest 100.
How many different species could there actually be?

The smallest number that rounds to 3700 is 3650
The largest number that rounds to 3700 is 3749
So there are between 3650 and 3749 different species
of cockroach in the world.

Exercise 1F

1   Round these numbers to the nearest 100:

   (**a**) 483   (**b**) 164   (**c**) 736
   (**d**) 452   (**e**) 84   (**f**) 708
   (**g**) 2438   (**h**) 1483   (**i**) 12 514
   (**j**) 984   (**k**) 3108   (**l**) 9974

2   For each calculation:

   ●   Round each number to the nearest 100 then add or
       subtract to find an approximate answer.

   (**a**) $463 + 347$ (**b**) $353 + 284$ (**c**) $737 - 391$
   (**d**) $760 - 284$ (**e**) $647 + 583$ (**f**) $872 - 314$
   (**g**) $917 - 284$ (**h**) $502 - 83$ (**i**) $593 - 543$
   (**j**) $1718 - 473$ (**k**) $2453 - 607$ (**l**) $1863 - 382$

3   Write each number correct to the nearest 1000:

   (**a**) 3732   (**b**) 8426   (**c**) 7378
   (**d**) 6052   (**e**) 3543   (**f**) 13 842
   (**g**) 37 602   (**h**) 123 740   (**i**) 9744
   (**j**) 832   (**k**) 475   (**l**) 99 612

4   For each calculation:

   ●   Round each number to the nearest 1000 then add or
       subtract to find an approximate answer.

   (**a**) $9256 - 4624$ (**b**) $8941 - 2486$
   (**c**) $6514 - 2069$ (**d**) $7499 + 2503$
   (**e**) $9443 - 3276$ (**f**) $7612 - 941$
   (**g**) $3076 + 6532$ (**h**) $9847 - 3543$
   (**i**) $13 734 - 3833$ (**j**) $19 346 + 9511$
   (**k**) $27 614 - 13 278$ (**l**) $39 641 + 8304$

5 Becca, Edward and Narinder have been collecting
signatures on a petition.
They have approximated their numbers to the nearest
100.
How many signatures could they each have
collected?

I've collected about 1000 signatures

I've collected about 700 signatures

Narinder

Becca

I've collected about 900 signatures

Edward

6 The table shows the distances in miles
of some cities from Cardiff.
Write each number rounded to the
nearest 100.

City	Distance in miles
York	245
Norwich	266
Southampton	141
Hull	252

7 The table shows the air distances in
kilometres of some cities from Paris,
rounded to the nearest 1000.
For each city:

(a) Write down the least distance it could
be from Paris.
(b) Write down the greatest distance it
could be from Paris.

City	Distance in km
Beijing	5000
Honolulu	7000
Montreal	3000
Sydney	10 000

8   The table shows the heights of the five tallest mountains in the world.

Mountain	Height in feet
Everest	29 030
K2	28 250
Kangchenjunga	28 170
Lhotse	27 890
Makalu 1	27 800

For each mountain:

(a) Write the height rounded to the nearest 100 feet.

(b) Write the height rounded to the nearest 1000 feet.

1.6 Checking answers by estimation

Jared used his calculator to work out
$674 + 412 + 720$

He checked the calculation in his head by rounding each number to the nearest 100 and doing
$700 + 400 + 700 = 1800$.

He realised he had made a mistake on his calculator.

■   **You can check to see if a calculator answer is correct by rounding and adding or subtracting to get an approximate answer.**

Example 11

Which number in the cloud is the correct answer to
$482 + 347$?

1189

595   829

429

Round each number in $482 + 347$ to the nearest 100 and add.

$500 + 300 = 800$

So 829 must be the correct answer.

Exercise 1G

1 Which number in the cloud is the correct answer?

(a) 574 + 236

(b) 427 + 378

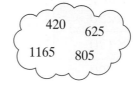

(c) 716 − 359

(d) 926 − 578

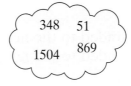

(e) 826 + 765

(f) 1356 − 481

2 Use rounding to choose which calculator shows the correct answer.

(a) 4682 + 2453

(b) 8952 − 3217

(c) 7428 + 6384

(d) 9245 − 4162

(e) 13 513 + 7612

(f) 23 613 − 7031

1.7 Mental maths with 2-digit numbers

You need to be able to add and subtract 2-digit numbers mentally.

You can do $67 + 25$ in two different ways:

```
67 + 25
  ↙   ↘
67 + 20 + 5
   ↓↓
  87 + 5
   = 92
```

```
67 + 25
  ↙   ↘
67 + 5 + 20
   ↓↓
  72 + 20
   = 92
```

You can do $87 - 38$ in three ways:

```
87 − 38
  ↙   ↘
87 − 30 − 8
   ↓↓
  57 − 8
   = 49
```

```
87 − 38
  ↙   ↘
87 − 8 − 30
   ↓↓
  79 − 30
   = 49
```

Start at 38 and work out how much you must add to get to 87

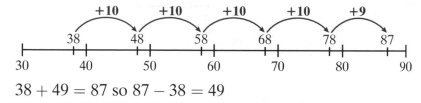

$38 + 49 = 87$ so $87 - 38 = 49$

Exercise 1H

Work out all your answers in your head. Don't write any working.

1 (a) $54 + 25$ (b) $45 + 32$ (c) $53 + 14$ (d) $45 + 23$
   (e) $47 + 28$ (f) $37 + 55$ (g) $36 + 28$ (h) $49 + 24$
   (i) $37 + 47$ (j) $38 + 38$ (k) $23 + 49$ (l) $46 + 27$

2 (a) $72 + 54$ (b) $83 + 35$ (c) $88 + 43$
    (d) $65 + 73$ (e) $94 + 64$ (f) $78 + 56$
    (g) $69 + 57$ (h) $97 + 37$ (i) $48 + 84$
    (j) $39 + 74$ (k) $89 + 96$ (l) $87 + 69$

3 (a) $57 - 14$ (b) $48 - 23$
    (c) $69 - 43$ (d) $84 - 23$
    (e) $75 - 32$ (f) $63 - 25$
    (g) $82 - 47$ (h) $64 - 29$
    (i) $76 - 28$ (j) $93 - 42$
    (k) $68 - 39$ (l) $76 - 38$

4 (a) $27 + 38 + 13$ (b) $24 + 45 + 27$
    (c) $58 + 36 - 42$ (d) $34 + 27 + 38$
    (e) $45 + 38 - 52$ (f) $85 - 23 + 35$
    (g) $98 - 34 - 23$ (h) $46 + 37 - 25$
    (i) $87 - 25 - 48$ (j) $76 - 49 + 26$

5 Ellie has £100 to spend.

  (a) She could buy the skirt, the jeans and the T-shirt.
       How much would these three cost in total?
  (b) What other sets of clothes could she afford to buy?
       How much does each set cost?

6   The table shows the scores of four pupils in three tests.

Name	History 1	History 2	History 3
Ted	37	28	56
Kathleen	46	53	78
Graham	23	85	56
Ian	35	46	74

(a) What is the total score of each pupil?
(b) What is the difference between the best score and the worst score in each test?

1.8 Adding numbers on paper

You need to be able to add larger numbers on paper.

Example 12

Work out $574 + 687 + 98$.

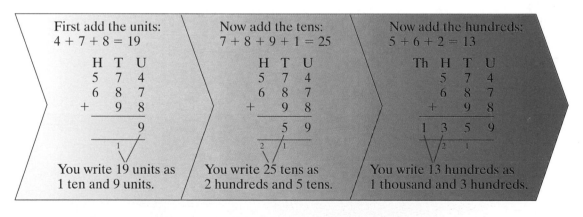

First add the units:
$4 + 7 + 8 = 19$

```
  H  T  U
  5  7  4
  6  8  7
+    9  8
_____
        9
```

You write 19 units as 1 ten and 9 units.

Now add the tens:
$7 + 8 + 9 + 1 = 25$

```
  H  T  U
  5  7  4
  6  8  7
+    9  8
_____
     5  9
```

You write 25 tens as 2 hundreds and 5 tens.

Now add the hundreds:
$5 + 6 + 2 = 13$

```
Th H  T  U
   5  7  4
   6  8  7
+     9  8
_____
 1 3  5  9
```

You write 13 hundreds as 1 thousand and 3 hundreds.

Exercise 1I

1 (a) $465 + 274$ (b) $348 + 423$
    (c) $387 + 546$ (d) $637 + 21$
    (e) $768 + 493$ (f) $629 + 784$
    (g) $527 + 284 + 87$ (h) $748 + 254 + 45$
    (i) $473 + 834 + 476$ (j) $593 + 469 + 626$
    (k) $485 + 780 + 338$ (l) $505 + 628 + 983$

2 The table shows the number of people using a Fitness Centre during a week in October.
   (a) How many people used the centre each day?
   (b) What was the total number of people using the centre on weekend afternoons?
   (c) What was the total number of people using the centre on Wednesday, Thursday and Friday evenings?

Day	Morning	Afternoon	Evening
Monday	67	103	218
Tuesday	74	147	189
Wednesday	134	85	243
Thursday	87	134	218
Friday	112	128	242
Saturday	246	268	138
Sunday	134	374	Closed

1.9 Subtracting numbers on paper

You need to be able to subtract larger numbers.

Example 13

Work out $625 - 473$.

First subtract the units: $5 - 3 = 2$	You can't subtract 7 from 2 …	… so change 1 hundred into 10 tens: $12 - 7 = 5$	Now subtract the hundreds: $5 - 4 = 1$

H T U
6 2 5
− 4 7 3
―――
    2
	H T U
	6 2 5
	− 4 7 3
	―――
	  ? 2
		H T U
		^{5}6 ^{1}2 5
		− 4 7 3
		―――
		  5 2
			H T U
			^{5}6 ^{1}2 5
			− 4 7 3
			―――
			1 5 2

You can use the same method to subtract a 2-digit number from a 3-digit number. Always remember to line up the units.

	H	T	U
	^{7}8	^{14}8	^{1}3
−		6	7
	7	8	6

Exercise 1J

1   (a) 485 − 243   (b) 674 − 312
    (c) 869 − 435   (d) 546 − 218
    (e) 874 − 436   (f) 583 − 147
    (g) 836 − 462   (h) 748 − 382
    (i) 562 − 271   (j) 845 − 376
    (k) 623 − 256   (l) 904 − 486

2   The table shows an animal dealer's records.
    It shows the price at which he bought and sold each animal.

    (a) How much profit did he make on each animal?

    (b) He bought a pair of parrots for a total of £548.
        He later sold one of them for £450 and the other for £480.
        What was his total profit on the parrots?

    (c) He bought a flamingo for £763 and a pheasant for £185.
        He later sold them together for £1500.
        What was his profit?

Animal	Bought for	Sold for
Snake	£56	£160
Iguana	£79	£185
Macaw	£380	£855
Falcon	£528	£765
Owl	£386	£764

Profit is:
selling price − buying price

Summary of key points

1   A place value diagram can help you read large numbers.

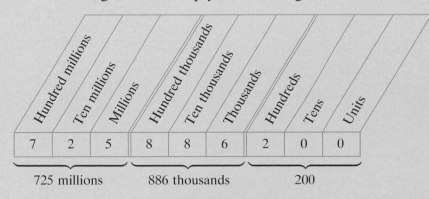

Hundred millions	Ten millions	Millions	Hundred thousands	Ten thousands	Thousands	Hundreds	Tens	Units
7	2	5	8	8	6	2	0	0

725 millions   886 thousands   200

You say:
Seven hundred and twenty five million, eight hundred and eighty six thousand, two hundred.

2 To order numbers less than a thousand:
- sort them by the hundreds digits,
- then sort them by the tens digits,
- then sort them by the units digits.

3 To order numbers larger than a thousand, sort them into a thousands only group and a millions group. Put each group in order.

4 To round to the nearest 10 look at the digit in the units column:
- If it is less than 5 round down.
- If it is 5 or more round up.

5 To round to the nearest 100 look at the digit in the tens column:
- If it is less than 5 round down.
- If it is 5 or more round up.

6 To round to the nearest 1000 look at the digit in the hundreds column:
- If it is less than 5 round down.
- If it is 5 or more round up.

7 You can check to see if a calculator answer is correct by rounding and adding or subtracting to get an approximate answer.

2 Angles

2.1 Acute and obtuse angles

Angles less than 90° are called **acute angles**.

Angles greater than 90° but less than 180° are called **obtuse angles**.

Remember: angles that are exactly 90° are called **right angles**.

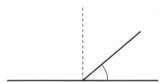

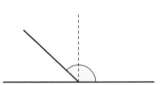

Exercise 2A

1   Without measuring, write down whether the angle is acute or obtuse:

(a)

(b)

(c)

(d)

2   Write down whether the angle is acute or obtuse:

(a) 136°   **(b)** 19°   **(c)** 89°   **(d)** 91°

3   For each angle:
   • Write down whether the angle is acute or obtuse.
   • Estimate the size of the angle.
   • Measure the angle using a protractor or angle measurer.

(a)

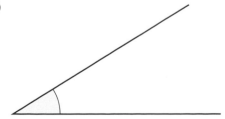

Remember: to estimate the size of an angle you can compare it to a right angle.

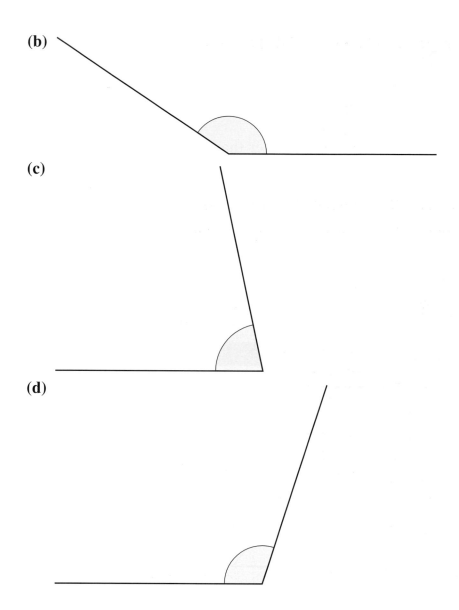

(b)

(c)

(d)

2.2 Reflex angles

Angles can be greater than 180°.

This angle is between 2 right angles (180°) and 3 right angles (270°).

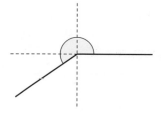

This angle is between 3 right angles (270°) and 4 right angles (360°).

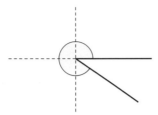

■ **An angle between 180° and 360° is called a reflex angle.**

You can measure a reflex angle easily using a circular protractor.

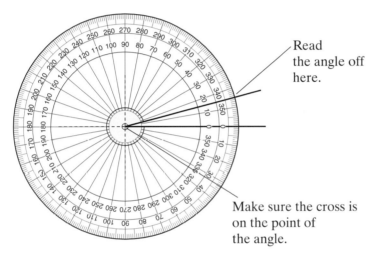

Read the angle off here.

Make sure the cross is on the point of the angle.

A semicircular protractor only goes up to 180°.
You need to:

1 Measure the angle that the reflex angle leaves from a full turn.

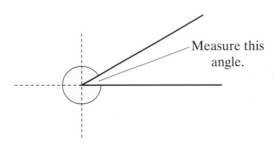

Measure this angle.

2 Subtract this angle from 360°.
The acute angle in the diagram measures 30°.
So the reflex angle is:

360° − 30° = 330°

Remember: angles that make a full turn add up to 360°.

Example 1

(a) Estimate the size of this reflex angle.
(b) Find its size using a protractor.

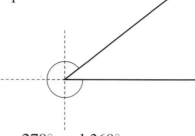

(a) The angle is between 270° and 360°.
A sensible estimate is 300°.

(b)

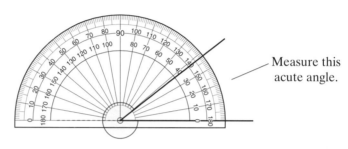

Measure this acute angle.

Acute angle = 38°
Reflex angle = 360° − 38°
= 322°

Drawing reflex angles

You can use a similar method to draw a reflex angle.

Example 2

Draw an angle of 213°.

1   Subtract 213° from 360°.
360° − 213° = 147°

2   Draw an angle of 147°.

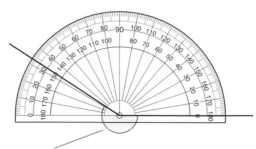

This angle is 213°

Exercise 2B

1   For each reflex angle:
   ● Estimate its size.
   ● Find its size using a protractor.

   (a)

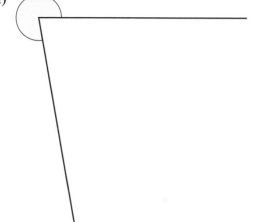

   (b)

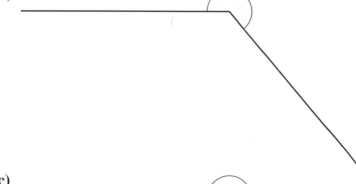

   (c)

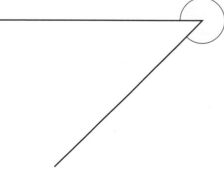

2   Draw these reflex angles:
   (a) 250°
   (b) 200°
   (c) 320°
   (d) 280°

3 Without measuring, write down whether the angle is acute, obtuse or reflex.

(a)    **(b)**    **(c)**

(d)   **(e)**   **(f)**

4 Write down whether the angle is acute, obtuse or reflex.

    (a) 263°   **(b)** 54°   **(c)** 175°   **(d)** 192°

2.3 Angle facts

You need to know these angle facts:

■ **A square corner of 90° is called a right angle.**

■ **You can put angles together to make a right angle. Angles that make a right angle always add up to 90°.**

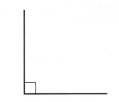

$a + b = 90°$
angles in a square corner

■ **You can put angles together to make a straight line. Angles that make a straight line always add up to 180°.**

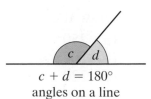

$c + d = 180°$
angles on a line

■ **You can put angles together at a point to make a full turn.**
  Angles that make a full turn always add up to 360°.

You can use these angle facts to find unknown angles.

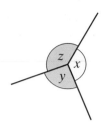

$x + y + z = 360°$
angles at a point

Example 3

Find the angles marked with letters:

(a)

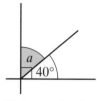

Using angles in a
square corner
$a + 40° = 90°$
So $a = 50°$

(b)

Using angles on a line
$140° + b = 180°$
So $b = 40°$

(c)

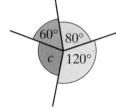

Using angles at a point
$c + 60° + 80° + 120° = 360°$
$c + 260° = 360°$
So $c = 100°$

Exercise 2C

1 Find the angles marked with letters. Say which angle
   fact you used.

(a)

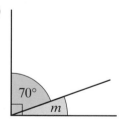

(b)

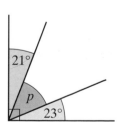

(c)

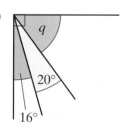

(d)

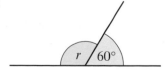

(e)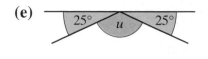

(f)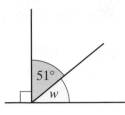

(g)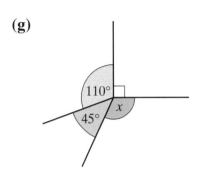

(h)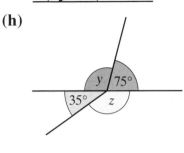

2.4 Opposite angles

■ **When two straight lines cross the opposite angles are equal.**

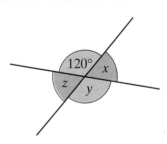

$$p = r$$
$$q = s$$

opposite angles are equal

Example 4

Find the angles marked with letters:

Using opposite angles

$$y = 120°$$

y and z are on a straight line

so $\qquad y + z = 180°$

so $\qquad 120° + z = 180°$

$$z = 60°$$

Using opposite angles

$$x = z = 60°$$

Exercise 2D

1 Find the angles marked with letters:

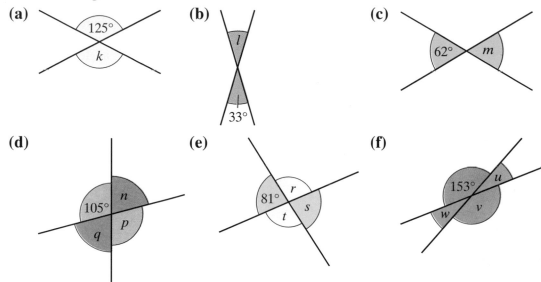

(a) 125° k

(b) l 33°

(c) 62° m

(d) n 105° p q

(e) r 81° s t

(f) 153° u w v

2.5 Angles between parallel lines

Lines are **parallel** if they are always the same distance apart. No matter how far you extend parallel lines, they never meet.

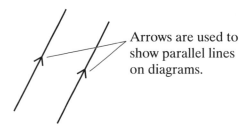

Arrows are used to show parallel lines on diagrams.

In the diagrams below, a straight line crosses two parallel lines. The pair of shaded angles are called **corresponding angles**. They are equal to each other.

Corresponding angles are sometimes called **F angles**. Looking for an F shape can sometimes help you find corresponding angles.

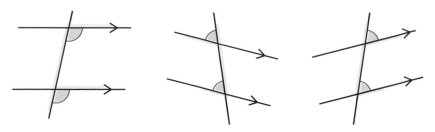

■ **Corresponding angles on parallel lines are equal**

These angles are called alternate angles. They are equal to each other.

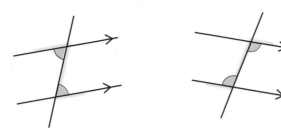

Alternate angles are sometimes called **Z angles**. Looking for a Z shape can sometimes help you find alternate angles.

■ **Alternate angles between parallel lines are equal**

Example 5

Write down the angle which is

(a) corresponding to the shaded angle
(b) alternate to the shaded angle.

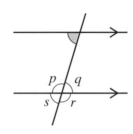

(a) s is the angle which is corresponding to the shaded angle.

(b) q is the angle which is alternate to the shaded angle.

Example 6

Find x. Give a reason for your answer.

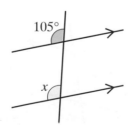

$x = 105°$ (corresponding angles)

Example 7

Find x and y. Give reasons for your answers.

$$x = 74° \qquad \text{(alternate angles)}$$
$$x + y = 180° \qquad \text{(angles on a straight line add to } 180°\text{)}$$
$$74° + y = 180°$$
$$y = 180° - 74°$$
$$y = 106°$$

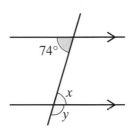

Exercise 2E

1 Write down the angle which is:

(i) corresponding to the shaded angle

(ii) alternate to the shaded angle.

(a)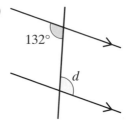

(b)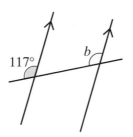

(c)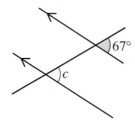

2 Find the missing angles and write which angle fact you used.

(a)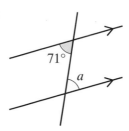

(b)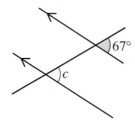

(c)

(d)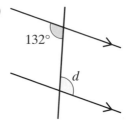

(e)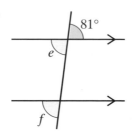

(f)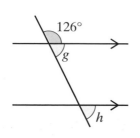

2.6 Angles in a triangle

1 Draw any triangle on a piece of paper.

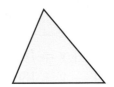

2 Tear the triangle into three pieces so you have three angles.

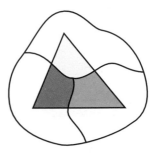

3 Put the pieces together again so that the points of the angles are together.

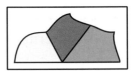

The three angles together make a half turn.

$0°$ ——— $180°$

The three angles together add up to $180°$.
This will work for any triangle.

■ **The three angles of any triangle add up to 180°.**

Example 8

What angles do these letters represent?

(a)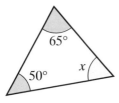

(b)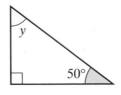

(c)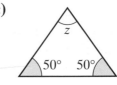

(a)
Angles add to $180°$
$x + 50° + 65° = 180°$
$x + 115° = 180°$
$x = 180° - 115°$
$x = 65°$

(b)
Angles add to $180°$
$y + 50° + 90° = 180°$
$y + 140° = 180°$
$y = 180° - 140°$
$y = 40°$

(c)
Angles add to $180°$
$z + 50° + 50° = 180°$
$z + 100° = 180°$
$z = 180° - 100°$
$z = 80°$

Exercise 2F

What angles do these letters represent?

1

2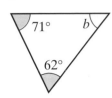

3

4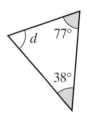

5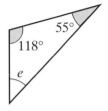

6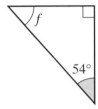

7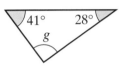

8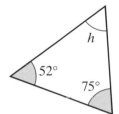

9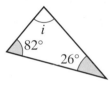

10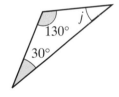

11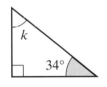

12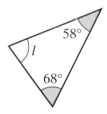

2.7 Isosceles triangles

■ An isosceles triangle has two sides of equal length.
The angles opposite the equal sides are equal.

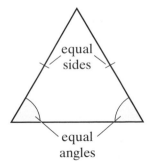

Example 9

This is an isosceles triangle.
Find the angles marked a and b.

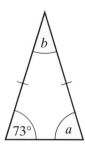

$a = 73°$ because the angles opposite the equal sides are equal.

The angles of a triangle add up to $180°$

So
$$b + 73° + 73° = 180°$$
$$b + 146° = 180°$$
$$b = 180° - 146°$$
$$b = 34°$$

Example 10

In this isosceles triangle, work out the size of the angle marked x.

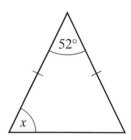

Angles opposite equal sides are equal.
So the unmarked angle is equal to x.

The angles of a triangle add up to $180°$.

So
$$x + x + 52° = 180°$$
$$x + x = 180° - 52°$$
$$x + x = 128°$$
$$2x = 128°$$
$$x = 64°$$

Exercise 2G

1. Find the angles marked with letters in these isosceles triangles:

(a)

(b)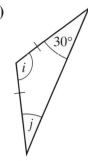

(c)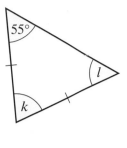

(d)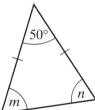

(e)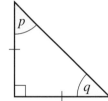

(f)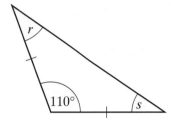

2.8 Solving problems using angle facts

You can combine angle facts to solve more difficult problems.

Example 11

Find the angles marked with letters.

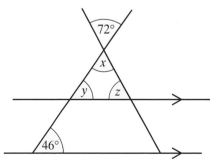

$$x = 72° \qquad \text{(opposite angles)}$$
$$y = 46° \qquad \text{(corresponding angles)}$$
$$x + y + z = 180° \qquad \text{(angles of a triangle)}$$
$$72° + 46° + z = 180°$$
$$118° + z = 180°$$
$$z = 180° - 118°$$
$$z = 62°$$

Exercise 2H

Find the angles marked with letters. Looking back through the information given in the chapter, say which angle facts you used.

1

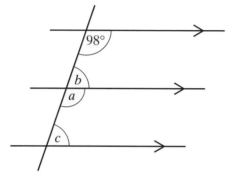

2

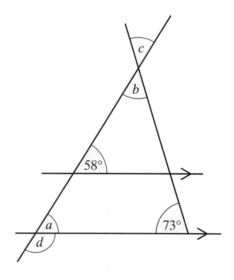

3

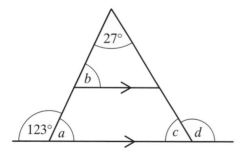

4

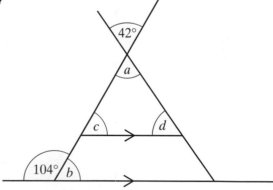

5

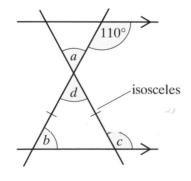

6

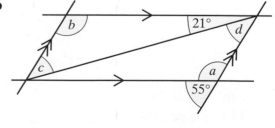

Summary of key points

1   An angle between $180°$ and $360°$ is called a reflex angle.

2   A square corner of $90°$ is called a right angle.

3   Angles that make a right angle always add up to $90°$.

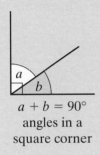

$a + b = 90°$
angles in a
square corner

4   Angles that make a straight line always add up to $180°$.

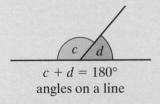

$c + d = 180°$
angles on a line

5   Angles that make a full turn always add up to $360°$.

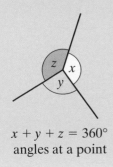

$x + y + z = 360°$
angles at a point

6 When two straight lines cross, the opposite angles are equal.

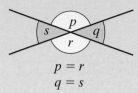

$p = r$
$q = s$

7 Corresponding angles on parallel lines are equal.

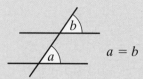

$a = b$

8 Alternate angles between parallel lines are equal.

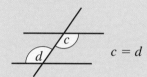

$c = d$

9 The three angles of any triangle add up to 180°.

10 An isosceles triangle has two sides of equal length. The angles opposite the equal sides are equal.

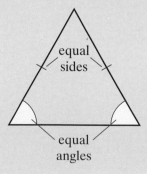

equal
sides

equal
angles

3 Working with algebra

Algebra is a part of mathematics where letters are used to represent numbers.

Algebra is used to estimate the amount of fuel needed for the journey.

3.1 Using letters

You can use letters in algebra to represent numbers you do not know.

Example 1

Bhavana has some CDs.
How many CDs has she got?
Using algebra you can say that Bhavana has x CDs.

She buys 3 more CDs.
How many does she have altogether?

Bhavana has

x CDs $+ 3$ CDs

Using algebra you can say that she has

$x + 3$ CDs

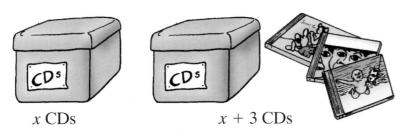

x CDs $x + 3$ CDs

Example 2

Roger collects postcards.
Each black and white postcard is
worth b pounds.
Each coloured postcard is worth c pounds.

b c

How much are Roger's postcards worth?

He has 3 black and white postcards

These are worth $b + b + b = 3b$ pounds

He also has 4 colour postcards

   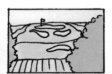

$c + c + c + c = 4c$ pounds

Altogether they are worth $3b + 4c$ pounds.

Example 3

Write in a shorter form:

(a) $a + a + a$

(b) $b + b + b + b + b$

> Remember:
> Using algebra you
> write $3 \times a$ as $3a$.

(a) $a + a + a = 3$ lots of a

$\quad\quad\quad = 3 \times a$

$\quad\quad\quad = 3a$

(b) $b + b + b + b + b = 5$ lots of b

$\quad\quad\quad\quad\quad\quad = 5 \times b$

$\quad\quad\quad\quad\quad\quad = 5b$

Example 4

Write in a longer form:

(a) $3d$

(b) $6e$

(a) $3d = 3$ lots of d

$\quad\quad = d + d + d$

(b) $6e = 6$ lots of e

$\quad\quad = e + e + e + e + e + e$

Exercise 3A

1 (a) Charlene has some books. You do not know how many books she has. Use algebra to say how many books she has.

(b) Charlene buys 5 more books. How many books has she now?

2 (a) Sam does not know how many stamps he has collected.
Use algebra to say how many stamps he has collected.

(b) Sam gives 8 stamps to his friend.
How many stamps are there now in Sam's collection?

3   Francis has x bars of chocolate and Melrose has y bars of chocolate.
How many bars of chocolate do they have altogether?

4   Robert has p pencils.
He buys 5 more pencils.
How many pencils does he have now?

5   Jane has p tokens and Mary has q tokens.
How many tokens do they have altogether?

6   Write in a shorter form:

(**a**) $x + x$ (**b**) $y + y + y$
(**c**) $a + a + a$ (**d**) $b + b + b + b$
(**e**) $r + r + r + r + r$ (**f**) $w + w$
(**g**) $s + s + s + s$ (**h**) $d + d + d + d + d$
(**i**) $e + e + e$ (**j**) $x + x + x + x + x + x$
(**k**) $m + m$ (**l**) $g + g + g$
(**m**) $v + v + v + v$ (**n**) $t + t + t + t + t$
(**o**) $x + x + x$ (**p**) $f + f + f + f$
(**q**) $y + y + y + y + y + y$ (**r**) $a + a$

7   Write in a longer form:

(**a**) $2x$ (**b**) $3a$ (**c**) $4b$
(**d**) $5c$ (**e**) $3s$ (**f**) $4t$
(**g**) $7w$ (**h**) $5g$ (**i**) $3m$
(**j**) $6n$ (**k**) r (**l**) $4k$

3.2 Collecting like terms

Roger's postcards are worth $3b + 4c$ pounds.

■   **$3b + 4c$ is an algebraic expression.**

     Each part is called a term.

Terms that use the same letter are called **like terms**.

You can often make an algebraic expression **simpler** by collecting like terms together.

You can collect like terms by adding or subtracting:

$3x + 4x$ $3x$ and $4x$ are both terms in x.

$7x$ Collect terms in x.

■ **Bringing terms together is called 'collecting like terms'.**

Example 5

Simplify by collecting like terms:
(a) $2x + 3x$
(b) $6d - 4d$
(c) $5a + 3b$
(d) $5f - f$

(a) $2x$ and $3x$ are both terms in x.
2 lots of x + 3 lots of x = 5 lots of x
So $2x + 3x = 5x$

$2x$ and $3x$ are called terms in x because they both use the letter x.

(b) $6d$ and $4d$ are both terms in d.
6 lots of d − 4 lots of d = 2 lots of d
So $6d - 4d = 2d$

(c) $5a$ and $3b$ use different letters.
So $5a + 3b$ cannot be simplified.

$5a$ and $3b$ are not like terms.

(d) $5f$ and f are both terms in f
5 lots of f − 1 lot of f = 4 lots of f
So $5f - f = 4f$

Remember f means 1 lot of f

Exercise 3B

1 Simplify these expressions by collecting like terms:
(a) $2x + 4x$ (b) $3y + 5y$
(c) $4a + 4a$ (d) $t + 3t$
(e) $5a - 2a$ (f) $7g - g$
(g) $6b - 5b$ (h) $8c + 5c$
(i) $11d + 5d$ (j) $6r - 6r$
(k) $3b + b$ (l) $4c + 5c$
(m) $3x + 2x + 4x$ (n) $4b - 3b + 5b$
(o) $3a + 5b$ (p) $9w + 3w - 9w$
(q) $15b - 3b - 8b$ (r) $10y - 6y - 4y$
(s) $11a + 3b - 11a$ (t) $3x + x - 2x$
(u) $4d - 3d + 2d$ (v) $5c - 2c - 3c$

2 Make up five questions that simplify to $6a$.

3 Which expression has each pupil chosen from the white board?

$3a - 2a$

$7a - 2a + 3a$

$a + a + a + a$

$8a - 5a$

My expression is 3a

Jamilla

My expression is a

Ben

My expression is 8a

Sally

My expression is 4a

Desmond

3.3 Simplifying expressions

Roger has 3 black and white postcards and 4 colour postcards. They are worth $3b + 4c$ pounds.

At a sale Roger buys 2 black and white postcards and 5 colour postcards.
So Roger's new postcards are worth

$2b + 5c$ pounds

How much are Roger's cards now worth in total?

Altogether he has

$3b + 4c + 2b + 5c$

Collect the like terms and then add them.

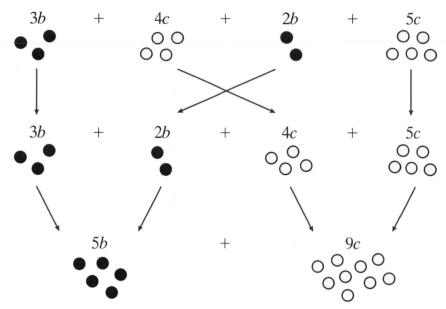

So all his postcards together are worth

$5b + 9c$ pounds

■ **Making an expression simpler is called simplifying**
e.g. $2a + 3b + 4a = 6a + 3b$

Example 6

Simplify:

(a) $2a + 3b + 5a + b$ **(b)** $4x - 2y + 3x + 5y$

(a) Collect like terms:

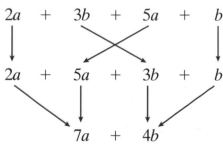

Remember b means
1 lot of b

(b) Collect like terms:

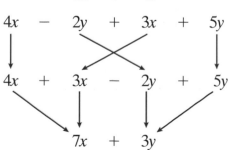

Notice that the + or
− sign is part of
each term.

Exercise 3C

Simplify:

(a) $2a + 4b + 2a + 3b$ (b) $3c + 5d + 5c + 3d$
(c) $4f + 3g - 2f + 3g$ (d) $6m + 2n - 5m + 3n$
(e) $r + 3s + 5r + 4s$ (f) $9x + 3y - 3y + 6x$
(g) $3t + 2t - t + 4t$ (h) $5p - 2q + 3p + 2q$
(i) $7r + 7s - 7r - 7s$ (j) $3a + 2 + 3a + 4$
(k) $5b - 3 - 5b + 4$ (l) $6x - 3y + 4x + 5y$
(m) $4a + 3b + 5a + 4b$ (n) $11y + 15w + y + w$
(o) $3a + 4a - a + b - 2a$ (p) $10x + 3y - 8x - 3y$
(q) $4m + 2n + 6m + 2n$ (r) $11r + 3t - 10r + 2t - r$
(s) $5d + 5f + 6d - 5f + 1$ (t) $8d + 4g - 3 + 2d - 3g$

3.4 Multiplying terms together

At Katie's bakery they need to work out how much
icing to make for slab cakes.

Each slab cake is divided into
slices x wide and y long.

Then the whole slab cake is:

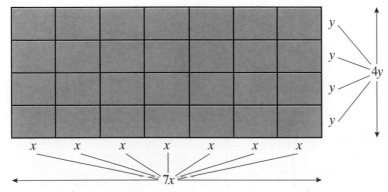

Area of icing $= 7x \times 4y$

Example 7

Work out the areas of these rectangles:

(a)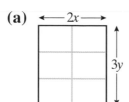

(b)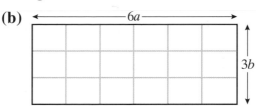

(a) Area $= 2x \times 3y$
$$= 2 \times x \times 3 \times y$$
Multiply the numbers first:
$$2 \times 3 = 6$$
Then multiply the letters:
$$x \times y = xy$$
So $2x \times 3y = 6 \times xy$
$$= 6xy$$

Remember:
area of a rectangle
$=$ length $\times$ width

(b) Area $= 6a \times 3b$
$$= 6 \times a \times 3 \times b$$
Multiply the numbers first:
$$6 \times 3 - 18$$
Then multiply the letters:
$$a \times b = ab$$
So $6a \times 3b = 18 \times ab$
$$= 18ab$$

Example 8

Work out:
(a) $3a \times 2b$

(b) $3xy \times 4z$

(a) $3a \times 2b$
Multiply the numbers first:
$$3 \times 2 = 6$$
Then multiply the letters:
$$a \times b = ab$$
So $3a \times 2b = 6 \times ab$
$$= 6ab$$

(b) $3xy \times 4z$
Multiply the numbers first:
$$3 \times 4 = 12$$
Then multiply the letters:
$$xy \times z = xyz$$
So $3xy \times 4z = 12 \times xyz$
$$= 12xyz$$

Exercise 3D

1 Work out the areas of these rectangles:

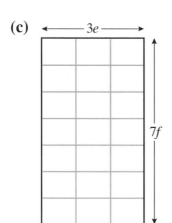

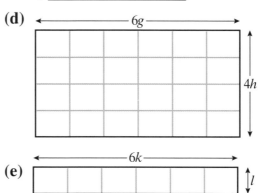

2 Multiply these:

(a) $3a \times 4b$	**(b)** $2x \times 3y$	**(c)** $5p \times 4q$	**(d)** $2g \times 2f$
(e) $3c \times 6d$	**(f)** $5x \times 2y$	**(g)** $4r \times 2s$	**(h)** $3s \times 4p$
(i) $7a \times 3b$	**(j)** $9c \times 4d$	**(k)** $2m \times 4n$	**(l)** $5b \times 3c$
(m) $3a \times 2bc$	**(n)** $3x \times 4yz$	**(o)** $2c \times 3de$	**(p)** $3a \times bc$
(q) $5m \times 2np$	**(r)** $4cd \times 2e$	**(s)** $3mn \times 2p$	**(t)** $3x \times 8yz$
(u) $abc \times d$	**(v)** $pq \times rs$	**(w)** $3ab \times 2cd$	**(x)** $4mn \times 3pq$
(y) $2abc \times 3de$	**(z)** $5pqr \times mn$		

3.5 Brackets in algebra

Brackets are used in algebra to help write expressions.
For example:

$3 \times (a + b)$ means multiply each term in the bracket by 3.

We usually write $3(a + b)$ without the $\times$ sign.
So $3(a + b)$ means $3 \times a + 3 \times b = 3a + 3b$
This is called **expanding the brackets**.

■ **Removing the brackets in an expression is called
expanding the brackets,**
e.g. $3(2a + 3) = 6a + 9$

Example 9

Expand the brackets in these expressions:

(a) $2(4a + 1)$
(b) $3(2x - 4y)$
(c) $4(2a - b)$

(a) $2(4a + 1)$
$$= 2 \times 4a + 2 \times 1$$
$$= 8a + 2$$

(b) $3(2x - 4y)$
$$= 3 \times 2x - 3 \times 4y$$
$$= 6x - 12y$$

(c) $4(2a - b)$
$$= 4 \times 2a - 4 \times b$$
$$= 8a - 4b$$

$4 \times b$
$= 4 \times 1b$
$= 4b$

Exercise 3E

1 Expand the brackets in these expressions:

(a) $2(2a + 3)$ (b) $3(3b + 1)$
(c) $4(3c + 2d)$ (d) $2(3x - 4y)$
(e) $5(a + 2b)$ (f) $3(2x - 3y)$
(g) $2(x - 3y)$ (h) $6(2c + 3d)$
(i) $7(2a - b)$ (j) $4(a + 3b)$
(k) $2(a + 2b + 3c)$ (l) $5(2x + 3y + 5z)$
(m) $3(2c - 3d + 5e)$ (n) $4(2a - 3b - 2c)$

3.6 Powers in algebra

You can use powers to multiply numbers that are the same:

	You write:	You say:
3×3	3^2	3 squared
$3 \times 3 \times 3$	3^3	3 cubed
$3 \times 3 \times 3 \times 3$	3^4	3 to the 4th or 3 to the power of 4
$3 \times 3 \times 3 \times 3 \times 3$	3^5	3 to the 5th or 3 to the power of 5

You can also use powers to multiply letters that are the same:

	You write:	You say:
$y \times y$	y^2	y squared
$y \times y \times y$	y^3	y cubed
$y \times y \times y \times y$	y^4	y to the 4th or y to the power of 4
$y \times y \times y \times y \times y$	y^5	y to the 5th or y to the power of 5

Example 10

Write in a simpler form:
(a) 5×5

(b) $4 \times 4 \times 4 \times 4$

(c) $2 \times 2 \times 2$

(d) $7 \times d \times d \times d$

(a) 5^2

(b) 4^4

(c) 2^3

(d) $7d^3$

Example 11

Write without powers:
(a) 4^2

(b) 3^6

(c) a^3

(d) $3b^4$

(a) 4×4

(b) $3 \times 3 \times 3 \times 3 \times 3 \times 3$

(c) $a \times a \times a$

(d) $3 \times b \times b \times b \times b$

Exercise 3F

1 Write these in a simpler form:
The first one has been done for you.

(a) $5 \times 5 = 5^2$

(b) $7 \times 7 \times 7$

(c) 8×8

(d) $4 \times 4 \times 4 \times 4 \times 4$

(e) $a \times a$

(f) $x \times x \times x$

(g) $w \times w \times w \times w \times w$

(h) $5 \times 5 \times 5 \times 5 \times 5$

(i) $3 \times 3 \times 3 \times 3 \times 3 \times 3 \times 3$

(j) $y \times y \times y \times y$

(k) $r \times r \times r \times r \times r \times r$

(l) $m \times m$

(m) $p \times p \times p$

(n) $5 \times y \times y$

(o) $3 \times r \times r \times r \times r$

(p) $2 \times b \times b \times b \times b \times b$

(q) $2 \times 3 \times a \times a$

(r) $3 \times 5 \times b \times b \times b$

2 Write these without powers.
The first one has been done for you.

   (a) $2^3 = 2 \times 2 \times 2$ **(b)** 3^2
   (c) 4^3 **(d)** 7^5
   (e) 5^3 **(f)** c^2
   (g) a^3 **(h)** f^2
   (i) d^5 **(j)** r^4
   (k) s^3 **(l)** y^8
   (m) r^5 **(n)** $5y^2$
   (o) $2x^3$ **(p)** $4p^4$
   (q) $3y^2$ **(r)** $2r^3$

Summary of key points

1 $3b + 4c$ is an algebraic expression.

    Each part is called a term.

2   Bringing terms together is called collecting like terms,

    e.g. $3x + 4x = 7x$

3   Making an expression simpler is called simplifying,

    e.g. $2a + 3b + 4a = 6a + 3b$

4   Removing the brackets in an expression is called expanding the brackets,

    e.g. $3(2a + 3) = 6a + 9$

4 Multiplication and division

4.1 Multiples and factors

Jules buys three boxes of popcorn. They cost £2 each. Altogether she pays $3 \times £2 = £6$.
6 is a **multiple** of 3.

The multiples of 3 are 3, 6, 9, **12**, 15, 18, 21, **24**, ...

The multiples of 4 are 4, 8, **12**, 16, 20, **24**, 28, ...

■ **Numbers that are multiples of two separate numbers are called common multiples.**

12 and 24 are both common multiples of 3 and 4.

■ **The lowest common multiple of two numbers is the lowest number that is a multiple of them both. Lowest common multiple is sometimes written as LCM.**

The lowest common multiple of 3 and 4 is 12.

Example 1

(a) What are the first three common multiples of 4 and 6?
(b) What is the LCM of 4 and 6?

(a) Write out the multiples of 4:   4, 8, <u>12</u>, 16, 20, <u>24</u>, 28, 32, <u>36</u>, 40, ...
    Write out the multiples of 6:   6, <u>12</u>, 18, <u>24</u>, 30, <u>36</u>, 42, ...

   The first three common multiples of 4 and 6 are <u>12</u>, <u>24</u>, <u>36</u>.
(b) The lowest common multiple of 4 and 6 is **12**.

Exercise 4A

1   What are the first three common multiples of:
   (a) 2 and 5   **(b)** 5 and 4   **(c)** 3 and 5   **(d)** 3 and 7
   (e) 6 and 9   **(f)** 3 and 9   **(g)** 8 and 6   **(h)** 15 and 20

2 What is the lowest common multiple of:

(a) 4 and 7   (b) 4 and 10   (c) 3 and 9   (d) 8 and 12

(e) 20 and 30   (f) 10 and 15   (g) 2, 3 and 4   (h) 3, 6 and 9

3 Find as many pairs of numbers as you can which have an LCM of:

(a) 20   (b) 18   (c) 12   (d) 24

4 Which pairs of numbers have the following common multiples? There may be more than one answer for each question.

(a) 4, 8, 12, 16, ...   (b) 6, 12, 18, 24, ...

(c) 7, 14, 21, 28, ...   (d) 10, 20, 30, ...

(e) ..., 20, 24, 28, ...   (f) ..., 32, 40, 48, ...

(g) ..., 25, 30, 35, ...   (h) ..., 40, 60, 80, ...

5 Complete the following statements. There may be more than one answer for each question.

(a) The LCM of 3 and __ is 12.

(b) The LCM of 5 and __ is 15.

(c) The LCM of 6 and __ is 24.

(d) The LCM of 10 and __ is 30.

(e) The LCM of __ and 7 is 28.

(f) The LCM of __ and 9 is 18.

(g) The LCM of __ , 4 and __ is 20.

(h) The LCM of __ , __ and 14 is 28.

> You can find the LCM of three numbers in the same way as for two. Write out the multiples and look for the common numbers.

Common factors

Jared's birthday cake is cut into 6 slices. If he shares it between 3 people each person gets 2 slices. If he shares it between 6 people each person gets 1 slice. 1, 2, 3 and 6 are all **factors** of 6.

The factors of 18 are 1, 2, 3, 6, 9, 18.

The factors of 24 are 1, 2, 3, 4, 6, 8, 12, 24.

■ **Numbers that are factors of two separate numbers are called common factors.**

> 1, 2, 3 and 6 are common factors of 18 and 24.

■ **The highest common factor of two numbers is the highest number that is a factor of them both. Highest common factor is sometimes written as HCF.**

> The highest common factor of 18 and 24 is **6**.

Example 2

(a) Find the common factors of 30 and 45.
(b) What is the HCF of 30 and 45?

(a) The factors of 30 are <u>1</u>, 2, <u>3</u>, <u>5</u>, 6, 10, <u>15</u>, 30.
The factors of 45 are <u>1</u>, <u>3</u>, <u>5</u>, 9, <u>15</u>, 45.

The common factors are **1, 3, 5, 15**.
(b) The HCF is **15**.

Exercise 4B

1   What are the common factors of:
   (a) 6 and 8   (b) 15 and 20   (c) 9 and 15   (d) 6 and 12
   (e) 8 and 12   (f) 12 and 16   (g) 16 and 24   (h) 18 and 27

2   What is the highest common factor of:
   (a) 12 and 18   (b) 6 and 9   (c) 8 and 20   (d) 14 and 21
   (e) 20 and 30   (f) 16 and 28   (g) 6, 12 and 15   (h) 12, 16 and 24

3   Each of these pupils has chosen a pair of numbers from the blackboard.
   Which pair of numbers has each pupil chosen?

4   Can the LCM and the HCF of two numbers ever be the same? Explain your answer.

5   Investigation
Choose two numbers and find their LCM and their HCF.
Multiply the two numbers together.
Multiply their LCM and HCF together.
What do you notice?
Try this for other pairs of numbers.

4.2 Prime numbers

Jared has another birthday cake divided into 7 slices. It is impossible to divide the cake equally between 2, 3, 4, 5 or 6 people. The only factors of 7 are 1 and 7. 7 is called a prime number.

■   **A prime number is a whole number with exactly two factors: itself and 1.**

1 is not a prime number: it has only one factor.

Prime numbers are sometimes just called **primes**.

Example 3

Say whether these are prime numbers:

(a) 5
(b) 6
(c) 9

(a) Factors of 5 are 1, 5.
5 has two factors so it is a prime number.
(b) Factors of 6 are 1, 2, 3, 6.
6 has four factors so it is not a prime number.
(c) Factors of 9 are 1, 3, 9.
9 has three factors so it is not a prime number.

Exercise 4C

1   Activity   You will need a 100 square.
One way to find prime numbers is to use the **sieve of Eratosthenes**.

~~1~~	②	③	~~4~~	⑤	~~6~~	7	~~8~~	~~9~~	~~10~~
11	~~12~~	13	~~14~~	~~15~~	~~16~~	17	~~18~~	19	~~20~~
~~21~~	~~22~~	23	~~24~~	~~25~~	~~26~~	~~27~~	~~28~~	29	~~30~~

Eratosthenes was a Greek mathematician who lived in the third century BC. He was a librarian in Alexandria in Egypt.

- On your hundred square cross out 1 because it is not a prime number.
- Circle 2 then cross out all other multiples of 2.
- The next number that is not crossed out is 3. Circle 3 then cross out all other multiples of 3.
- The next number that is not crossed out is 5. Circle 5 then cross out all other multiples of 5.

Continue like this until all the numbers in your hundred square are either circled or crossed out.

The circled numbers are the prime numbers less than 100.

2   Find two prime numbers that add up to:
(**a**) 9 (**b**) 10 (**c**) 12 (**d**) 14
(**e**) 15 (**f**) 18 (**g**) 19 (**h**) 24

3   Find three prime numbers that add up to:
(**a**) 10 (**b**) 12 (**c**) 14 (**d**) 15
(**e**) 20 (**f**) 21 (**g**) 22 (**h**) 25

4   2 and 3 are a pair of prime numbers.
$2 + 3 = 5$ and 5 is a prime number.

(**a**) Find other pairs of prime numbers whose sum is a prime number.
(**b**) What do you notice about your answers?

17 + 2 = 19
41 + 2 = 43

5   Find three prime numbers whose total is a prime number. How many different answers can you find to this question?

6   Can every number be written as the sum of two prime numbers?

Prime factors

The factors of 12 are 1, 2, 3, 4, 6, 12.
The numbers 2 and 3 are prime numbers.
12 can be written as $2 \times 2 \times 3$
This is called writing 12 as a product of
its prime factors.

■ **Any number can be written as a
product of its prime factors.**

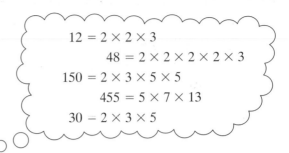

$12 = 2 \times 2 \times 3$
$48 = 2 \times 2 \times 2 \times 2 \times 3$
$150 = 2 \times 3 \times 5 \times 5$
$455 = 5 \times 7 \times 13$
$30 = 2 \times 3 \times 5$

Example 4

Write 20 as a product of its prime factors.

The factors of 20 are 1, 2, 4, 5, 10, 20.
The prime factors of 20 are 2 and 5.
Multiply 2s and 5s to make 20: $2 \times 2 \times 5 = 20$

20 written as a product of its prime factors is $2 \times 2 \times 5$

Alternatively:
Start with the lowest
prime number first.
$20 = 2 \times 10$
$ = 2 \times 2 \times 5$

Exercise 4D

1   Write each of these numbers as a product of its prime
factors.

(a) 15   (b) 18   (c) 16
(d) 21   (e) 25   (f) 28
(g) 30   (h) 35

2   Here are the rules for growing magic number seeds:
● the stalk splits if you can find a pair of factors
neither of which is 1.
● a leaf grows when you reach a prime number.

Plant the number
18 seed …

… the stalk splits into 2
and 9 because $2 \times 9 = 18$
The 2 stalk grows a leaf …

… the 9 stalk splits into 3
and 3 because $3 \times 3 = 9$
The 3 stalks grow leaves …

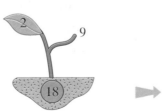

(a) There is another plant that can grow from a number 18 seed. Draw it.

(b) Draw a plant that can grow from each of these number seeds.

Hint: make the first split 3×6

(c) What do you notice about the numbers in the leaves of each plant?

4.3 Multiplying and dividing by 10, 100 and 1000

Multiplying whole numbers by 10 is easy.

For example: 32×10

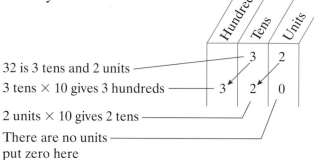

32 is 3 tens and 2 units

3 tens $\times$ 10 gives 3 hundreds

2 units $\times$ 10 gives 2 tens

There are no units put zero here

So $32 \times 10 = 320$

■ **To multiply a whole number by 10 move each digit one column to the left then put 0 in the units column.**

There is also a quick way to multiply whole numbers by 100:

$$100 = 10 \times 10$$

So $32 \times 100 = 32 \times 10 \times 10$

$$= 320 \times 10$$

$$= 3200$$

So $32 \times 100 = 3200$

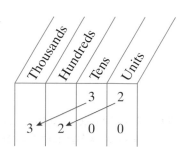

■ **To multiply a whole number by 100 move each digit two columns to the left, then put 0 in the tens and units columns.**

■ **To multiply a whole number by 1000 move each digit three columns to the left, then put 0 in the hundreds, tens and units columns.**

For example: $32 \times 1000 = 32\,000$

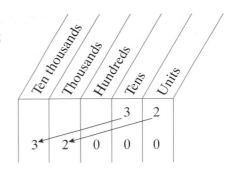

You can also use place value diagrams to divide numbers by 10, 100 or 1000.

■ **To divide a whole number by 10 move each digit one column to the right.**

For example: $240 \div 10 = 24$

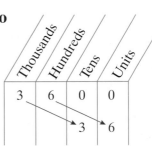

■ **To divide a whole number by 100 move each digit two columns to the right.**

For example: $3600 \div 100 = 36$

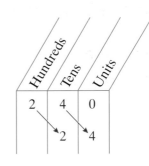

■ **To divide a whole number by 1000 move each digit three columns to the right.**

For example: $48\,000 \div 1000 = 48$

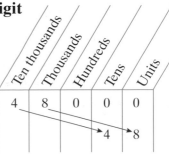

Exercise 4E

1
  (a) 35×10 **(b)** 26×10 **(c)** 39×100

  (d) 76×10 **(e)** 48×100 **(f)** 100×89 ⎯⎯ Think of this as
89×100

  (g) 10×465 **(h)** 100×321 **(i)** 10×725

  (j) 100×42 **(k)** 89×100 **(l)** 842×1000

2
  (a) $76 \times 10 \times 10$ **(b)** $48 \times 10 \times 100$

  (c) $57 \times 100 \times 10$ **(d)** $456 \times 100 \times 10$

  (e) $97 \times 1000 \times 10$ **(f)** 100×10

  (g) 100×100 **(h)** 1000×10 ⎯ Hint: think of this as
$8 \times 100 \times 10$

  (i) $10 \times 100 \times 100$ **(j)** $100 \times 8 \times 10$

3
  (a) $430 \div 10$ **(b)** $870 \div 10$ **(c)** $6800 \div 100$ **(d)** $7200 \div 100$

  (e) $3400 \div 10$ **(f)** $9600 \div 10$ **(g)** $2000 \div 100$ **(h)** $87\,000 \div 100$

4
  (a) $4000 \div 1000$ **(b)** $17\,000 \div 1000$ **(c)** $171\,000 \div 1000$

  (d) $90\,000 \div 1000$ **(e)** $237\,000 \div 1000$ **(f)** $66\,000 \div 1000$

5
  (a) $29 \times 100 \div 10$ **(b)** $46 \times 100 \div 10$ **(c)** $380 \div 10 \times 100$

  (d) $780 \div 10 \times 100$ **(e)** $960 \times 10 \div 100$ **(f)** $120 \times 10 \div 100$

Multiples of 10 and 100

You know how to multiply a 2- or 3-digit number by a
1-digit number. You can use this to multiply by multiples of 10.

Example 5

Work out 53×70

Think of 70 as 7×10

$53 \times 70 = 53 \times 7 \times 10$

$\qquad\quad = \mathbf{371} \times 10$

$\qquad\quad = 3710$

$$
\begin{array}{r}
53 \\
\times\ \ 7 \\
\hline
371 \\
{}_2
\end{array}
$$

You can set it out like this:

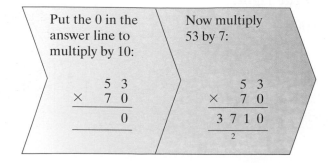

Put the 0 in the answer line to multiply by 10:	Now multiply 53 by 7:
$\begin{array}{r} 5\ 3 \\ \times\ \ 7\ 0 \\ \hline 0 \end{array}$	$\begin{array}{r} 5\ 3 \\ \times\ \ 7\ 0 \\ \hline 3\ 7\ 1\ 0 \\ {}_{2} \end{array}$

■ To multiply by 70, first multiply by 7 then multiply your answer by 10.
To multiply by 700, first multiply by 7 then multiply your answer by 100.

Exercise 4F

1 (a) 32×20 (b) 21×30 (c) 24×30
(d) 32×40 (e) 23×40 (f) 30×42 _____ Hint: think of this as
(g) 50×38 (h) 53×40 (i) 30×73 42×30
(j) 49×50 (k) 20×72 (l) 69×40

2 (a) 24×60 (b) 36×70
(c) 47×60 (d) 84×70
(e) 90×85 (f) 60×58
(g) 29×90 (h) 53×70
(i) 90×84 (j) 64×70

3 (a) 23×200 (b) 35×300
(c) 54×500 (d) 37×400
(e) 400×75 (f) 500×48
(g) 69×200 (h) 57×300
(i) 500×74 (j) 87×400

4 (a) 523×20 (b) 354×40 (c) 674×50
(d) 862×60 (e) 564×200 (f) 352×400
(g) 482×300 (h) 475×80 (i) 787×70
(j) 708×40 (k) 570×30 (l) 700×30

4.4 Multiplying 2- or 3-digit numbers by 2-digit numbers

This section shows you a way to do harder multiplications on paper.

Example 6

Work out 753×76

Think of 76 as $70 + 6$

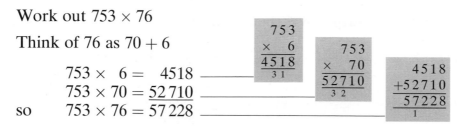

$$753 \times 6 = 4518$$
$$753 \times 70 = \underline{52\,710}$$
so $\quad 753 \times 76 = \overline{57\,228}$

You can set out 753×76 like this:

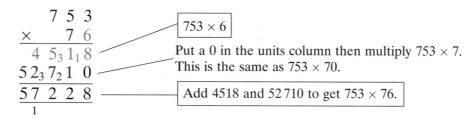

753×6

Put a 0 in the units column then multiply 753×7. This is the same as 753×70.

Add 4518 and 52 710 to get 753×76.

Exercise 4G

1
(a) 32×21 (b) 43×32
(c) 38×23 (d) 543×34
(e) 473×45 (f) 544×43
(g) 407×63 (h) 540×59
(i) 738×72 (j) 828×44
(k) 754×71 (l) 654×97

2
(a) 196×12 (b) 311×27
(c) 49×91 (d) 13×696 —— Hint: this is the same as 696×13.
(e) 44×112 (f) 98×461
(g) 812×19 (h) 21×402
(i) 399×66 (j) 809×71
(k) 207×43 (l) 36×909

3 (a) Choose any four digits, for example 2, 3, 4, and 6. Write them as a 2-digit $\times$ 2-digit multiplication and work out the answer.
Try other arrangements of your four digits.
Which arrangement gives the largest answer?
Which arrangement gives the smallest answer?
(b) Repeat part (a) but choose five digits and make a 3-digit $\times$ 2-digit multiplication.

4.5 Dividing 3-digit numbers by 1- or 2-digit numbers

1-digit numbers

This section shows you how to do divisions such as $864 \div 5$ on paper.

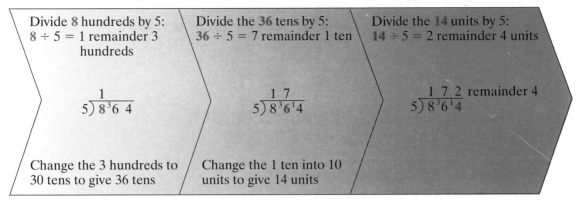

Divide **8** hundreds by 5:
$8 \div 5 = 1$ remainder 3 hundreds

$$\begin{array}{r} 1 \\ 5\overline{)\,8\,{}^3 6\ \ 4} \end{array}$$

Change the 3 hundreds to 30 tens to give 36 tens

Divide the **36** tens by 5:
$36 \div 5 = 7$ remainder 1 ten

$$\begin{array}{r} 1\ 7 \\ 5\overline{)\,8\,{}^3 6\,{}^1 4} \end{array}$$

Change the 1 ten into 10 units to give 14 units

Divide the **14** units by 5:
$14 \div 5 = 2$ remainder 4 units

$$\begin{array}{r} 1\ 7\ 2\ \text{remainder 4} \\ 5\overline{)\,8\,{}^3 6\,{}^1 4} \end{array}$$

So $864 \div 5 = 172$ remainder 4

Exercise 4H

1   (a) $84 \div 3$ (b) $76 \div 3$ (c) $86 \div 5$ (d) $974 \div 4$
    (e) $873 \div 3$ (f) $876 \div 4$ (g) $835 \div 5$ (h) $644 \div 4$
    (i) $796 \div 5$ (j) $896 \div 3$ (k) $838 \div 4$ (l) $563 \div 5$

2   (a) $764 \div 6$ (b) $987 \div 7$ (c) $957 \div 8$ (d) $826 \div 6$
    (e) $787 \div 6$ (f) $989 \div 8$ (g) $943 \div 9$ (h) $400 \div 8$
    (i) $427 \div 6$ (j) $111 \div 7$ (k) $653 \div 8$ (l) $478 \div 9$

2-digit numbers

This section shows you how to do divisions such as $851 \div 31$ on paper.

You cannot divide 8 hundreds by 31
So divide **85** tens by 31:
$85 \div 31 = 2$ remainder 23 tens

$$\begin{array}{r} 2 \\ 31\overline{)\,8\ 5\ 1} \\ \underline{6\ 2} \\ 2\ 3 \end{array}$$

Change the 23 tens into 230 units and bring down the **1** unit to make 23**1** units

$$\begin{array}{r} 2 \\ 31\overline{)\,8\ 5\ 1} \\ \underline{6\ 2} \\ 2\ 3\ \mathbf{1} \end{array}$$

Divide **231** units by 31:
$231 \div 31 = 7$ remainder 14 units

$$\begin{array}{r} 2\ 7 \\ 31\overline{)\,8\ 5\ 1} \\ \underline{6\ 2} \\ 2\ 3\ 1 \\ \underline{2\ 1\ 7} \\ 1\ 4 \end{array}$$

$31 \times 7 = 217$

So $851 \div 31 = 27$ remainder 14

Exercise 4I

1 (a) $457 \div 21$ (b) $596 \div 26$ (c) $796 \div 32$ (d) $896 \div 42$
    (e) $786 \div 56$ (f) $546 \div 17$ (g) $682 \div 18$ (h) $682 \div 57$
    (i) $765 \div 31$ (j) $687 \div 16$

2 (a) $226 \div 19$ (b) $780 \div 12$ (c) $906 \div 47$
    (d) $792 \div 31$ (e) $301 \div 18$ (f) $565 \div 35$
    (g) $806 \div 22$ (h) $961 \div 62$ (i) $196 \div 11$

4.6 Checking answers by approximation (rounding to 1 significant figure)

In section 1.6 **Checking answers by estimation**, you used rounding to estimate the answers to addition and subtraction problems. Each time you rounded the numbers to the nearest 100, or to the nearest 1 000, before adding or subtracting to get an approximate answer. An easier way to say this is that you rounded each number to one significant figure.

```
873 rounds to    900
418 rounds to    400
450 rounds to   +500
                1 800
```

so $873 + 418 + 450$ is about 1 800

- **The first significant figure of a whole number is the digit (or figure) on the left of the number.**

- **The first significant figure in   6 is 6**
  The first significant figure in   364 is 3.
  The first significant figure in   2 541 is 2.

- **62 rounded to 1 significant figure is   60.**
  364 rounded to 1 significant figure is   400.
  2 541 rounded to 1 significant figure is   3 000.

- **1 s.f. means to one significant figure.**

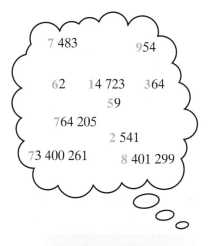

The first significant figure in each number is shown in blue.

Example 7

Round each number to 1 significant figure to get an approximate answer to:

(a) 43×271

(a) 40×300
   $- 120 \times 100$
   $= 12\,000$

Remember: to multiply by 300 multiply by 3 then multiply by 100

(b) $784 \div 35$

(b) $800 \div 40$
   $= 80 \div 4$
   $= 20$

To divide by 40 do the opposite of multiplying by 40: divide by 10 then divide by 4

Exercise 4J

Do not use a calculator for this exercise.

1 Round each number to 1 significant figure:
    (a) 73   **(b)** 48   **(c)** 29   **(d)** 75
    (e) 84   **(f)** 97   **(g)** 482   **(h)** 745
    (i) 861   **(j)** 348   **(k)** 874   **(l)** 963
    (m) 3 643   **(n)** 8 365   **(o)** 6 548   **(p)** 9 802
    (q) 45 432   **(r)** 83 413

2 Round each number to 1 significant figure to get an approximate answer to:
    (a) 53×26 **(b)** 35×64 **(c)** 6×43
    (d) 18×45 **(e)** 563×25 **(f)** 273×53
    (g) 282×72 **(h)** 464×493 **(i)** 843×115
    (j) 632×464

3 Round each number to 1 significant figure to get an approximate answer to:
    (a) $57 \div 26$ **(b)** $92 \div 28$ **(c)** $76 \div 43$
    (d) $946 \div 323$ **(e)** $752 \div 207$ **(f)** $573 \div 34$
    (g) $823 \div 38$ **(h)** $935 \div 30$ **(i)** $5 843 \div 291$
    (j) $7 543 \div 39$

4 By rounding to 1 s.f. find the correct answer in the cloud for each calculation.
    (a) $13 281 \times 2 641$ **(b)** $8 724 \times 254$
    (c) $19 648 \div 4 912$ **(d)** $42 714 \div 189$
    (e) $76 834 \times 913$ **(f)** $598 884 \div 286$

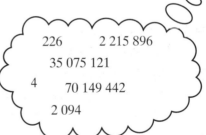

226   2 215 896
35 075 121
4   70 149 442
2 094

5 **(a)** Copy the table but round each number to 1 significant figure.
    (b) Decide which of the following statements are true and which are false:
    (i) The Arabian Sea is about twice the size of the Bay of Bengal.
    (ii) The Coral Sea is about ten times the size of the Black Sea.
    (iii) The Bay of Bengal is about ten times bigger than the Baltic Sea.
    (c) Make up a statement like this of your own.

Sea	Area km^2
Coral Sea	4 791 352
Arabian Sea	3 863 377
Bay of Bengal	2 304 243
Philippine Sea	1 036 739
Sea of Japan	978 000
Black Sea	508 964
Baltic Sea	414 352
Persian Gulf	238 312

4.7 Powers of whole numbers

In chapter 3 you used powers to simplify algebraic expressions. You can also write large numbers using powers.

$10^{100} = 1\,000\,000\,000\,000\,000\,000$

The number 10^{100} is called a googol. It is 1 followed by a hundred zeros.

Example 8

Write a million as a power.

$$1\,000\,000 = 10 \times 10 \times 10 \times 10 \times 10 \times 10 = 10^6$$

You can also find the exact value of numbers written as powers.

Example 9

Find the value of 5^4.

$$5^4 = 5 \times 5 \times 5 \times 5 = 625$$

■ **5^4 means $5 \times 5 \times 5 \times 5$. The number 4 is called the power or index.**

Exercise 4K

1 Write 125 as a power of 5.

2 Write $10\,000\,000$ as a power of 10.

3 Work out 6^3.

4 Write:
   (a) 9 as a power of 3
   (b) 25 as a power of 5
   (c) 1000 as a power of 10
   (d) 8 as a power of 2
   (e) 27 as a power of 3
   (f) 16 as a power of 2
   (g) $1\,000\,000\,000$ as a power of 10
   (h) 512 as a power of 2
   (i) $100\,000\,000$ as a power of 10
   (j) 81 as a power of 3
   (k) 64 as a power of 4
   (l) 729 as a power of 9

5 Work out:
   (a) 2^5
   (b) 3^5
   (c) 4^2
   (d) 5^4
   (e) 1^4
   (f) 10^4
   (g) 9^2
   (h) 0^3
   (i) 6^4
   (j) 100^3
   (k) 8^3
   (l) 7^3

6 Match up pairs of numbers from the cloud
that have the same value.

For example: $2^6 = 4^3$

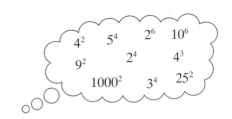

4^2 5^4 2^6 10^6
9^2 2^4 4^3
1000^2 3^4 25^2

Squaring and cubing

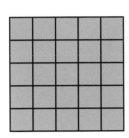

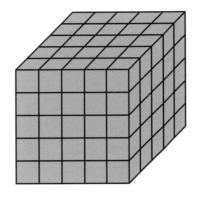

5^2 is also called 5 squared
because it is the number of
small squares in a 5×5 square.

5^3 is also called 5 cubed
because it is the number of
small cubes in a $5 \times 5 \times 5$ cube.

- ■ **5^2 or '5 to the power of 2' is also called '5 squared'.
  25 is called a square number because $25 = 5^2$ (5 squared).
  5 is called the square root of 25.**

- ■ **5^3 or '5 to the power of 3' is also called '5 cubed'.
  125 is called a cube number because $125 = 5^3$ (5 cubed).
  5 is called the cube root of 125.**

Example 10

Work out 6 cubed.

6 cubed is $6^3 = 6 \times 6 \times 6 = 216$.

Example 11

What is the square root of 9?

$9 = 3 \times 3 = 3^2$.

3 is the square root of 9.

Exercise 4L

1 Work out:
   (a) 2 squared   (b) 3 cubed   (c) 5 squared
   (d) 2 cubed   (e) 4 cubed   (f) 10 squared
   (g) 10 cubed   (h) 7 squared (i) 8 squared
   (j) 100 squared (k) 0 squared (l) 1 cubed

2 Which is larger:
   (a) 2 cubed or 3 squared   (b) 100 squared or 10 cubed
   (c) 4 cubed or 8 squared   (d) 6 cubed or 9 squared?

3 What is the:
   (a) square root of 36   (b) square root of 16
   (c) cube root of 8   (d) cube root of 27
   (e) square root of 49   (f) cube root of 64
   (g) square root of 100   (h) square root of 81
   (i) square root of 64
   (j) cube root of 1000
   (k) cube root of 1
   (l) square root of 1

4 John picked a number from each cloud. He found that the squares of the first two numbers added up to the square of the third number.

   (a) Find three other numbers that do the same.
   (b) How many ways can you do this?

5 Which numbers up to 20 can be written as the sum or difference of two square numbers?

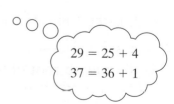

$$13 = 9 + 4$$
$$15 = 16 - 1$$

6 Which primes less than 50 can be written as the sum of two square numbers?

$$29 = 25 + 4$$
$$37 = 36 + 1$$

Using powers to write large numbers

Astronomers have to deal with very large distances.

You can use powers to write down the distances to the stars in a shorter form:

$$\text{distance to the Sun} = 95\,000\,000$$
$$= 95 \times 1\,000\,000$$
$$= 95 \times 10^6 \text{ miles}$$

$$\text{distance to Proxima Centauri} = 25\,000\,000\,000\,000$$
$$= 25 \times 10^{12} \text{ miles}$$

$$\text{distance to the edge of the Universe} = 83\,000\,000\,000\,000\,000\,000\,000\,000$$
$$= 83 \times 10^{21} \text{ miles}$$

Example 12
Write 57×10^7 in full.

10^7 will have seven zeros
so $57 \times 10^7 = 57 \times 10\,000\,000$
so $57 \times 10^7 = 570\,000\,000$

Example 13
Write in a shorter form $23 \times 10^5 \times 10^3$

$10^5 \times 10^3 = 100\,000 \ \times 1000$
$ = 100\,000\,000$
$ = 10^8$
$23 \times 10^5 \times 10^3 = 23 \times 10^8$

Exercise 4M

1   Use powers of ten to write these numbers in a shorter form:
   (a) $43\,000\,000$ (b) $28\,000\,000\,000$ (c) $3\,400\,000$
   (d) $1\,800\,000\,000$ (e) $530\,000\,000$ (f) $104\,000\,000$
   (g) $80\,600\,000$ (h) $7\,030\,000\,000$

2   Write in full:
   (a) 23×10^6 (b) 49×10^3 (c) 5×10^7 (d) 76×10^5
   (e) 204×10^7 (f) 8×10^8 (g) 537×10^4 (h) 743×10^9

3   Write in a shorter form:
   (a) $4 \times 10^3 \times 10^4$ (b) $34 \times 10^4 \times 10^5$ (c) $6 \times 10^6 \times 10^3$
   (d) $27 \times 10^5 \times 10^3$ (e) $25 \times 10^7 \times 10^2$ (f) $8 \times 10^8 \times 10^3$
   (g) $457 \times 10^3 \times 10^4$ (h) $753 \times 10^9 \times 10^3$

4.8 Using inverse operations to check solutions

You will need a calculator for this section.
In section 6 the idea of rounding to 1 significant figure was
used to check calculations done on calculators.
Another way is by the use of inverse operations.

Suppose you wish to do a calculation such as:

$$984 \times 67$$

It is very easy to press a wrong key and get an answer
which is approximately right but not exactly correct.
For example by rounding to 1 s.f. you get

$$1\,000 \times 70 \cong 70\,000$$

If you entered the digits of the last number in reverse
order on your calculator you would get:

$$984 \times 76 = 74\,784$$

The answer is
approximately right
but not exactly
correct.

The correct answer is:

$$984 \times 67 = 65\,928$$

You can think of the calculation as a number machine:

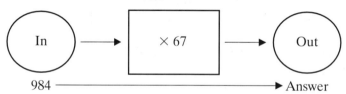

984 ——————————————————→ Answer

Think of the inverse number machine:

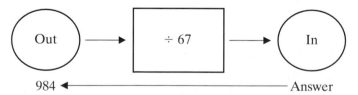

984 ←—————————————————— Answer

So to check if your answer is correct you do:
Answer $\div 67 =$ and you should get back to 984.

■ **To check if a calculation such as   984 × 67 = Answer**
is correct you do: Answer ÷ 67 =
If you get back to 984 your answer is probably correct.
If you do not then your answer is probably wrong and
you should do the calculation again.
This is called checking by use of inverse operations.

Example 14

Julie worked out 592×72 using a calculator.
She got the answer $43\,216$
Check her answer by the method of inverse operations.
$43\,216 \div 72 = 600.222$ so her answer is wrong.

Example 15

Ann worked out $15\,904 \div 28$ using a calculator.
She got the answer 568
Check her answer by the method of inverse operations.
$568 \times 28 = 15\,904$
so her answer is correct.

Exercise 4N

1   Use the method of inverse operations to check which
   of the following calculations are correct:
   (a) $36 \times 48 = 1\,728$ **(b)** $293 \times 75 = 21\,945$
   (c) $128 \times 436 = 55\,308$ **(d)** $397 \times 58 = 23\,026$
   (e) $4\,386 \times 48 = 210\,528$ **(f)** $25\,286 \times 439 = 11\,100\,554$

2   Use the method of inverse operations to check which
   of the following calculations are correct:
   (a) $46\,455 \div 57 = 815$ **(b)** $8\,896 \div 64 = 139$
   (c) $29\,687 \div 329 = 82$ **(d)** $9\,198 \div 219 = 42$
   (e) $247\,536 \div 764 = 324$ **(f)** $766\,445 \div 635 = 1237$

3   Use the method of inverse operations to work out the
   missing numbers in the following calculations:
   (a) $\ldots\ldots \times 63 = 3\,024$ **(b)** $\ldots\ldots \div 84 = 64$
   (c) $\ldots\ldots \times 497 = 325\,038$ **(d)** $\ldots\ldots \div 678 = 14$
   (e) $\ldots\ldots \div 531 = 169$ **(f)** $\ldots\ldots \times 568 = 532\,216$

Summary of key points

1   Numbers that are multiples of two separate
   numbers are called common multiples.

12 and 24 are both
common multiples of
3 and 4.

2 The lowest common multiple of two numbers is the lowest number that is a multiple of them both. Lowest common multiple is sometimes written as LCM.

The lowest common multiple of 3 and 4 is 12.

3 Numbers that are factors of two separate numbers are called common factors.

1, 2, 3 and 6 are common factors of 18 and 24.

4 The highest common factor of two numbers is the highest number that is a factor of them both. Highest common factor is sometimes written as HCF.

The highest common factor of 18 and 24 is 6.

5 A prime number is a whole number with exactly two factors: itself and 1.
1 is not a prime number, it has only one factor.

Prime numbers are sometimes just called **primes**.

6 Any number can be written as a product of its prime factors.

$12 = 2 \times 2 \times 3$
$150 = 2 \times 3 \times 5 \times 5$

7 To multiply a whole number by 10 move each digit one column to the left, then put 0 in the units column.

8 To multiply a whole number by 100 move each digit two columns to the left, then put 0 in the tens and units columns.

9 To multiply a whole number by 1000 move each digit three columns to the left, then put 0 in the hundreds, tens and units columns.

10 To divide a whole number by 10 move each digit one column to the right.

11 To divide a whole number by 100 move each digit two columns to the right.

12 To divide a whole number by 1000 move each digit three columns to the right.

13 To multiply by 70, first multiply by 7 then multiply your answer by 10.
To multiply by 700, first multiply by 7 then multiply your answer by 100.

14 The first significant figure of a whole number is the digit (or figure) on the left of the number.

15 The first significant figure in   62 is 6
The first significant figure in   364 is 3
The first significant figure in   2 541 is 2

16   62 rounded to 1 significant figure is   60
364 rounded to 1 significant figure is   400
2 541 rounded to 1 significant figure is 3 000

17 1 s.f. means to one significant figure.

18 5^4 means $5 \times 5 \times 5 \times 5$. The number 4 is called the power or index.

19 5^2 or '5 to the power of 2' is also called '5 squared'.
25 is called a square number because $25 = 5^2$
(5 squared).
5 is called the square root of 25.

20 5^3 or '5 to the power of 3' is also called '5 cubed'.
125 is called a cube number because $125 = 5^3$
(5 cubed).
5 is called the cube root of 125.

21 To check if a calculation such as $984 \times 67 = $ Answer
is correct you do: Answer $\div 67 =$
If you get back to 984 your answer is probably correct.
If you do not then your answer is probably wrong and you should do the calculation again.
This is called checking by use of inverse operations.

5 Averages

Deenita is of average height.

A centre forward averages a goal a game.

Teenagers in Britain spend an average of £8 a month on CDs.

The word average means that something is typical, or describes something that typically happens.

5.1 Some revision

- **There are three different types of average:**
  - **the mean**
  - **the mode**
  - **the median**

You will need to know how to work out these different averages.

The mean

- **The mean of a set of data is the sum of all the values divided by the number of values:**

$$\text{mean} = \frac{\text{sum of values}}{\text{number of values}}$$

Example 1

The number of goals Pat scored in ten games of water polo were:

   2   3   1   0   3   5   2   0   1   2

Work out the mean number of goals scored per match.

$$\text{Mean} = \frac{2+3+1+0+3+5+2+0+1+2}{10} = \frac{19}{10} = 1.9$$

The mean is often not a whole number.

The mode

■ **The mode of a set of data is the value which occurs most often. The mode is sometimes called the modal value.**

Remember:
- There can be more than one mode.
- Sometimes there is no mode.
- The mode does not have to be a number.

Example 2

Aaron owns twelve pairs of shoes. The colours of the shoes are:

   Black   Brown   Black   Blue   White   Black
   Brown   White   Silver   Grey   Black   Brown

Black is the colour which occurs the most often so the modal colour is black.

Example 3

The number of shots needed to score a basket for a group of pupils is shown in the bar chart.

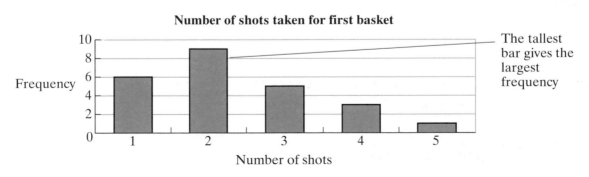

Number of shots taken for first basket

The tallest bar gives the largest frequency

Frequency

Number of shots

The mode is the value with the largest frequency.
The mode is 2 shots. ————————————————

Give the units or refer back to the problem to make sure the answer makes sense.

The median

■ **The median is the middle value when the data is arranged in order of size.**
When there is an even number of values the median is the average (mean) of the middle two values.

Example 4

During the week Natasha spends a different amount of money for her lunch each day.

Monday	Tuesday	Wednesday	Thursday	Friday
£1.25	£0.95	£1.40	£1.05	£1.65

What is the median amount she spent?

Arrange these in order:

  £0.95   £1.05   £1.25   £1.40   £1.65

The middle value is £1.25

The median amount Natasha spent on lunch is £1.25.

Example 5

The number of pupils in ten Year 9 tutor groups is shown in the table.

9L	9I	9G	9H	9T	9S	9O	9U	9N	9D
27	29	31	26	30	28	31	32	25	30

What is the median number of pupils in a group?

Arrange these in order.

  25   26   27   28   29   30   30   31   31   32

To find the median of an even number of values, add the 2 middle values and divide by 2.

There are two middle values so the median $= \dfrac{29 + 30}{2} = \dfrac{59}{2} = 29.5$

The median number of pupils in a form is 29.5.

The median does not have to be a whole number.

The range

■ **The range of a set of data is the difference between the highest and lowest values:**

range = largest value − smallest value

Example 6

The number of phone calls Jennie received during a week were:

Monday	Tuesday	Wednesday	Thursday	Friday	Saturday	Sunday
12	17	5	21	8	31	16

Calculate the range.

The largest value is 31. The smallest value is 5.

The range $-31 - 5 = 26$ calls.

Example 7

In a local football league Mostyn Rangers have the highest goal difference of +25 goals and Kidder Harriers have the lowest of −31 goals.
Work out the range.

The range = largest value − smallest value = $+25 - -31 = 56$ goals.

Exercise 5A

1   Calculate for each set of data:

  (i) the mode
  (ii) the median
  (iii) the mean
  (iv) the range

  (a) 4, 2, 3, 4, 6, 4, 3, 6, 7, 2, 4
  (b) £12, £18, £20, £10, £20
  (c) 2.4, 3.6, 1.3, 3.7, 2.4, 1.6, 0.9, 3.1, 2.4, 2.0, 3.6

2 The number of times Philip's computer crashes per month is shown in the table.

Jan	23	Jly	43
Feb	34	Aug	51
Mar	17	Sep	30
Apr	36	Oct	23
May	18	Nov	32
Jun	23	Dec	42

Calculate:

(a) the mode   **(b)** the median   **(c)** the mean   **(d)** the range.

3 Dave spins a six-sided spinner 20 times. His scores are:

1 2 1 4 3 5 6 3 2 6
2 4 3 5 3 2 3 6 4 3

Calculate:

(a) the mean   **(b)** the median   **(c)** the mode   **(d)** the range.

4 The number of guests staying at the Bay View Guest House is shown in the graph.

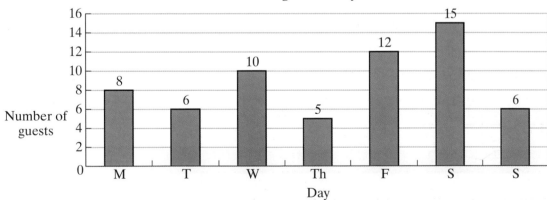

Number of guests at Bay View

(a) Copy and complete the table:

Day	M	T	W	Th	F	Sa	Su
Number of guests							

(b) Using the data, calculate:

(i) the mode   **(ii)** the median   **(iii)** the mean   **(iv)** the range.

5 The smallest shoe size in a class is size 5. The range is 9. Work out the size of the largest shoe in the class.

6 During a round of golf the worst score is 8 above par (+8) and the best score is 6 below par (−6). Work out the range for the scores.

5.2 Finding the mean from a frequency table

You can use a frequency table to work out the mean.

Example 8

The table shows the number of bedrooms in the houses in a street.

Number of bedrooms	Frequency
1	2
2	9
3	23
4	15
5	1

> This means 23 houses each have 3 bedrooms. Because it is the largest frequency we know the mode is 3 bedrooms.

$$\text{Mean} = \frac{\text{total number of bedrooms}}{\text{total number of houses}}$$

Extend the table to find the total number of bedrooms.

Add a new column.

Number of bedrooms	Frequency	Number of bedrooms × frequency
1	2	$1 \times 2 = 2$
2	9	$2 \times 9 = 18$
3	23	$3 \times 23 = 69$
4	15	$4 \times 15 = 60$
5	1	$5 \times 1 = 5$
Total	50	154

The total number of houses is 50.

Total number of bedrooms is 154.

$$\text{Mean} = \frac{\text{total number of bedrooms}}{\text{total frequency}} = \frac{154}{50}$$

Mean $= 3.08$

The mean number of bedrooms per house is 3.08

■ **When using a frequency table:**

$$\text{mean} = \frac{\text{total of (each value} \times \text{frequency)}}{\text{total frequency}}$$

Exercise 5B

1 The frequency table shows the number of attempts needed to dial-up an internet connection.

Number of attempts	Frequency
1	20
2	15
3	6
4	5
5	4

(a) What is the modal number of attempts needed to get through to the internet?
(b) Copy the table and add an extra column to calculate the mean number of attempts needed to get through to the internet.

2 The table shows the number of call-outs a week made by an in-shore lifeboat during the season.

(a) What is the modal number of call-outs a week the in-shore lifeboat makes?
(b) Copy the table and add an extra column to calculate the mean number of call-outs a week the inshore lifeboat makes.

Number of callouts	Frequency
0	5
1	4
2	5
3	2
4	4
5	2
6	1
7	3
8	1

3 A golfer records the number of shots she takes for two rounds of golf (36 holes).

Number of shots	Frequency
2	2
3	5
4	10
5	11
6	8

(a) What is the mode of the number of shots she takes?
(b) Copy the table and add an extra column to calculate the mean of the number of shots she takes.

4 Sibfain kept a record of the number of phone calls he answered an hour. The frequency table shows his results for one week.

Number of calls	Frequency
0	2
1	4
2	5
3	6
4	8
5	5
6	2
7	1
8	1

(a) Calculate the mean number of calls he answered per hour.
(b) State the modal number of calls he answered per hour.

5 The frequency table shows the number of packets of crisps eaten by each pupil during one week at school.

Number of packets of crisps	Frequency
0	31
1	53
2	59
3	98
4	120
5	66
6	31
7	28
8	14

(a) Calculate the mean number of packets of crisps eaten by each pupil.

(b) State the modal number of packets of crisps by each pupil.

5.3 Finding the median from a frequency table

Sometimes you need to find the median from a frequency table.

Example 9

The number of eggs in 25 birds' nests was counted and recorded in this table.

Number of eggs	Frequency
0	1
1	2
2	5
3	7
4	5
5	3
6	2

To find the median add a cumulative frequency column to the table.

■ **The cumulative frequency is the running total of all the frequencies so far.**

Number of eggs	Frequency	Cumulative frequency
0	1	1
1	2	$2 + 1 = 3$
2	5	$5 + 3 = 8$
3	7	$7 + 8 = 15$
4	5	$5 + 15 = 20$
5	3	$3 + 20 = 23$
6	2	$2 + 23 = 25$

There are 25 values in total

The median is the middle value.

To find the middle value add 1 to the total number of values then divide the result by 2.

$$\frac{25 + 1}{2} = \frac{26}{2} = 13$$

The median is the 13th value.

Number of eggs	Frequency	Cumulative frequency
0	1	1
1	2	3
2	5	8
3	7	15
4	5	20
5	3	23
6	2	25

The first 8 values are all 2 or less.

The 9th to the 15th values are all 3.

The median is 3 eggs.

■ **The median is the value halfway along the cumulative frequency.**

Example 10

Rhys records the shoe size for 50 children. He ignores half sizes. His results are shown in the table below.

Shoe size	Frequency
4	6
5	8
6	11
7	12
8	9
9	4

Find the median of this data.

Redraw the table with the cumulative frequency column.

Shoe size	Frequency	Cumulative frequency	
4	6	6	
5	8	14	
6	11	25	—— 25th value is 6.
7	12	37	—— 26th value is 7.
8	9	46	
9	4	50	

$$\text{The median value} = \frac{\text{total number of values} + 1}{2}$$

$$= \frac{50 + 1}{2}$$

$$= 25\tfrac{1}{2}\text{th value}$$

To find the $25\tfrac{1}{2}$th value you have to add the 25th and the 26th values and divide by 2.

$$\frac{6 + 7}{2} = 6\tfrac{1}{2}$$

So the median shoe size is $6\tfrac{1}{2}$.

Exercise 5C

1 The table below shows the fines collected by a library, for late returns of books, in a week.

Fine	20p	40p	60p	80p	100p	120p
Frequency	20	18	10	6	4	2

(a) Work out the median value.
(b) State the mode.
(c) Work out the mean.

2 The table below shows the number of pictures spoilt when developing a film.

Number spoilt	0	1	2	3	4
Frequency	18	12	9	6	3

(a) Work out the median. (b) State the mode.
(c) Work out the mean. (d) State the range.

3 The number of bookings made on each Saturday during the football season is shown in the table below.

Bookings	0	1	2	3	4	5
Frequency	12	23	32	22	10	1

(a) Work out the median. (b) State the mode.
(c) Work out the mean. (d) State the range.

4 The table below shows the number of days absent per pupil for two forms.

Frequency for Form 9A	Number of absences	Frequency for Form 9B
16	0	15
8	1	3
3	2	1
0	3	5
1	4	0
2	5	4

(a) For each form work out:
    (i) the median   **(ii)** the mean
    (iii) the mode   **(iv)** the range
(b) Which form do you think has the best attendance?
    Give your reasons.

5.4 Using stem and leaf diagrams to find the median

Frequency tables are very useful when your data is in separate groups. If you have a lot of different data values it is usually more useful to draw a **stem and leaf diagram**.

Example 11

The number of customers at an all-night petrol station are recorded each hour for 24 hours. The results are:

    18, 21, 5, 33, 35, 49, 37, 7, 12, 29, 24, 19, 41, 43, 38, 23, 48, 12, 31, 16, 31, 20, 39, 31

(a) Represent this data on a stem and leaf diagram.
(b) Use your stem and leaf diagram to find the median and mode.

(a) You can record this data in groups called **stems**. The values from 10–19 all have stem 1 because they start with the digit 1.

The stems for this data are:

    0
    1
    2
    3
    4

You can add the data one at a time. You record 18 like this:

    0
    1 | 8
    2
    3
    4

This is the complete stem and leaf diagram:

```
0 | 5 7
1 | 8 2 9 2 6
2 | 1 9 4 3 0
3 | 3 5 7 8 1 1 9 1
4 | 9 1 3 8
```

For the value 7, the stem is 0 and the leaf is 7.

Stem = 10 customers

This shows you that to read values off the diagram you have to multiply the stem by 10 and add the leaf.

You should always write the leaves in order of size on your finished stem and leaf diagram:

```
0 | 5 7
1 | 2 2 6 8 9
2 | 0 1 3 4 9
3 | 1 1 1 3 5 7 8 9
4 | 1 3 8 9
```

Stem = 10 customers

It is easiest to record your values in the order they are given, then rewrite your diagram like this.

(b) There are 24 values in the data set. The median will be half way between the 12th and 13th values.

```
0 | 5 7
1 | 2 2 6 8 9
2 | 0 1 3 4 9
3 | 1 1 1 3 5 7 8 9
4 | 1 3 8 9
```

The 12th value is 29.

The 13th value is 31.

$$\text{median} = \frac{29 + 31}{2} = 30$$

You can see from the stem and leaf diagram that the mode is 31.

Exercise 5D

1 The scores for an American football team are shown in this stem and leaf diagram.

(a) Work out the median.
(b) State the mode.

```
0 | 5 6 6 9
1 | 2 2 3 5 6 8 9
2 | 0 0 3 4 7 7 8 8 9
3 | 1 2 2 3 3 4 4 4
4 | 0 2 4 6
```

Stem = 10 points

Hint: count the number of values first.

2 Katie recorded the length of time she spent on her homework each day for 20 days:

> 1 h 25 min, 2 h 35 min, 3 h 10 min, 4 h 20 min,
> 1 h 15 min, 30 min, 3 h 20 min, 2 h 10 min,
> 1 h 35 min, 2 h 10 min, 55 min, 2 h 10 min,
> 1 h 40 min, 2 h 0 min, 1 h 20 min, 1 h 40 min,
> 3 h 50 min, 2 h 20 min, 1 h 50 min, 2 h 15 min

(a) Show this data on a stem and leaf diagram.

(b) Work out the median and the mode for the data.

3 The graph shows the mathematics test results for a class.

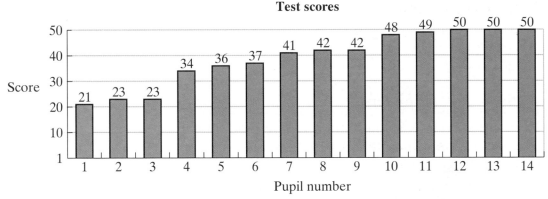

(a) Draw a stem and leaf diagram to show this data.

(b) Work out the median and mode.

(c) Say which of the two averages is not representative of the data and explain your answer.

(d) State what you think the maximum mark available for the test was?

Summary of key points

1 There are three different types of average:
- the mean
- the mode
- the median

2 The mean of a set of data is the sum of all the values divided by the number of values:

$$\text{mean} = \frac{\text{sum of valucs}}{\text{number of values}}$$

3 The mode of a set of data is the value which occurs most often.

4 The median is the middle value when the data is arranged in order of size.
When there is an even number of values the median is the average (mcan) of the middle two values.

5 The range of a set of data is the difference between the highest and lowest values:

range = largest value − smallest value

6 When using a frequency table:

$$\text{mean} = \frac{\text{total of (each value} \times \text{frequency)}}{\text{total frequency}}$$

7 The cumulative frequency is the running total of all the frequencies so far.

8 The median is the value halfway along the cumulative frequency.

6 Graphs

6.1 Coordinates

The map shows the plan of a motor racing circuit.

The lookout tower is in the middle.

You can describe the position of other objects and places on the circuit using coordinates.

Remember:
Always go across first

⟷

The coordinates of the TV camera are (−9, 8). From the lookout tower go across to −9 and up to 8.

This is the *x*-coordinate

(−9, 2)

This is the *y*-coordinate

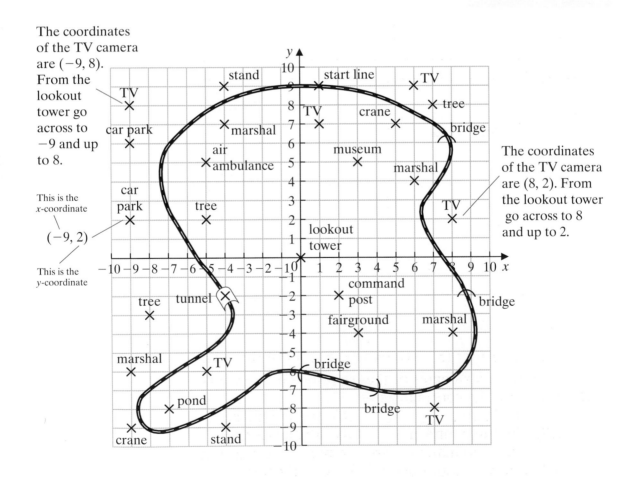

The coordinates of the TV camera are (8, 2). From the lookout tower go across to 8 and up to 2.

Exercise 6A

1 Look at the plan of the racing circuit.
What is at:

(**a**) $(-4, 9)$ (**b**) $(7, 8)$ (**c**) $(-9, -9)$
(**d**) $(-4, -2)$ (**e**) $(0, 0)$ (**f**) $(-9, 2)$
(**g**) $(-7, -8)$ (**h**) $(2, -2)$?

2 What are the coordinates of:

(**a**) the fairground   (**b**) the air ambulance
(**c**) the start line   (**d**) the museum
(**e**) the six TV cameras   (**f**) the four marshals
(**g**) the four bridges   (**h**) the three trees?

3 The diagram is an enlargement of the racing circuit
showing the start position of each car.

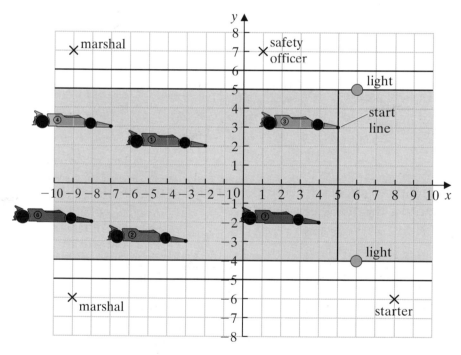

Car number 3 is at $(5, 3)$ (look at the front of the car).

(**a**) Give the coordinates of the front of the other cars.
(**b**) What are the coordinates of:

    (**i**)   the lights   (**ii**) the marshals
    (**iii**) the safety officer   (**iv**) the starter?

(**c**) Give the coordinates of three points on the start line.
What do you notice about the x-coordinates of
your points?

4 The grid shows a go-kart track.
To get from start to finish a possible route begins:
$(-4, 5)$ to $(3, 5)$ to $(7, 7)$ to $(10, 5)$

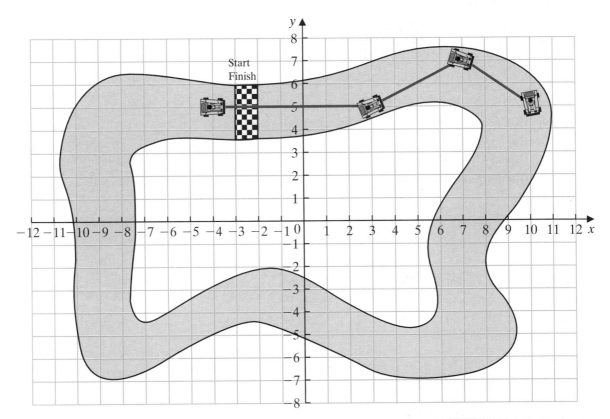

Write down a sequence of moves for the go-kart
to complete a circuit of the track. The go-kart
mustn't touch the sides of the track.

Race game
In pairs, write down a
sequence of moves to
take your go-kart
round the track.
Whoever uses the least
number of moves is the
winner.

5 Draw a coordinate grid from -8 to 8 on both axes.
Plot these sets of points and join them up in order:
   (a) $(8, 5)$ $(8, 8)$ $(2, 8)$ $(2, 5)$ $(8, 5)$
   (b) $(-8, 3)$ $(-6, 8)$ $(-4, 5)$ $(-8, 3)$
   (c) $(1, 6)$ $(1, -1)$ $(-2, -1)$ $(-2, 6)$ $(1, 6)$
   (d) $(-6, -2)$ $(-8, -6)$ $(-5, -6)$ $(-3, -2)$ $(-6, -2)$
   (e) $(3, -7)$ $(5, -7)$ $(5, -5)$ $(7, -5)$ $(7, -3)$ $(5, -3)$
       $(5, -1)$ $(3, -1)$ $(3, -3)$ $(1, -3)$ $(1, -5)$ $(3, -5)$
       $(3, -7)$
Name as many of the shapes as you can.

Using fractions in coordinates **97**

6   Draw a coordinate grid from −8 to 8 on both axes. The
grid is to show the layout of an exhibition.
Mark points with a '×' and label with the correct code
from the key.

(a) fire exits at: $(6, 8)$, $(8, -5)$, $(-8, -7)$ and $(-8, 7)$

(b) security posts at: $(2, 3)$ and $(-4, -6)$

(c) cloakrooms at: $(6, 2)$, $(-6, -2)$ and $(-6, 5)$

(d) children's play area at: $(2, -1)$

(e) ticket office at: $(0, 4)$

(f) entrances at: $(0, -7)$, $(8, -2)$, $(-8, 1)$ and $(-8, -2)$

(g) food stalls at: $(4, 4)$, $(3, -4)$ and $(-4, 3)$

(h) lost and found at: $(7, -6)$

(i) stalls at: $(-4, 7)$, $(-6, 3)$, $(-5, -3)$, $(1, -5)$, $(5, -1)$, $(3, 5)$ and $(0, 7)$

Key:		
FE	–	fire exit
SP	–	security
PA	–	children's play area
TO	–	ticket office
E	–	entrance
C	–	cloakroom
FS	–	food stall
LF	–	lost and found
S	–	stall

6.2 Using fractions in coordinates

Sometimes positions do not have whole-number
coordinates.

The coordinate grid shows the layout of a group of five
villages.

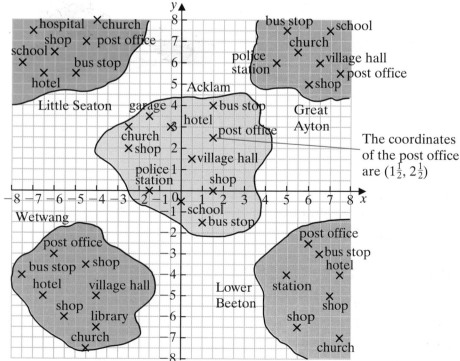

The coordinates of the post office are $(1\frac{1}{2}, 2\frac{1}{2})$

The *x*-coordinate of the post office at Acklam is halfway between 1 and 2. It has *x*-coordinate $1\frac{1}{2}$.

The *y*-coordinate of the post office at Acklam is halfway between 2 and 3. It has *y*-coordinate $2\frac{1}{2}$.

Exercise 6B

1 For each village give the coordinates of:
   (a) church (5 answers)
   (b) bus stop (6 answers)
   (c) shop (8 answers).

2 Write down the coordinates of:
   (a) the school in Great Ayton
   (b) the hotel in Lower Beeton
   (c) the station in Lower Beeton
   (d) the library in Wetwang
   (e) the hotel in Little Seaton
   (f) the police station in Acklam.

3 What can be found at:
   (a) $(4\frac{1}{2}, 6)$
   (b) $(-4, -5)$
   (c) $(\frac{1}{2}, 1\frac{1}{2})$
   (d) $(7\frac{1}{2}, -4)$
   (e) $(0, -\frac{1}{2})$
   (f) $(-7\frac{1}{2}, 6)$
   (g) $(-6\frac{1}{2}, -5)$
   (h) $(-1\frac{1}{2}, 0)$
   (i) $(-1\frac{1}{2}, 3\frac{1}{2})$?

6.3 Lines on graphs

You can describe straight lines on a graph using equations.

The equation of a line tells you which points can be on the line.

The coordinate grid shows a dancing team at the start of their dance routine.

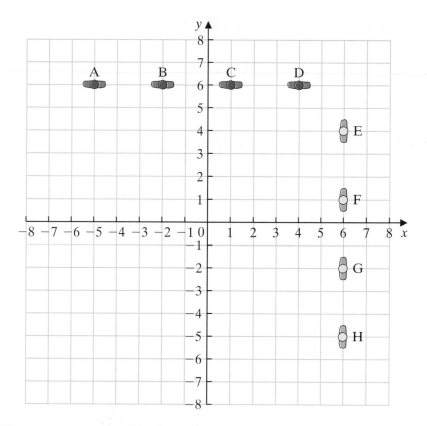

The men are standing in a line.

The coordinates of the men are:

$(-5, 6)$ $(-2, 6)$ $(1, 6)$ $(4, 6)$

The y-coordinates are all 6.

The equation of the line is $y = 6$. Any points on this line must have a y-coordinate of 6.

The women are also standing in a line.

The coordinates of the women are:

$(6, 4)$ $(6, 1)$ $(6, -2)$ $(6, -5)$

The x-coordinate of each point is 6.

The equation of the line is $x = 6$.

■ **You can use an equation to describe a straight line.**

■ **Vertical lines all have equation $x = \boxed{}$**

■ **Horizontal lines all have equation $y = \boxed{}$.**

Remember:
——— horizontal
| vertical

Exercise 6C

1   At the end of the
    routine the dancers
    are in these positions.
    Find the equations
    of the lines joining
    these points.
    (*Hint*: write down the
    coordinates of each
    point first.)

    (a) B and C
    (b) A and E
    (c) B and H
    (d) C and F
    (e) H and F
    (f) D and G
    (g) A and D
    (h) E and G.

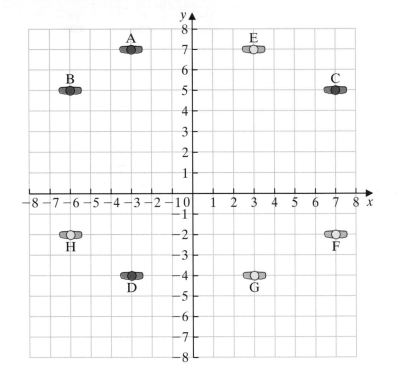

2   Write down the equations of the lines on this grid:

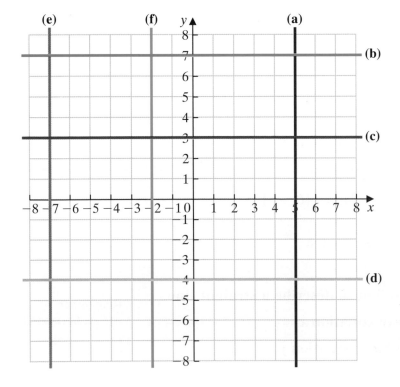

3 The cheerleaders for the Cleveland Bombers Ice Hockey Team plan their routines very carefully. Part way through a routine they are in these positions:

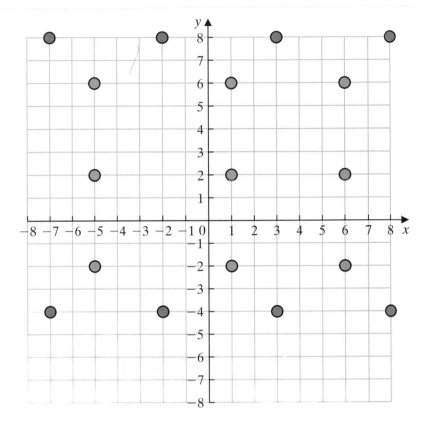

(a) Name 2 horizontal red lines.
(b) Name 3 vertical blue lines.
(c) Name 3 horizontal blue lines.
(d) Name 4 vertical red lines.

4 Look carefully at these sets of coordinates. Write down the equations of the lines joining these points:

(a) $(-4, 3) (2, 3) (6, 3)$
(b) $(5, -4) (5, -2) (5, 6)$
(c) $(-1, -6) (-1, -2) (-1, 4)$
(d) $(-3, -4) (4, -4) (7, -4)$
(e) $(-6, 0) (2, 0) (5, 0)$
(f) $(\frac{1}{2}, \frac{1}{2}) (\frac{1}{2}, 2) (\frac{1}{2}, 3)$
(g) $(-4, -1\frac{1}{2}) (1, -1\frac{1}{2}) (7, -1\frac{1}{2})$
(h) $(0, \frac{1}{2}) (0, 1) (0, 2)$
(i) $(-1, 6) (0, 6) (1, 6)$
(j) $(0, -\frac{1}{2}) (1, -\frac{1}{2}) (2, -\frac{1}{2})$

5 This hut has been drawn using straight lines.
Give the equation of each line in the drawing.

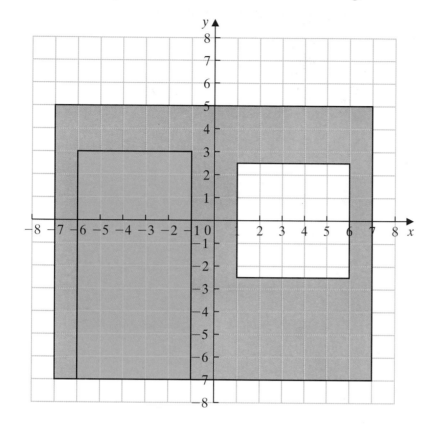

6 Draw a coordinate grid and label each axis from −8 to 8.
Draw and label these lines on your grid:

(a) $x = 4$ (b) $y = -1$ (c) $y = 4$ (d) $x = 6$
(e) $y = 8$ (f) $x = -5$ (g) $y = 0$ (h) $x = 3$

6.4 Equations of sloping lines

When a line on a graph is sloping you can find its equation
by finding the rule that links the coordinates of the points.

The points A, B, C, D and E on the diagram make a
straight line.
Look at the coordinates:

$$(-7, -3) \qquad (-5, -1) \qquad (-2, 2) \qquad (0, 4) \qquad (3, 7)$$

$+4 \qquad\qquad +4 \qquad\qquad +4 \qquad\qquad +4 \qquad\qquad +4$

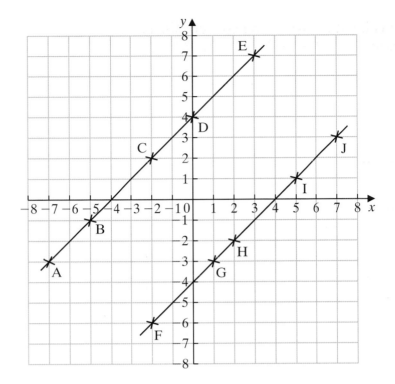

The rule to find the y-coordinate is add 4 to the x-coordinate.

The equation of the line is $y = x + 4$.

Example 1

The points F, G, H, I and J are on a straight line. Find the equation of the line.

Write down the coordinates of the points on the line:

$$(-2, -6) \qquad (1, -3) \qquad (2, -2) \qquad (5, 1) \qquad (7, 3)$$
$$\underset{-4}{} \qquad \underset{-4}{} \qquad \underset{-4}{} \qquad \underset{-4}{} \qquad \underset{-4}{}$$

The rule to find the y-coordinate is 'subtract 4 from the x-coordinate'.

The equation of the line is $y = x - 4$.

■ **To find the equation of a sloping line find a rule connecting the x-coordinate and the y-coordinate.**

For example $y = x + 3$
$ y = x - 7$

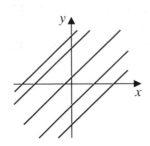

Exercise 6D

1 Find the equation of each line on the diagram.

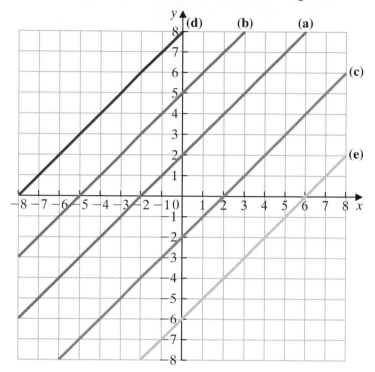

2 For each of these lines:

   (i) Write down the coordinates of four points on the line.

   (ii) Find a rule connecting the *x*-coordinate and the *y*-coordinate.

   (iii) Write down the equation of the line.

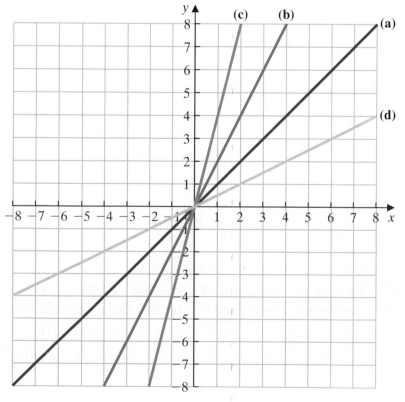

6.5 Drawing sloping lines

You can draw sloping lines from a table of values.

Example 2

Draw the line with equation $y = 3x - 2$.

Choose a set of values for x:

$$-4, \quad -3, \quad -2, \quad -1, \quad 0, \quad 1, \quad 2, \quad 3, \quad 4$$

Show them in a table:

x	y
-4	
-3	
-2	
-1	
0	
1	
2	
3	
4	

Work out $y = 3x - 2$ for each value of x.

For example, for $x = -4$

$$y = 3 \times -4 - 2$$
$$= -12 - 2$$
$$= -14$$

Remember:
    BIDMAS
You always
$\left. \begin{array}{c} \times \\ \div \end{array} \right\}$ before $\left\{ \begin{array}{c} + \\ - \end{array} \right.$

Complete the table:

x	-4	-3	-2	-1	0	1	2	3	4
y	-14	-11	-8	-5	-2	1	4	7	10

The coordinate of the points on the line are:

$$(-4, -14), (-3, -11), (-2, -8), (-1, -5), (0, -2), (1, 1), (2, 4), (3, 7), (4, 10)$$

You must draw and label your axes so that they can contain all the coordinates from the table.

For this line you need:

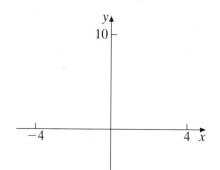

Plot the points.
Draw and label the line:

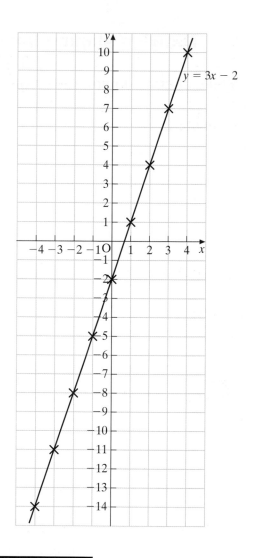

$y = 3x - 2$

Exercise 6E

1 For each equation:
  - copy and complete the table of values.
  - plot the points on a coordinate grid
  - draw and label the line.

(a) $y = x + 5$

x	−4	−3	−2	−1	0	1	2	3	4
y		2						8	

(b) $y = x - 4$

x	−4	−3	−2	−1	0	1	2	3	4
y		−7							0

(c) $y = 2x + 5$

x	−4	−3	−2	−1	0	1	2	3	4
y		1					9		

(d) $y = 3x - 4$

x	−4	−3	−2	−1	0	1	2	3	4
y									

(e) $y = 5x + 2$

x	-4	-3	-2	-1	0	1	2	3	4
y									

(f) $y = 2x - 5$

x	-4	-3	-2	-1	0	1	2	3	4
y									

(g) $y = 4 - x$

x	-4	-3	-2	-1	0	1	2	3	4
y									

(h) $y = 3 - 2x$

x	-4	-3	-2	-1	0	1	2	3	4
y									

6.6 Information graphs

Graphs can be used to show information about real-life events.

This graph shows the Brown family's journey from their home to Aunty Margaret's house.
The graph is made up of 5 straight lines.
Each line tells the story of part of the journey

The vertical axis gives information about distance. Each square stands for 5 miles.

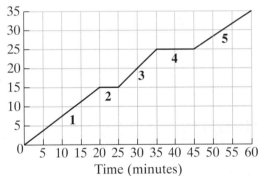

Distance from home (miles)

Time (minutes)

The horizontal axis gives information about time. Each square stands for 5 minutes.

■ **On information graphs always look to see what information each axis gives and what one square represents.**

■ **This graph shows the relationship between distance travelled and time taken. It is called a distance-time graph.**

On the graph:

Section **1** 15 miles are covered in 20 minutes.
The line is straight so the car travelled
at a constant speed.

Section **2** A horizontal line means no distance
is covered – the car has stopped.
Mrs Brown is putting petrol in the car.

Section **3** The Browns travel 10 miles in
10 minutes.

Section **4** They've stopped again – a puncture.
It took 10 minutes to fix.

Section **5** They do the final 10 miles in 15 minutes.

Example 3

Look at the Browns' distance-time graph.

(a) How far does Aunty Margaret live from the Browns?
(b) How long did it take them to get there?
(c) How long did they have for breaks, in total?
(d) Which part of the journey did they travel the fastest?

(a) The line starts at $(0,0)$ and finishes at $(60,35)$.
Aunty Margaret lives 35 miles away.

(b) The whole journey took 60 minutes.

(c) They had two breaks:
one of 5 minutes and one of 10 minutes.
So they had 15 minutes in breaks in total.

(d) The line with the steepest slope shows when they went
the fastest.

From the graph:

Section 3, from 25 to 35 minutes, was when they
travelled the fastest.

Exercise 6F

1 Look at this distance-time graph of a car journey.
Use it to answer these questions.

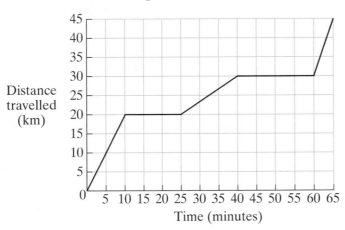

(a) What does each square stand for
- on the horizontal axis
- on the vertical axis?
(b) How many stages are there in the journey?
(c) How long did the car stop in total?
(d) How many minutes was the car moving in total?
(e) How long was the journey in kilometres?
(f) How long did the journey take?
(g) Which stage did the car travel fastest?
(h) Which stage did the car travel slowest?

2 This graph shows the flight of a hot air balloon.
Use it to answer these questions.

(a) What does each square stand for
- on the horizontal axis
- on the vertical axis?
(b) Describe what is happening to the balloon at each of the 8 stages of the journey.
(c) How long did the flight last?
(d) How high did the balloon get?
(e) During which stage did the balloon:
- rise most quickly
- fall most quickly?

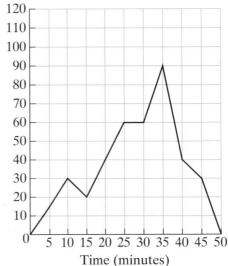

3 The graph shows the depth of water in Sanjay's bath.

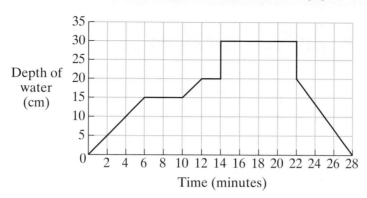

(a) When did Sanjay first turn the taps off?
(b) How deep was the water then?
(c) He turned the taps on again after 10 minutes. For how long?
(d) When did Sanjay get into the bath?
(e) How deep was the water once he was in the bath?
(f) How long did Sanjay stay in the bath?
(g) When did he take the plug out?
(h) How long did it take for the water to run out?

4 Draw your own bath graph and describe each stage of your bath.

5 The graph shows a rocket flight.

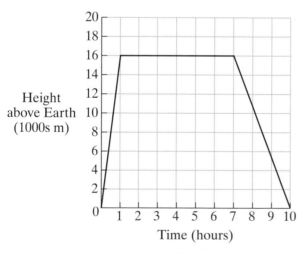

(a) What does each square represent horizontally?
(b) What does each square represent vertically?
(c) How high above the Earth did the rocket reach?
(d) At its maximum height the rocket orbited the Earth.
    For how many hours did it orbit the Earth?
(e) How long did the rocket take to come back down to Earth?
(f) Which was fastest: the rocket going up or the rocket coming down?

Summary of key points

1 You can use an equation to describe a straight line.

2 Vertical lines all have equation $x = \boxed{}$.

3 Horizontal lines all have equation $y = \boxed{}$.

4 To find the equation of a sloping line find a rule connecting the x-coordinate and the y-coordinate.

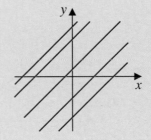

   For example $y = x + 3$
   $y = x - 7$

5 On information graphs you should always look to see what information each axis gives and what one square represents.

6 A distance-time graph shows the relationship between distance travelled and time taken.

7 Shape, space and measure

7.1 Points, lines and shapes

You can use capital letters to name points, lines and shapes.

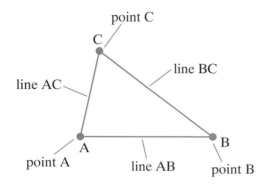

The whole shape is triangle ABC

Parallel lines
are lines which never meet.

Perpendicular lines
are lines which meet at right angles.

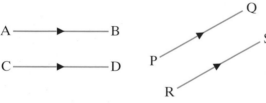

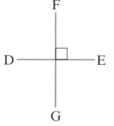

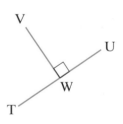

line AB and line CD
are parallel

line PQ and line RS
are parallel

line DE and line FG
are perpendicular

line TU and line VW
are perpendicular

Exercise 7A

1   Name all the points and lines on this quadrilateral.

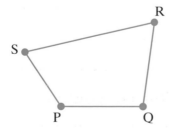

2 The diagram shows trapezium ABCD. Write down:

(a) a pair of parallel lines

(b) a pair of perpendicular lines.

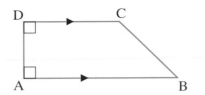

3 The diagram shows rhombus DEFG.

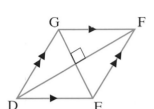

(a) Name four triangles.

(b) Write down the names of

  (i)   two diagonals

  (ii) two pairs of parallel lines

  (iii) a pair of perpendicular lines.

7.2 Solids and nets

Many everyday objects are made from mathematical shapes. The photograph shows an igloo sculpture.

You should be able to identify cubes, cuboids, pyramids and prisms.

You also need to know these solids:

	A prism with a circular cross section is called a **cylinder**.
	A pyramid with a circular base is called a **cone**.
	A ball shape is called a **sphere**.
	Half a sphere is called a **hemisphere**.

You can imagine 'opening out' any solid to make a flat shape.

This cube can be opened out ...

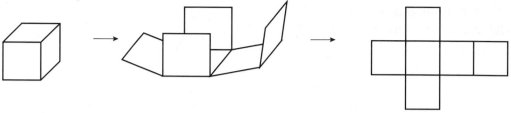

... to give this flat shape

■ **A shape that you can fold to make a solid is called a *net* of the solid.**

Exercise 7B

1 Write down the name of each of these solids.

(a) **(b)** **(c)**

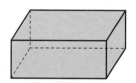 

2 Draw a triangular prism.
Show where hidden lines are with dotted lines.

3 Which of these is a net of a cube?

(a) **(b)** **(c)**

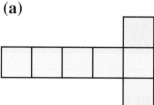 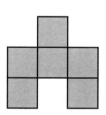 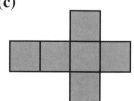

4 For each of these incomplete nets:
- complete the net
- write down the name of the solid.

(a) **(b)**

 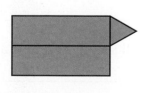

5 A cuboid is 4 cm long, 3 cm wide and 2 cm high.
Draw **two** different nets of the cuboid.

7.3 Tessellations

Equilateral triangles fit
together without any gaps
and without any overlap.
You say that shapes like this
tessellate and the patterns they
make are called **tessellations**.

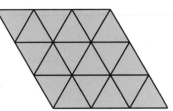

These words come
from *tessera*, the
Latin word for the
small tiles used to
make mosaic
patterns.

Isosceles triangles also
tessellate.

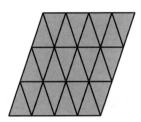

■   **Shapes tessellate if they fit together without any gaps
    and without any overlap. The patterns they make are
    called tessellations.**

■   *All* **triangles tessellate and** *all* **quadrilaterals
    tessellate.**

Not all shapes
tessellate. For
example, circles do
not tessellate.

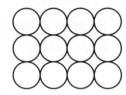

Example 1

Draw a diagram to show how this shape tessellates.

Fit the shape together
without any gaps:

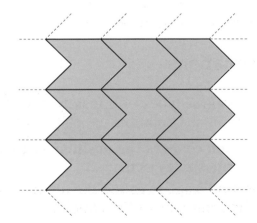

Exercise 7C

1   Draw a diagram to show how each of these shapes tessellates.

   (a)

   Rectangle

   (b)

   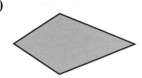
   Kite

   (c)

   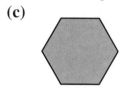
   Regular hexagon

2   This shape is made from three squares.
    On squared paper, draw a diagram to show how it
    tessellates.

3   This shape is made from four squares.
    On squared paper, draw a diagram to show how it
    tessellates.

4   Draw a diagram to show that regular pentagons do *not*
    tessellate.

5   **(a)** Draw a diagram to show that regular octagons do
        not tessellate.
    (b) What shape is needed to fill the gaps?

7.4 Transformations

This section covers three types of transformation –
translation, reflection and rotation.

■   **A transformation changes the position of a shape.
    Some change the size as well.**
    ● **The original shape is called the object**
    ● **The transformed shape is called the image**

Translation

■ **A translation is a sliding movement.**

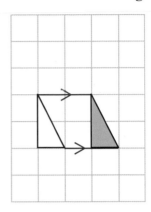

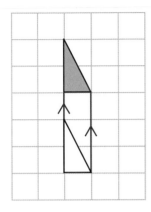

A translation of 2 squares to the *right* moves the white triangle to the green triangle.

A translation of 3 squares *up* moves the white triangle to the green triangle.

In each case, the white triangle is the **object** and the green triangle is the **image**.

A single translation can move a shape *both* horizontally *and* vertically.

Example 2

Describe the transformation which moves the white shape to the green shape.

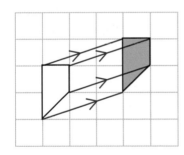

The transformation is a translation of 3 squares to the right and 1 up.
Notice that each corner of the shape moves 3 squares to the right and 1 up.

Reflection

This diagram shows a triangle and its reflection in a mirror.

■ **The reflection of a shape is the same distance behind the mirror as the original shape is in front.**

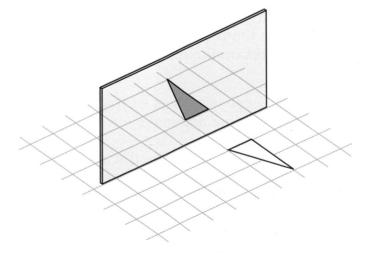

The diagram below shows the mirror line, the triangle and its reflection viewed from above.

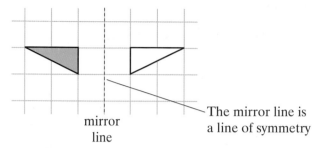

If the paper is folded along the mirror line, the original shape fits exactly on top of its reflection.

Example 3

Reflect the parallelogram in the mirror line.

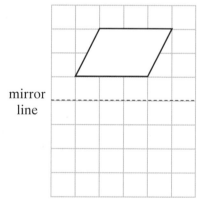

To mark the corners:

Method 1

- Count the number of squares from each corner to the mirror line.
- Draw in the reflection the same number of squares on the other side of the mirror line.

Method 2

- Put the edge of a sheet of tracing paper on the mirror line and make a tracing of the parallelogram.
- Keeping the edge of the tracing paper on the mirror line, turn the tracing paper over.
- Mark the reflections of the corners with a pencil or a compass point.

Then use a ruler to draw in the edges of the parallelogram.

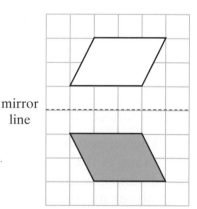

This method is useful for awkward shapes or if the shapes are not drawn on a grid.

Rotation

- **A rotation is a turn.**

- **The point about which a shape is rotated is called the centre of rotation.**

The white triangle has been rotated to form the green triangle by $\frac{1}{4}$ turn anticlockwise about the centre of rotation shown.

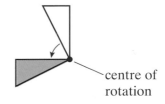

centre of rotation

You can check a rotation using tracing paper:

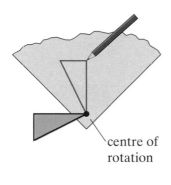

centre of rotation

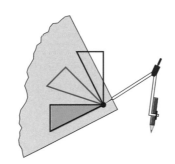

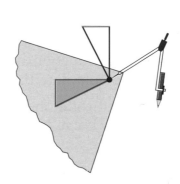

Trace the white triangle (the **object**).

Keep the centre of rotation fixed using a compass or sharp pencil.

Turn the tracing until it fits exactly on top of the green triangle (the **image**).

Angles of turn may be given in degrees, instead of fractions of a turn.

There is more on degrees and turns on page 25.

clockwise $\frac{1}{4}$ turn = 90°   **clockwise $\frac{1}{2}$ turn = 180°**

clockwise $\frac{3}{4}$ turn = 270°

Example 4

Rotate the triangle 90° clockwise about A.

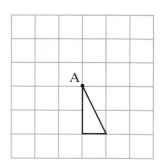

- Make a tracing of the object.
- Keeping A fixed with a pencil point, rotate the triangle 90° clockwise.
- Mark the new positions of the corners with a pencil or a compass point and draw in the lines to complete the image.

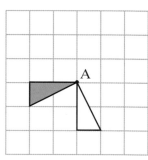

The centre of rotation is not always at a corner of the shape. It can be anywhere.

Example 5

Rotate the shape through 180° about B.

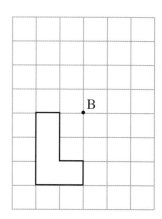

- Make a tracing of the object.
- Keeping B fixed with a pencil point, rotate the shape through 180°.
- Mark the positions of the corners with a pencil or a compass point and draw in the lines to complete the image.

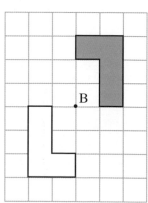

Exercise 7D

1   Describe the translation of the white triangle to the green triangle.

(a)   **(b)**   **(c)**

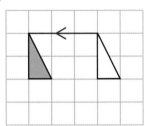   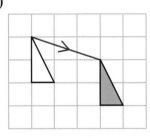   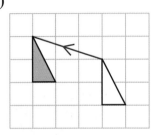

2   Copy the diagrams on squared paper and translate each shape by the amount shown.

(a)   **(b)**   **(c)**

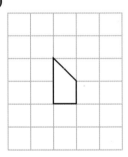   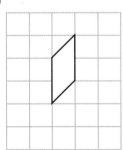   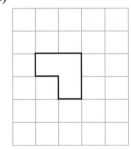

    2 squares down   2 squares to the left   2 squares to the right
                              and 1 square down   and 1 square up

3   Copy the diagrams on squared paper and reflect each shape in the mirror line.

(a)   **(b)**   **(c)**

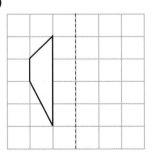   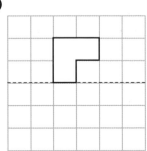   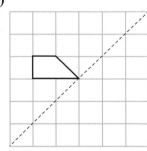

4 Copy the diagrams on squared paper. Each diagram shows a shape and its reflection. Draw in the mirror lines.

(a)

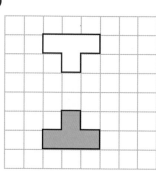

(b)

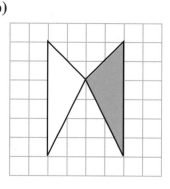

(c)

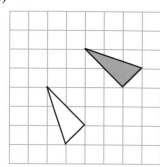

5 Copy the diagrams on squared paper and rotate each triangle through a $\frac{1}{2}$ turn about C.

Hint: use tracing paper to help.

(a)

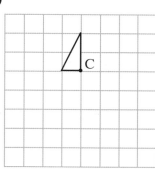

(b)

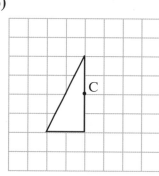

(c)

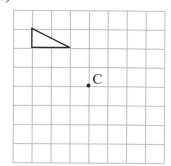

6 Copy the diagrams on squared paper and rotate each shape by the given angle about C.

(a)

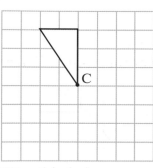

90° anticlockwise

(b)

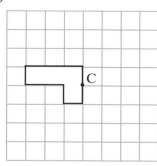

90° clockwise

(c)

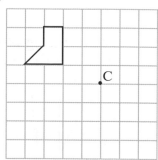

90° anticlockwise

7   Each diagram shows a rotation about C of the white
     triangle to the coloured triangle. For each diagram:
  ● State the angle of the rotation, in degrees
    and as a fraction of a turn.
  ● State whether the rotation is clockwise or
    anticlockwise.

(a)   **(b)**   **(c)**

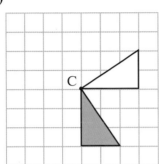   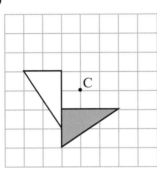   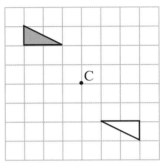

8   For each diagram:
  ● Is the transformation a translation, a reflection or a rotation?
  ● Describe the transformation fully.

(a)   **(b)**   **(c)**

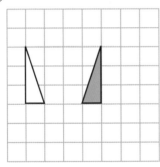   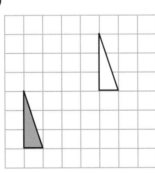   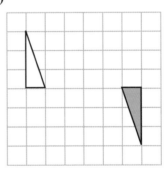

7.5 Congruence

Activity 1

● Make a tracing of one of the four quadrilaterals below.
● Check that the tracing fits exactly on top of the other three quadrilaterals.

- Turn the tracing paper over.
- Check that the tracing fits exactly on top of each of the four quadrilaterals below.

  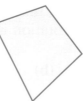 

All eight quadrilaterals are exactly the same shape and size.

You say that they are **congruent**.

■ **Congruent means exactly the same shape and size. Congruent shapes can be transformed into each other using only rotation, reflection and translation.**

Example 6

Which of these triangles are congruent?

A    B 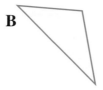   C 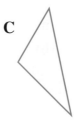   D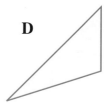

Make a tracing of triangle **A**.
The tracing fits exactly on top of triangle **B**, but not on top of **C** or **D**.
Turn the tracing paper over.
The tracing now fits exactly on top of triangle **C**, but not on top of **B** or **D**.
Triangles **A**, **B** and **C** are congruent.

Exercise 7E

1 Use tracing paper to say which of these triangles are congruent.

  (a)   **(b)**   **(c)** 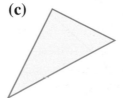   **(d)**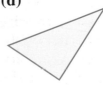

2 Write down the letters of the pairs of shapes which are congruent.

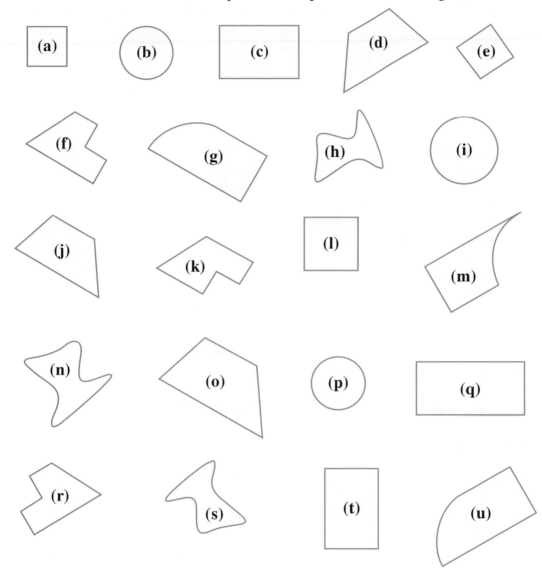

Activity 2

1 Diagram 1 shows an object and its image after a translation.

(a) Measure the lengths of the sides of the object and its image.
What do you notice?

(b) Measure the sizes of the angles at the corners of the object and its image. What do you notice?

(c) The object and its image are congruent. Explain why.

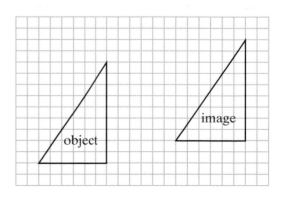

2   Diagram 2 shows an object and its image after a
    reflection.

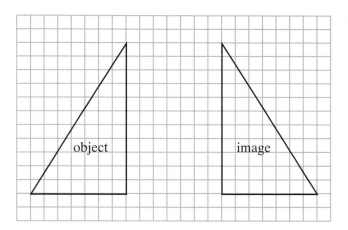

(a) Measure the lengths of the sides of the object and its
    image. What do you notice?
(b) Measure the sides of the angles at the corners of the
    object and its image. What do you notice?
(c) Are the object and its image congruent? Explain your
    answer.

3   Diagram 3 shows an object and its image after a
    rotation.

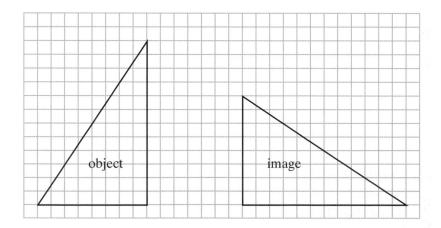

(a) Measure the lengths of the sides of the object and its
    image. What do you notice?
(b) Measure the sides of the angles at the corners of the
    object and its image. What do you notice?
(c) Are the object and its image congruent? Explain your
    answer.

7.6 Plans and elevations

The diagram shows a solid made from three cubes.

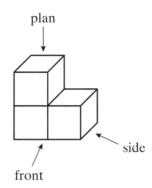

plan

front

side

| This is the view from above and is called the **plan**. | This is the view from the front and is called the **front elevation**. | This is the view from the right-hand side and is called the **right side elevation**. |

- **A plan of a solid is the view from above.**
- **The front elevation of a solid is the view from the front.**
- **The side elevation of a solid is the view from the side.**

Activity 3

You will need four multilink cubes.

For each of the following plan and elevation descriptions:
- Make the solid.
- Draw the solid using Activity Sheet 6. (The first one has been drawn for you.)

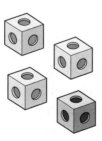

	Plan	Front elevation	Right side elevation
(a)			
(b)			
(c)			
(d)			
(e)			
(f)			

Example 7

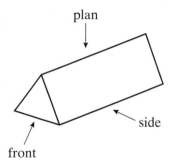

plan

side

front

The diagram shows a triangular prism. Its ends are equilateral triangles. Draw the plan and elevations of the prism.

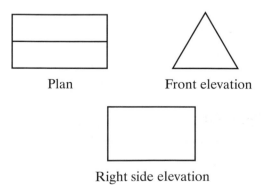

Plan   Front elevation

Right side elevation

Exercise 7F

Draw the plan and elevations of each of these solids.

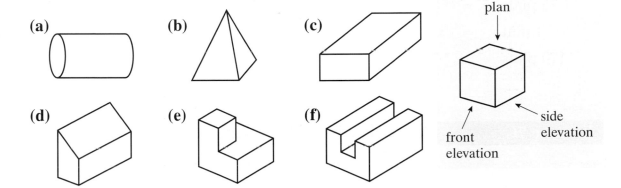

(a) **(b)** **(c)**

(d) **(e)** **(f)**

7.7 Metric and imperial measure

Most measurements taken today are in metric units. It is important to be able to convert metric units into old style imperial units like miles and pints.

In September 1999 the NASA Mars Climate Orbiter was lost in space because some of the designers forgot to convert metric to imperial units. It was worth $125 million.

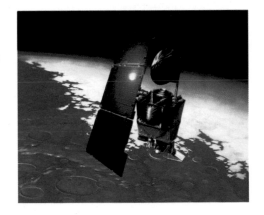

Metric		Imperial
8 kilometres	=	5 miles
1 kilogram	=	2.2 pounds
1 litre	=	1.75 pints
2.54 centimetres	=	1 inch

You can write lb for pounds and ″ for inches.

Example 8

Katie weighs 68 kg. What is her weight in pounds?

$1\,kg = 2.2\,lb$

$68\,kg = 68 \times 2.2 = 149.6\,lb$

Example 9

A bathtub holds 170 pints of water. How much can it hold in litres? Give your answer to one decimal place.

$$1.75 \text{ pints} \quad = \quad 1 \text{ litre}$$
$$1 \text{ pint} \quad = \quad 1 \div 1.75 \text{ litres}$$
$$170 \text{ pints} \quad = \quad 170 \times (1 \div 1.75) = 97.1 \text{ litres}$$

Exercise 7G

1 Change these distances to miles.
   (**a**) 32 km   (**b**) 208 km
   (**c**) 3680 km   (**d**) 136 km
   (**e**) 9776 km   (**f**) 2400 km

2 The radius of the earth is 6360 km. What is this in miles?

3 Change these distances to kilometres.
   (**a**) 25 miles   (**b**) 1275 miles
   (**c**) 1000 miles   (**d**) 220 miles
   (**e**) 600 miles   (**f**) 445 miles

4 A reservoir holds 11 million litres of water. How much can it hold in pints?

5 An African elephant weighs 12 800 lb. What is its weight in kilograms? Give your answer to the nearest 10 kg.

6 Change these lengths to centimetres. Give your answers to 2 decimal places.
   (**a**) 12″   (**b**) 2″
   (**c**) $6\frac{1}{2}''$ (**d**) 3 ft
   (**e**) 1 ft 6″   (**f**) $2\frac{2}{3}$ ft

There are 12 inches in a foot.

7 Change these lengths to feet and inches. Give your answers to the nearest inch.
   (**a**) 8 cm   (**b**) 110 cm
   (**c**) 12 cm   (**d**) 30 cm
   (**e**) 68 cm   (**f**) 80 cm

8   Copy and complete this table showing the top speeds of some creatures in miles per hour and kilometres per hour.

Animal	Top speed (mph)	Top speed (kph)
Penguin		40
Peregrine falcon	225	
Greyhound	38	
Cheetah		110
Swordfish	56	
Bumblebee		12

Summary of key points

1   A shape that you can fold to make a solid is called a *net* of the solid.

2   Shapes tessellate if they fit together without any gaps and without any overlap. The patterns they make are called tessellations.

3   *All* triangles tessellate and *all* quadrilaterals tessellate.

4   A transformation changes the position and sometimes the size of a shape.
   ● The original shape is called the object
   ● The transformed shape is called the image

5   Translation, reflection and rotation are all transformations which change only the *position* of a shape. They do *not* change its size.

6   Translation is a sliding movement.

7   The reflection of a shape is the same distance behind the mirror as the original shape is in front.

8 A rotation is a turn.

9 The point about which a shape is rotated is called the centre of rotation.

10 Congruent means exactly the same shape and size. Congruent shapes can be transformed into each other using only rotation, reflection and translation.

11 A plan of a solid is the view from above.

12 The front elevation of a solid is the view from the front.

13 The side elevation of a solid is the view from the side.

8 Fractions and ratio

8.1 Mixed numbers and improper fractions

Jan, Tim and Sue are at Pizza House for a meal. They choose the special offer: 4 pizzas for the price of 3. How much pizza do they each get?

Sue says: 'Each of us can have 1 whole pizza. Then cut the last pizza into 3. Then we will have $1\frac{1}{3}$ each.'

Jan says: 'Cut each pizza into 3 and share out the slices. Then we will have $\frac{4}{3}$ each.

So each friend gets $1\frac{1}{3} = \frac{4}{3}$ of a pizza.

- ■ $1\frac{1}{3}$ is a mixed number – it has a whole number part and a fraction part.

- ■ $\frac{4}{3}$ is an improper fraction – its numerator is greater than its denominator.

- ■ You can write a mixed number as an improper fraction. For example: $1\frac{1}{3}$ is equal to $\frac{4}{3}$.

Remember:
The top number is called the numerator.
The bottom number is called the denominator.

Example 1

Write $2\frac{1}{4}$ as an improper fraction.

$$2\frac{1}{4} = 1 + 1 + \frac{1}{4}$$
$$= \frac{4}{4} + \frac{4}{4} + \frac{1}{4}$$
$$= \frac{4+4+1}{4} = \frac{9}{4}$$

Remember:
Any fraction with its numerator and denominator the same is equal to 1:

$$1 = \frac{2}{2} = \frac{3}{3} = \frac{4}{4} = \ldots$$

To add fractions with the same denominator, add the numerators. Write the result over the same denominator.

Example 2

Change $\frac{12}{5}$ to a mixed number.

$$\frac{12}{5} = \frac{5+5+2}{5}$$
$$= \frac{5}{5} + \frac{5}{5} + \frac{2}{5}$$
$$= 1 + 1 + \frac{2}{5} = 2\frac{2}{5}$$

You can also do it like this:

$12 \div 5 = 2$
remainder 2 parts (fifths)
So $\frac{12}{5} = 2\frac{2}{5}$

Exercise 8A

1 Change these improper fractions into mixed numbers:

(a) $\frac{14}{5}$ (b) $\frac{10}{3}$

(c) $\frac{7}{4}$ (d) $\frac{11}{7}$

2 Change these mixed numbers into improper fractions:

(a) $3\frac{1}{2}$ (b) $1\frac{7}{8}$

(c) $2\frac{2}{3}$ (d) $4\frac{6}{7}$

3 Five friends share seven pizzas.
How much pizza do they each get?
Write your answer as:

(a) a mixed number
(b) an improper fraction.

8.2 Equivalent fractions

Equivalent fractions are used in all sorts of fraction calculations.

Remember:
Equivalent fractions are fractions that have the same value.

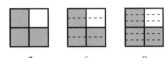

$\frac{3}{4} = \frac{6}{8} = \frac{9}{12}$ are equivalent fractions.

$\frac{3}{4}$ is the **simplest form** of this set of fractions.

■ **You can find equivalent fractions by multiplying or dividing the numerator and denominator by the same number.**

■ **A fraction is in its simplest form if there is no equivalent fraction with smaller numbers on the top and bottom.**

Example 3

Find an equivalent fraction for $\frac{2}{3}$

(a) in sixths **(b)** in fifteenths

Hint: For **(a)**
$6 \div 3 = 2$ so multiply top and bottom by 2.

(a)

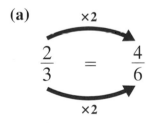

(b)

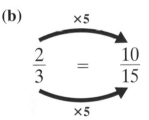

Example 4

Write $\frac{18}{21}$ in its simplest form.

Factors of 18: 1, 2, **3**, 6, 9, 18
Factors of 21: 1, **3**, 7, 21

3 is the highest common factor of 18 and 21:

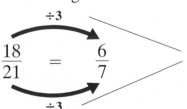

To reduce a fraction to its simplest form, you divide the numerator and denominator by the highest common factor.

There is more about highest common factors on page 58.

$\frac{18}{21} = \frac{6}{7}$ in its simplest form.

■ **To find the simplest form of a fraction, divide the numerator and the denominator by the highest common factor.**

1 Find an equivalent fraction in twentieths for:

   (a) $\frac{2}{5}$ **(b)** $\frac{3}{10}$ **(c)** $\frac{3}{4}$ **(d)** $\frac{1}{2}$

2 Find an equivalent fraction in twenty-fourths for:

   (a) $\frac{2}{3}$ **(b)** $\frac{3}{4}$ **(c)** $\frac{5}{6}$ **(d)** $\frac{3}{8}$

3 Write each of these as an equivalent fraction in sevenths:

   (a) $\frac{15}{21}$ **(b)** $\frac{30}{42}$ **(c)** $\frac{20}{28}$ **(d)** $\frac{35}{49}$

   What do you notice about your answers?

4 Copy this table and complete it. The first row has been done for you as an example.

Fraction	Factors of the numerator	Factors of the denominator	Highest common factor	Simplest form of the fraction
$\frac{7}{21}$	1, 7	1, 3, 7, 21	7	$\frac{1}{3}$
$\frac{3}{12}$	1, ☐	1, 2, ☐, 4, ☐, 12	☐	$\frac{1}{4}$
$\frac{10}{15}$	1, ☐, 5, ☐	☐, 3, ☐, 15	☐	☐
$\frac{6}{9}$	☐, 2, ☐, ☐	1, ☐, ☐	☐	☐
$\frac{4}{28}$	☐, ☐, ☐	1, 2, ☐, 7, 14, 28	☐	☐

5 Write each of these fractions in its simplest form:

   (a) $\frac{9}{12}$ **(b)** $\frac{15}{27}$ **(c)** $\frac{16}{32}$ **(d)** $\frac{10}{25}$ **(e)** $\frac{6}{21}$

6 Cancel these fractions where possible:

   (a) $\frac{18}{36}$ **(b)** $\frac{17}{51}$ **(c)** $\frac{11}{12}$ **(d)** $\frac{25}{28}$ **(e)** $\frac{22}{33}$

7 Write these improper fractions as mixed numbers in their simplest form:

   (a) $\frac{24}{20}$ **(b)** $\frac{50}{8}$ **(c)** $\frac{63}{49}$ **(d)** $\frac{28}{14}$ **(e)** $\frac{20}{12}$

8.3 Putting fractions in order of size

You can use equivalent fractions to put fractions in order.

Example 5

Which is larger, $\frac{1}{3}$ or $\frac{2}{5}$?

Change the fractions so that they have the same denominator:

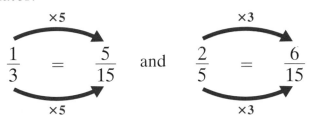

$$\frac{1}{3} = \frac{5}{15} \quad \text{and} \quad \frac{2}{5} = \frac{6}{15}$$

$\frac{6}{15}$ is larger than $\frac{5}{15}$

so $\frac{2}{5}$ is larger than $\frac{1}{3}$.

15 is the smallest number that is a multiple of 3 and 5. It is called the **lowest common multiple** of 3 and 5. There is more about lowest common multiples (LCM) on page 56.

■ **To put fractions in order of size, change them to equivalent fractions with the same denominator. That denominator is the lowest common multiple of the original denominators.**

Exercise 8C

1   (a) Change these fractions into twenty-fourths:

$$\frac{2}{3} \quad \frac{3}{4} \quad \frac{5}{12} \quad \frac{3}{8}$$

(b) Write them in order, starting with the smallest.

2   Use equivalent fractions to put these fractions in order, starting with the smallest.

$$\frac{2}{5} \quad \frac{7}{10} \quad \frac{4}{15} \quad \frac{5}{6} \quad \frac{1}{3}$$

Hint: Try using 30 as the denominator.

3   (a) Put the following fractions in ascending order.

$$\frac{5}{8} \quad \frac{1}{2} \quad \frac{3}{4} \quad \frac{7}{16} \quad \frac{9}{32}$$

(b) Now put them in descending order.

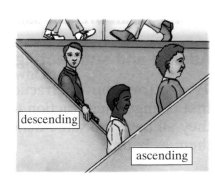

Example 11

Tony wants to know the difference between the two distances $1\frac{1}{2}$ miles and $2\frac{1}{5}$ miles.

He needs to subtract $1\frac{1}{2}$ from $2\frac{1}{5}$.

Change the mixed numbers into improper fractions:

$$2\frac{1}{5} = \frac{11}{5} \quad \text{and} \quad 1\frac{1}{2} = \frac{3}{2}$$
$$2\frac{1}{5} - 1\frac{1}{2} = \frac{11}{5} - \frac{3}{2} = \frac{22}{10} - \frac{15}{10} = \frac{7}{10}$$

The difference between the two distances is $\frac{7}{10}$ mile.

Example 12

Ben and Levi ran an 800 metre race. Ben's time was $3\frac{1}{5}$ minutes and Levi's time was $1\frac{3}{4}$ minutes. How much slower was Ben than Levi? Write your answer as a mixed number.

To find the difference in their times subtract:

$$3\frac{1}{5} - 1\frac{3}{4}$$
$$3\frac{1}{5} = \frac{15}{5} + \frac{1}{5} = \frac{16}{5} \qquad 1\frac{3}{4} = \frac{4}{4} + \frac{3}{4} = \frac{7}{4}$$
$$3\frac{1}{5} - 1\frac{3}{4} = \frac{16}{5} - \frac{7}{4} = \frac{64}{20} - \frac{35}{20} = \frac{29}{20} = 2\frac{9}{20}$$

4 and 5 are both factors of 20.

Ben was slower than Levi by $2\frac{9}{20}$ minutes.

Exercise 8E

1   Work out:
   (a) $1\frac{3}{4} + 2\frac{2}{3}$
   (b) $3\frac{1}{5} - 1\frac{1}{2}$
   (c) $2\frac{7}{8} - \frac{9}{10}$
   (d) $3\frac{1}{7} + 4\frac{1}{4}$
   (e) $2\frac{1}{7} + 1\frac{5}{14} - 3\frac{1}{2}$

2 Karen used $1\frac{1}{2}$ lbs of flour and $2\frac{1}{4}$ lbs of apples in her
Celebration Pudding.

(a) What did these ingredients weigh altogether?

Malcolm thought Karen used $\frac{1}{4}$ lb of flour more than
necessary.

(b) How much flour did he think she should have used?

(c) How much would the ingredients then have weighed?

3 Match the questions to the answers in the clouds
below. Write down all of your working.

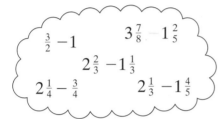
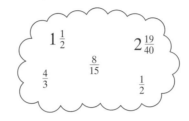

4 Andrew drives $5\frac{1}{3}$ miles to the Park and Ride. He then
travels $8\frac{1}{4}$ miles by coach. From the coach he walks for
half a mile to reach his office.

(a) How far does he travel by coach and car?

(b) How much further does he travel by coach than by
car?

(c) How far does he travel altogether?

(d) What is the difference between the distance he
walks and the distance he drives?

5 **(a)** What should be subtracted from $4\frac{4}{5}$ to give $1\frac{1}{3}$?

(b) Which is bigger:

$$2\frac{4}{9} \text{ or } 2\frac{7}{12}?$$

6 Anastasia, Mairead and Helena went shopping.
Anastasia bought $1\frac{1}{2}$ lbs of carrots and $3\frac{1}{2}$ lbs of
potatoes. Mairead bought $\frac{3}{4}$ lb of cheese and $\frac{1}{2}$ lb of
dates. Helena bought $2\frac{1}{2}$ lbs of apples and $1\frac{3}{4}$ lbs of
pears. Which of these statements are true?

(a) Anastasia's shopping weighed more than Mairead's
and Helen's altogether.

(b) Mairead's shopping weighed $2\frac{1}{4}$ lbs.

(c) Helena's shopping was heavier than Anastasia's.

(d) The apples weighed less than the dates, cheese and
carrots altogether.

8.5 Multiplying fractions

Sehan bought $\frac{3}{4}$ lb of cheese. She gave half of her cheese to her friend. To find out the weight of half of the cheese you need to find $\frac{1}{2}$ of $\frac{3}{4}$ lb.

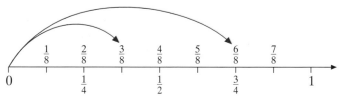

$\frac{1}{2}$ of $\frac{3}{4}$ is $\frac{3}{8}$. $\frac{1}{2}$ of $\frac{3}{4}$ means $\frac{1}{2} \times \frac{3}{4}$.

$\frac{3}{4}$ is equivalent to $\frac{6}{8}$.
$\frac{6}{8}$ is $\frac{3}{8} + \frac{3}{8}$ so half of $\frac{6}{8}$ is $\frac{3}{8}$.

Multiplying two fractions

Example 13

Work out $\frac{4}{5} \times \frac{2}{5}$

The shaded area represents $\frac{4}{5} \times \frac{2}{5}$

The shaded area is $\frac{8}{25}$.

$$\frac{4}{5} \times \frac{2}{5} = \frac{8}{25}$$

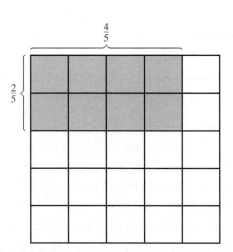

■   **To multiply two fractions, multiply the numerators and multiply the denominators.**

Example 14

Work out $\frac{1}{2}$ of $\frac{3}{5}$

$\frac{1}{2}$ of $\frac{3}{5}$ means $\frac{1}{2} \times \frac{3}{5}$

$\frac{1}{2} \times \frac{3}{5} = \frac{1 \times 3}{2 \times 5} = \frac{3}{10}$

Example 15

Work out $\frac{4}{5} \times \frac{5}{12}$

$\frac{4}{5} \times \frac{5}{12} = \frac{4 \times 5}{5 \times 12} = \frac{20}{60} = \frac{1}{3}$

$\frac{20}{60}$ simplifies to $\frac{1}{3}$. Always write your answers in simplest form.

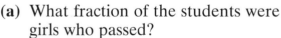

Exercise 8F

1   Work out the following. Give each answer in its simplest form.

(a) $\frac{1}{2} \times \frac{1}{3}$ (b) $\frac{6}{7} \times \frac{1}{5}$ (c) $\frac{3}{4} \times \frac{5}{8}$

(d) $\frac{3}{10} \times \frac{10}{13}$ (e) $\frac{8}{9} \times \frac{3}{4}$ (f) $\frac{1}{4} \times \frac{1}{8}$

2   Three-quarters of the students at Newton High School passed their mathematics exams. Two-thirds of these students were girls.

(a) What fraction of the students were girls who passed?

(b) What fraction of the students were boys who passed?

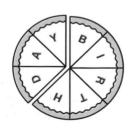

3   Twins Stella and Daniel were celebrating their birthday with friends. Stella had five-eighths of the cake. Her friends ate only four-fifths of her share.

(a) What fraction of the whole cake did they eat?

Daniel's friends ate two-thirds of his share.

(b) What fraction of the whole cake did they eat?

4 Ravi travels seven-eighths of a mile to school by bike.
Halfway there he gets a puncture. What distance had
he travelled before the puncture happened?

5 Christabel's food dish contains half of a tin
of Purrfeast cat food. She eats three-
quarters of it.

    (a) What fraction of the whole tin did she
       eat?

    (b) What fraction of the original tin was still
       in her food dish?

Multiplying a fraction by a whole number

$$5 \times 3 = 15$$

$$5 \times 2 = 10$$

$$5 \times 1 = 5$$

$$5 \times \tfrac{1}{2} = \tfrac{5}{2}$$

$$5 \times \tfrac{1}{4} = \tfrac{5}{4}$$

5 lots of a quarter is 5 quarters, or $\tfrac{5}{4}$.

You can write 5 as a fraction, $\tfrac{5}{1}$, and then multiply in the
normal way.

$$5 \times \tfrac{1}{4} = \tfrac{5}{1} \times \tfrac{1}{4} = \tfrac{5}{4}$$

- **To multiply a fraction by a whole number:**
  Write the whole number as a fraction over one.
  Multiply the numerators, and multiply the
  denominators.

For example, 5 is
written as $\tfrac{5}{1}$.

Example 16

Multiply $\tfrac{3}{10}$ by 7.

7 is the same as $\tfrac{7}{1}$ so $\tfrac{3}{10} \times 7 = \tfrac{3}{10} \times \tfrac{7}{1}$

$$\tfrac{3}{10} \times \tfrac{7}{1} = \frac{3 \times 7}{10 \times 1} = \frac{21}{10} = 2\tfrac{1}{10}$$

So $\tfrac{3}{10}$ multiplied by 7 is $2\tfrac{1}{10}$.

$\tfrac{21}{10} = \tfrac{10}{10} + \tfrac{10}{10} + \tfrac{1}{10}$
$= 2 + \tfrac{1}{10} = 2\tfrac{1}{10}$

Exercise 8G

1 Work out the following:

(a) $2 \times \frac{3}{4}$ (b) $\frac{5}{8} \times 3$ (c) $4 \times \frac{2}{3}$ (d) $\frac{7}{10} \times 3$

(e) $3 \times \frac{2}{3}$ (f) $\frac{5}{6} \times 2$ (g) $7 \times \frac{2}{5}$ (h) $\frac{3}{8} \times 4$

2 Use the number lines to find the missing numbers.

(a)

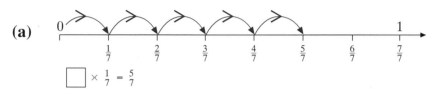

$$\boxed{} \times \frac{1}{7} = \frac{5}{7}$$

(b)

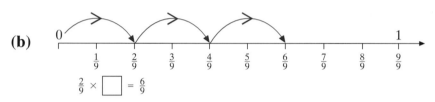

$$\frac{2}{9} \times \boxed{} = \frac{6}{9}$$

3 A recipe for two people uses $\frac{5}{8}$ of a pint of milk. Grace wants to make the recipe for six people. How much milk will she need?

4 Tabitha has 6 bars of chocolate. She gives $\frac{2}{7}$ of it to Emily. How much chocolate does Tabitha have left?

Multiplying mixed numbers

■ **To multiply mixed numbers, change them to improper fractions then multiply in the normal way.**

Example 17

Work out $2\frac{1}{4} \times 1\frac{3}{5}$.

Write the mixed numbers as improper fractions:

$$2\frac{1}{4} = \frac{9}{4} \qquad 1\frac{3}{5} = \frac{8}{5}$$

Now multiply in the normal way.

$$2\frac{1}{4} \times 1\frac{3}{5} = \frac{9}{4} \times \frac{8}{5} = \frac{9 \times 8}{4 \times 5} = \frac{72}{20} = 3\frac{3}{5}$$

Always write your answer in its simplest form.

Example 18

Carolyn soaks $2\frac{1}{4}$ kilograms of lentils to make soup. Each kilogram of lentils needs $1\frac{1}{2}$ litres of water. How much water does she require altogether?

To work out the total amount of water needed you need to multiply the fractions.

$$2\frac{1}{4} \times 1\frac{1}{2} = \frac{9}{4} \times \frac{3}{2} = \frac{9 \times 3}{4 \times 2} = \frac{27}{8} = 3\frac{3}{8}$$

Carolyn will need $3\frac{3}{8}$ litres of water.

Exercise 8H

1   Work these out, giving your answers in their simplest form:

    (a) $2\frac{1}{4} \times 1\frac{1}{10}$ **(b)** $2\frac{1}{2} \times 2\frac{1}{5}$ **(c)** $3\frac{1}{5} \times \frac{3}{8}$

    (d) $6\frac{1}{4} \times 1\frac{1}{5}$ **(e)** $1\frac{1}{4} \times \frac{9}{10}$ **(f)** $\frac{5}{6} \times 1\frac{1}{5}$

2   The base dimensions of Christian's rectangular hi-fi are $1\frac{1}{4}$ feet by $1\frac{3}{4}$ feet. He needs to work out the surface area he needs for it in his new flat. Show how he can do this and find the area of the base of the hi-fi.

3   Ami has bought a circular mirror. Its radius is $4\frac{1}{2}$ cm. Taking the value of π to be $3\frac{1}{7}$, work out the area of Ami's wall the mirror will cover.

Remember: the area of a circle is πr^2, or $\pi \times r \times r$.

4   A parallelogram has length $6\frac{4}{5}$ cm and perpendicular height $4\frac{1}{5}$ cm.

    (a) Work out the area of the parallelogram.

    Half of the parallelogram is red.

    (b) Work out the area of the shaded section.

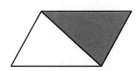

Hint:
Area of parallelogram
= length × perpendicular height

8.6 Dividing fractions

You will need to be able to solve problems by dividing fractions.

Example 19

Anna is baking muffins. She makes 4 lb of muffin mix. Each muffin uses $\frac{1}{5}$ lb of mix. How many muffins can Anna make?

Anna divides her 4 lb into $\frac{1}{5}$ portions:

$$4 \div \frac{1}{5}$$

There are 5 lots of $\frac{1}{5}$ in a whole so there are 4 lots of 5 fifths in 4 lb of muffin mix.

$$4 \times 5 = 20$$

Anna can make 20 muffins.

$4 \div \frac{1}{5}$ is the same as $4 \times \frac{5}{1}$ or 4×5.

■ **To find the reciprocal of a fraction turn it upside down.**

■ **To divide fractions replace the dividing fraction with its reciprocal and change the division sign to multiplication.**

The reciprocal of $\frac{1}{5}$ is $\frac{5}{1}$ or just 5.

Example 20

Work out $\frac{1}{4} \div 3$

$$3 = \frac{3}{1}$$

So the reciprocal of 3 is $\frac{1}{3}$.

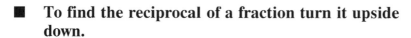

$$\frac{1}{4} \div 3 = \frac{1}{4} \times \frac{1}{3}$$

$$= \frac{1 \times 1}{4 \times 3}$$

$$= \frac{1}{12}$$

Example 21

Work out $\frac{2}{5} \div \frac{3}{4}$

The reciprocal of $\frac{3}{4}$ is $\frac{4}{3}$.

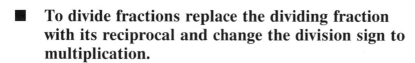

$$\frac{2}{5} \div \frac{3}{4} = \frac{2}{5} \times \frac{4}{3}$$

$$= \frac{2 \times 4}{5 \times 3}$$

$$= \frac{8}{15}$$

Exercise 8I

1   Find the reciprocal of each fraction.

(a) $\frac{3}{5}$ (b) $\frac{7}{8}$ (c) $\frac{5}{6}$ (d) $\frac{12}{5}$ (e) $1\frac{1}{2}$

2   Change the whole numbers to fractions over 1 to work out:

(a) $\frac{2}{3} \div 8$ (b) $\frac{4}{5} \div 16$ (c) $\frac{13}{15} \div 39$

(d) $\frac{7}{16} \div 14$ (e) $\frac{3}{4} \div 12$ (f) $\frac{9}{10} \div 18$

3   Work out:

(a) $\frac{2}{3} \div \frac{8}{9}$ (b) $\frac{3}{8} \div \frac{5}{7}$ (c) $\frac{7}{19} \div \frac{9}{14}$

(d) $\frac{6}{7} \div \frac{24}{35}$ (e) $\frac{3}{4} \div \frac{7}{12}$ (f) $\frac{2}{5} \div \frac{9}{17}$

4   Work out:

(a) $1\frac{1}{4} \div \frac{5}{6}$ (b) $2\frac{1}{2} \div 3\frac{1}{3}$ (c) $1\frac{1}{5} \div 2\frac{1}{10}$

(d) $3\frac{1}{5} \div 4$ (e) $6\frac{1}{4} \div 2\frac{1}{2}$ (f) $\frac{8}{9} \div 1\frac{1}{4}$

> To find the reciprocal of a mixed number first change it to an improper fraction. For example:
> $$1\frac{2}{3} = \frac{5}{3}$$
> the reciprocal of $\frac{5}{3}$ is $\frac{3}{5}$

> Hint: Change the mixed numbers to improper fractions first.

5   Ed buys a watermelon weighing $\frac{3}{4}$ kg. He divides it into equal pieces each weighing $\frac{3}{16}$ kg. How many pieces of melon does he have?

6   Jason is making rock cakes for a school fete. It takes him $\frac{2}{3}$ hour to make 24 cakes.

(a) What is the time taken per cake?

Keri took $\frac{3}{4}$ hour to make 36 rock cakes.

(b) What was Keri's time taken per cake?

7   True or false:

(a) The reciprocal of $1\frac{1}{7}$ is $\frac{8}{7}$.

(b) $\frac{2}{3} \div \frac{4}{5} < \frac{2}{3} \times \frac{3}{8}$.

(c) $\frac{3}{5} \div \frac{2}{3}$ is the same as $\frac{2}{3} \div \frac{3}{5}$.

(d) The area of a rectangular flower bed is $\frac{4}{5}$ square metres. The length of one side is $\frac{2}{3}$ metre. The length of the other side is $\frac{8}{15}$ metre.

> Remember: < means less than.

8   Mr Keane shares $2\frac{1}{2}$ lb of chocolate between a class of 12. How much chocolate does each pupil get?

9 The base area of Desire's rectangular playpen is $3\frac{1}{2}\,\text{m}^2$. If the width is $2\frac{1}{3}\,\text{m}$, find the length of the playpen in metres.

10 Cameron works steadily on his homework and completes $\frac{7}{8}$ in $1\frac{1}{2}$ hours. How much of his homework does he complete in 1 hour?

8.7 Ratio

The garden is divided into 9 equal parts.

Two parts are flowers and seven parts are grass. Describing this in fractions you would say that $\frac{2}{9}$ of the garden is flowers and $\frac{7}{9}$ of the garden is grass.

However, in ratios, you compare two quantities.

So in the garden you would say there are two parts flowers to seven parts grass, or that the ratio of flowers to grass is 2 to 7.

This is written as $2 : 7$.

You could also say that there are 7 parts grass to 2 parts flowers, or that the ratio of grass to flowers is 7 to 2. This is written as $7 : 2$.

■ **A ratio compares two or more quantities of the same kind.**

Example 22

(a) What fraction of the octagon is red?
(b) What fraction of the octagon is blue?
(c) Write the ratio of red parts to blue parts.
(d) Write the ratio of yellow parts to blue parts.
(e) Write the ratio of blue parts to red parts to yellow parts.

(a) There are eight parts in the whole shape and one is red, so $\frac{1}{8}$ of the octagon is red.
(b) Three parts are blue, so $\frac{3}{8}$ of the octagon is blue.
(c) There is one red part to three blue, so the ratio is 1 to 3, written as $1:3$.
(d) There are four yellow parts to three blue parts so the ratio is 4 to 3, written as $4:3$.
(e) There are three blue parts to one red part to four yellow parts. The ratio is 3 to 1 to 4, written as $3:1:4$.

> You can use ratios to compare three or more quantities in exactly the same way.

Example 23

Jane, Moira and Michael are comparing their weekly pocket money. Jane gets £3, Michael gets £4 and Moira gets £7. Write down the ratio of:

(a) Moira's pocket money to Michael's pocket money.
(b) Michael's pocket money to Jane's pocket money.
(c) Moira's pocket money to Michael's pocket money to Jane's pocket money.

(a) Moira gets £7. Michael gets £4. The ratio is $7:4$.
(b) Michael gets £4. Jane gets £3. The ratio is $4:3$.
(c) The ratio is $7:4:3$.

Simplifying ratios

There are six blue jerseys and three red jerseys on this line.
The ratio of red to blue is $3:6$.
For each red jersey there are two blue jerseys.
You can write the ratio of red to blue as $1:2$.

■ **You can simplify a ratio if you can divide its numbers by a common factor.**

■ **If the numbers in the ratio do not have a common factor the ratio is in its simplest form.**

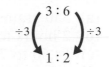

The ratio $1:2$ is the simplest form of the ratio $3:6$.

Example 24

Express these ratios in their simplest form:
(a) $80:50$
(b) $16:24$

(a) The highest common factor of 80 and 50 is 10:

$$\div 10 \left(\begin{array}{c} 80:50 \\ 8:5 \end{array} \right) \div 10$$

(b) The highest common factor of 16 and 24 is 8:

$$\div 8 \left(\begin{array}{c} 16:24 \\ 2:3 \end{array} \right) \div 8$$

Exercise 8J

1 Write these ratios in their simplest form:
(a) $5:15$ (b) $30:18$
(c) $14:49$ (d) $3:6:12$
(e) $56:24:16$ (f) $18:12:30$

2 Chris is sorting out his music and film collection. He has 80 CDs, 16 DVDs, 96 VHS tapes and 120 minidiscs.
(a) Write down the ratio of CDs to DVDs.
(b) Write down the ratio of VHS tapes to minidiscs.
(c) What is the ratio of CDs to VHS tapes to DVDs.
(d) Write down the ratio of minidiscs to VHS tapes to CDs to DVDs.

Always write your answers in their simplest form.

3   Write these ratios in their simplest form.

    (a) 350 grams to 7 kg

    (b) 2 hours to 180 minutes

    (c) £4.50 to 75p

    (d) 1 litre of milk to $\frac{1}{2}$ litre of milk

    (e) 8 years to 4 years 8 months

> Make the units the same before you write each ratio.

4   In a class there are 24 boys and 18 girls. Find the ratio of:

    (a) boys to girls

    (b) girls to boys

    (c) boys to the total number of students

    (d) girls to the total number of students

5   Paul and Ivalor are making chocolate mousse.
Paul uses 4 ounces of cream to 6 ounces of chocolate.
Ivalor uses 6 ounces of cream to 9 ounces of chocolate.
Which of the following statements are true?

    (a) The ratio of cream to chocolate is the same in both
Paul and Ivalor's recipes.

    (b) The ratio of chocolate to cream in Paul's mousse is
$3:2$

    (c) $\frac{6}{15}$ of Ivalor's mixture is cream.

    (d) $\frac{2}{3}$ of Paul's mixture is cream.

    (e) $\frac{3}{5}$ of Ivalor's mixture is chocolate.

8.8 Proportion

In a football team there are ten players and
one goalkeeper. The ratio of goalkeeper to
players is $1:10$.

In two football teams there are 20 players and
two goalkeepers. The ratio of goalkeepers to
players is $2:20$.

$1:10$ and $2:20$ are equivalent ratios.

The ratio of goalkeepers to players will be the same for any
number of football teams.

You say that the number of goalkeepers and the number of
players are in **direct proportion**.

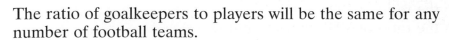

■ **Two or more quantities are in direct proportion if their ratio stays the same as the quantities increase or decrease.**

You sometimes say the quantities are **directly proportional** to each other.

Example 25

Petrol consumption and distance travelled are in direct proportion. Karla can drive 50 miles on 6 litres of petrol. How many litres of petrol will she need to drive 150 miles?

The ratio of miles to petrol is 50:6. The quantities are in direct proportion so the ratio for the longer journey will be equivalent:

120 miles is three times 40 miles... ×3

50 : 6

×3 ...so three times as much petrol is needed.

150 : 18

Karla needs 18 litres of petrol.

Exercise 8K

1   Say whether you think each of these quantities will be in direct proportion.

   (a) Number of identical chocolate bars bought and their cost.
   (b) Number of pupils in a class and their average height.
   (c) Area of a single tile and area of this whole patio.
   (d) Perimeter of a square and length of one side.

2   Derek's aquarium contains 3 frogs, 2 eels, 4 goldfish and 5 snails.

   (a) Write down the ratio of snails to goldfish to frogs to eels.

   He decides to increase the number of snails to 10. He wants to keep the numbers in the aquarium in direct proportion.

(b) How many more frogs does he need?

(c) How many more goldfish does he need?

(d) How many more eels does he need?

3 Colette makes a fruit punch. The ratio of orange juice to lemonade to grapefruit juice is $4:7:3$. She keeps the quantities in direct proportion. How much lemonade does she need if she uses:

(a) 400 ml of orange juice

(b) 6 l of grapefruit juice

(c) 120 ml of grapefruit juice?

4 A carpenter makes cabinets. The ratio of height to width to depth is $5:4:3$.

The carpenter keeps height, width and depth in direct proportion.

(a) How wide should a 105 cm tall cabinet be?

(b) Find the depth of a cabinet that is 88 cm wide.

(c) Find the width and depth of a cabinet that is 3 m tall.

5 Katherine and Ruth have rocking horses. The saddle height and the girls' heights are in direct proportion. Katherine is 60 cm tall and her horse's saddle is 48 cm high.

(a) Write down the ratio of Ruth's height to the height of her saddle.

(b) If Ruth is 75 cm tall, how high is her saddle?

8.9 Calculating with ratios

You will need to be able to solve more difficult ratio problems.

■ **You can solve ratio and proportion problems by reducing one side of the ratio to one.**

Example 26

Faith paints 48 m of fencing in 6 days.
How much fencing did she paint in 4 days?

The ratio of number of days to length of fencing painted is:

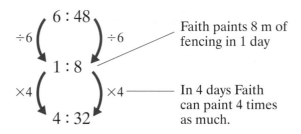

Faith paints 8 m of fencing in 1 day

In 4 days Faith can paint 4 times as much.

Faith painted 32 m of fencing in 4 days.

Example 27

A pancake recipe uses 120 grams of flour and 300 ml of milk for every 2 eggs. How much flour and milk are needed if you make pancakes with 7 eggs?

The ratio of the quantities is

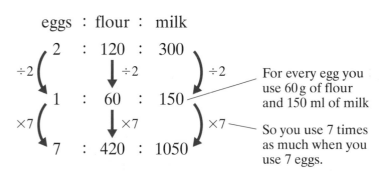

For every egg you use 60 g of flour and 150 ml of milk

So you use 7 times as much when you use 7 eggs.

You need 420 g of flour and 1050 ml, or 1.05 l of milk.

Exercise 8L

1   Peter walks 10 miles in 3 hours. How long would it take him to walk

    (a) 1 mile   **(b)** 12 miles

Hint: Write the time in minutes.

2   Aiden buys 3 CDs for £36. How much would it cost to buy

    (a) 1 CD   **(b)** 5 CDs

3   A grasshopper can leap 169 times in 13 minutes.
How many times can it leap in 11 minutes?

4   Pen wants her garden to contain flowers, vegetables
and grass in the ratio:

flowers : vegetables : grass
7   :   14   :   28

She designs a new plan that uses 12 square metres of
flowers. What area does she now need for:

(a) vegetables   **(b)** grass?

Summary of key points

1 A mixed number has a whole-number part and a
fraction part.
For example: $1\frac{1}{3}$, $9\frac{1}{2}$, $2\frac{1}{4}$.

2 An improper fraction has the numerator bigger than
the denominator.
For example: $\frac{5}{2}$, $\frac{8}{3}$, $\frac{19}{7}$.

3 You can write a mixed number as an improper
fraction.
For example: $1\frac{1}{3}$ is equal to $\frac{4}{3}$.

4 You can find equivalent fractions by multiplying or
dividing the numerator and denominator by the
same number.

5 A fraction is in its simplest form if there is no
equivalent fraction with smaller numbers on the top
and bottom.

6 To find the simplest form of a fraction, divide the numerator and the denominator by the highest common factor.

7 To put fractions in order of size, change them to equivalent fractions with the same denominator. That denominator is the lowest common multiple of the original denominators.

8 To add or subtract fractions with the same denominator, add or subtract the numerators. Write the result over the same denominator.

9 To add or subtract fractions with different denominators, first find equivalent fractions with the same denominators.

10 To add mixed numbers, add the whole-number part and then add the fractions.

11 To subtract mixed numbers, change them into improper fractions.

12 To multiply two fractions, multiply the numerators and multiply the denominators.

13 To multiply a fraction by a whole number:
Write the whole number as a fraction
(for example, $5 = \frac{5}{1}$).
Multiply the numerators and multiply the denominators.

14 To multiply mixed numbers, change them to improper fractions then multiply in the normal way.

15 To find the reciprocal of a fraction, turn it upside down.

16 To divide fractions, replace the dividing fraction with its reciprocal and change the division sign to multiplication.

17 A ratio compares two or more quantities of the same kind.

18 You can simplify a ratio if you can divide its numbers by a common factor.

19 If the numbers in a ratio do not have a common factor, the ratio is in its simplest form.

20 Two or more quantities are in direct proportion if their ratio stays the same as the quantities increase or decrease.

21 You can solve ratio and proportion problems by reducing one side of the ratio to one.

9 Handling data

9.1 Questionnaires

Questionnaires are a good way to collect information.
The questions should be simple and clearly worded.

| Are you | male? ☐ | female? ☐ |

Tick boxes are a useful way of getting information.

Certain types of questions can be difficult to answer, so try to avoid these.

| Classical music is boring isn't it? | Y N |

This question is unfair because it expects a certain answer.

| Have you ever cheated in a test? | Y N |

You may not get a truthful answer if your question is too personal or embarrassing to answer.

Exercise 9A

1   Decide whether these questions are suitable for a questionnaire. If not, give a reason and rewrite the question to make it more suitable.

   (a) What is your favourite food? (Ring the answer.)

   Cheesecake   fish and chips   cheese toastie   stir-fry   ice-cream

   (b) How many hours per day do you spend listening to music?

   1 hour ☐   2 hours ☐   3–4 hours ☐

   (c) Do you like ballet?

   Love it ☐   Hate it ☐

(d) Have you ever gone a whole day without brushing your teeth? Y N

(e) Music in the charts is rubbish, isn't it? Y N

2 Design a questionnaire to find out about different tastes in music in your class. You could ask questions about what type of music people like, how much time they spend listening to it, how much money they spend on music, or why they like it.

9.2 Sorting and presenting data

Presenting data in different ways helps to order the data, spot patterns or features and compare results for different sets of data.

The alphabetical order used in this dictionary helps to find a word quickly:

It is easy to see that forms 9H and 9S have done really well this term:

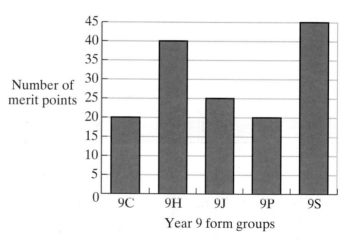

Year 9 form groups

Example 1

Alison asked 40 pupils how many hours they spent on their homework last week.
She wrote the replies in a list:

4, 6, 3, 4, 1, 7, 8, 6, 5, 6, 9, 5, 4, 7, 3, 2, 6, 5, 2, 4,
2, 4, 5, 1, 6, 3, 9, 5, 8, 0, 3, 4, 6, 3, 4, 5, 4, 6, 2, 8.

Alison decided to **sort** this data by using a frequency table:

Hours	Tally	Frequency
0	|	1
1	||	2
2	||||	4
3	⌊⊬⊤	5
4	⌊⊬⊤ |||	8
5	⌊⊬⊤ |	6
6	⌊⊬⊤ ||	7
7	||	2
8	|||	3
9	||	2

She used her frequency table to draw a bar chart:

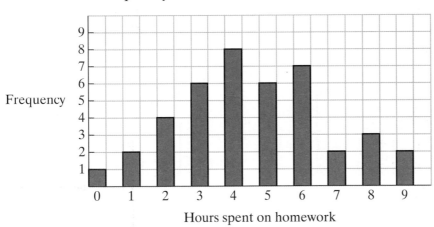

Hours spent on homework

It can sometimes be useful to group the data when there is a wide spread.

Example 2

A local bus company monitored the number of people who travelled on 40 of their buses. Here are the results for one day:

12	23	6	22	10	27	32	17	37	18
25	37	42	11	45	15	9	28	43	20
34	18	23	36	29	32	21	41	24	15
26	5	33	15	43	16	44	31	8	35

There are lots of ways of representing this data:

frequency table

Number of people	Tally	Frequency
0–9	||||	4
10–19	ⳆⳆⳆⳆⳆ ⳆⳆⳆⳆⳆ	10
20–29	ⳆⳆⳆⳆⳆ ⳆⳆⳆⳆⳆ |	11
30–39	ⳆⳆⳆⳆⳆ ||||	9
40–49	ⳆⳆⳆⳆⳆ |	6

The **intervals** (under 'Number of people') have been chosen so that their **boundaries** do not overlap.
If the intervals were 0–10, 10–20, and so on, we would not know where to put a value of 10, for example.

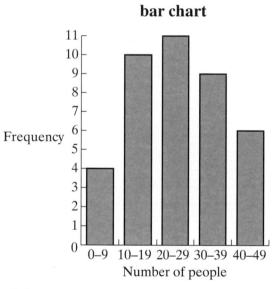

bar chart

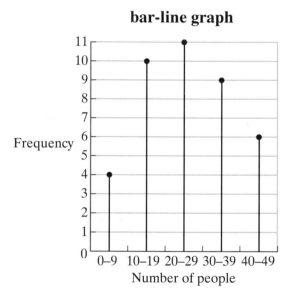

bar-line graph

pictogram

Number of people	
0–9	🚶🚶🚶🚶
10–19	🚶🚶🚶🚶🚶🚶🚶🚶🚶🚶
20–29	🚶🚶🚶🚶🚶🚶🚶🚶🚶🚶🚶
30–39	🚶🚶🚶🚶🚶🚶🚶🚶🚶
40–49	🚶🚶🚶🚶🚶🚶

Exercise 9B

1 Jamie noted down the colours of 50 cars that passed. The results were as follows:

B	G	R	Bl	G	Y	R	G	S	Bl
S	Y	B	S	Bl	S	B	S	Bl	S
R	S	G	Bl	B	S	R	Bl	R	G
S	Bl	B	G	S	Bl	B	S	B	Bl
G	B	S	B	Y	S	Bl	R	Y	Bl

Key	
Black	B
Blue	Bl
Red	R
Green	G
Yellow	Y
Silver	S

(a) Draw up a frequency chart.
(b) Draw a bar chart to illustrate the data.
(c) List the colours in order, most frequent first.

2 The table shows the number of letters delivered to a house one week:

Day	Mon	Tues	Wed	Thurs	Fri	Sat
Number of letters	8	12	4	6	10	5

Present this data as

(a) a bar chart,   **(b)** a pictogram.

3 The number of accidents recorded in Townley village in six months was as follows:

Month	Jan	Feb	Mar	Apr	May	June
Accidents	6	4	9	5	1	3

(a) Draw **(i)** a bar chart, **(ii)** a pictogram, **(iii)** a line graph.
(b) Which do you think is the most useful? Give a reason for your answer.

4 Fifty pupils' marks out of 40 in a geography test were:

10	16	26	17	29	20	9	32	12	23
22	34	3	20	18	27	15	27	24	17
19	14	21	28	33	12	18	7	39	28
35	7	18	11	22	5	24	33	22	26
22	22	15	21	36	24	27	18	31	11

(a) Using class intervals 0–4, 5–9 ... and so on, draw up a frequency table.
(b) Draw a bar chart to represent this data.
(c) In which class interval did most pupils' marks appear?

5 Here are some results for a history test:

Marks	1–10	11–20	21–30	31–40	41–50	51–60
Number of pupils	2	5	10	13	14	6

(a) Draw a bar chart to represent this data.

(b) Compare these results with those for the geography test in question **4**.

6 The age of players in a darts tournament were as follows:

Age	16–20	21–25	26–30	31–35	36–40	41–45	46–50
Number	2	8	10	7	3	5	1

Draw a horizontal bar graph.

7 The scores of the first sixty darts thrown were as follows:

```
20   60   10   18   22    5   60   60   60    3
57    8   36   10    1   60   60   57   36   60
 5   50   20   32   57   10   20   22    1   20
20    3   60   25   20   60   20   16   36   57
40   22   20    5   60    6   60    1   24    5
20   10   57   24   18   30   36   20   60   60
```

(a) Represent this data on a frequency chart.

(b) Draw a bar graph using this data.

8 'It is very important to be able to do simple calculations in your head without using a calculator. It is essential then that you know your tables.'

(a) Draw up a frequency table to show the number of times the vowels appear in the above sentences.

(b) Illustrate your answer by drawing a bar chart.

9 Ask 40 people which month their birthday is in.

(a) Record your results and draw a frequency chart.

(b) Present the data as (i) a pictogram, (ii) a bar chart.

10 Record the first letter on the number plate of 50 cars.

(a) Use your results to draw up a frequency chart.

(b) Illustrate your results by drawing a bar chart.

11 Collect some data of your own.

(a) Tabulate your result

(b) Illustrate your result.

(c) What deductions can you make?

9.3 Using bar charts to compare data

Bar charts can be used to compare different sets of data.

Example 3

Here are some exam results for 3 pupils:

	Music	RE	French
Alrik	75%	70%	65%
Ben	60%	70%	55%
Carl	55%	70%	90%

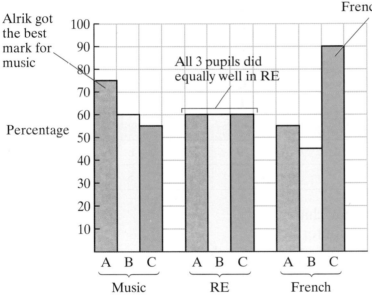

Alrik got the best mark for music

All 3 pupils did equally well in RE

Carl did very well in his French exams

It is easy to compare data presented in a bar chart.

Exercise 9C

1   The number of goals scored by two teams in six
    matches between them were as follows:

Tranmere United	2	5	3	1	6	4
Bicester Rovers	4	2	5	4	3	3

(a) Draw bar charts to illustrate this data.

(b) In which matches did Tranmere United score three more goals than Bicester Rovers?

(c) In how many matches were exactly seven goals scored?

2 This table shows the number of sightings of three types of butterfly one summer:

	April	May	June	July	August
Tortoiseshell	4	1	5	2	7
Holly Blue	5	4	2	0	6
Red Admiral	1	3	3	1	0

(a) Draw a bar chart to illustrate this data.

(b) Which butterfly had the most sightings?

(c) Which month had the least sightings?

3 The numbers of computers sold by two salespeople were as follows:

	March	April	May	June	July	August	September
Ms Finney	10	13	7	9	4	6	15
Ms O'Rahilly	11	6	10	8	7	8	12

(a) Present this data as a bar chart.

(b) Who sold the most computers?

(c) In which month were most computers sold?

(d) A £35 bonus is given for each computer sold. Calculate the bonuses Ms Finney and Ms O'Rahilly will receive during these seven months.

4 The maximum and minimum temperatures between March and September one year are as follows:

	March	April	May	June	July	August	September
Maximum (°C)	19	21	22	24	29	30	25
Minimum (°C)	10	12	13	15	18	21	17

(a) Draw a bar chart to represent this data.

(b) Compare the results by making three observations.

5 Thelma and Pamela's marks are given in the table:

	Maths	English	Science	History	Art	IT	Geography
Thelma	46	58	52	35	63	48	54
Pamela	62	47	68	44	48	56	36

(a) Draw bar charts to represent this data.
(Hint: start the frequency at 30.)
(b) Compare the results by making three observations.

6 The hockey results of two schools are shown in the table:

	Played	Won	Drawn	Lost	Goal difference	Points
Bluecoat	10	6	2	2	+7	14
Red Hill	12	8	1	3	+5	17

(a) Present this data as bar charts.
(b) Comment on anything you notice when comparing the results.
(c) Calculate the average points scored per match for each school.
(d) Which school had the better season? Give a reason for your answer.

9.4 Discrete and continuous data

Data can be **discrete** or **continuous**. It is important to know which type of data you are working with when representing information graphically.

■ **Data which can be counted is called discrete data.**

■ **Data which cannot take exact values and must be weighed or measured is called continuous data.**

Example 4

(a) This table shows the different numbers of people getting off a train at different times of the day:

	N	Cf	S	C
9 a.m. train	75	95	80	50
11 a.m. train	45	65	55	60

Key	
Newport	N
Cardiff	Cf
Swansea	S
Carmarthen	C

This data is **discrete**.
It can be shown in a bar-line graph:

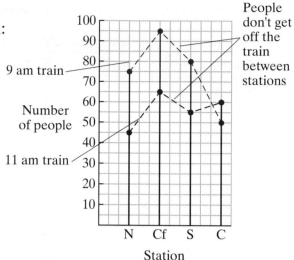

9 am train

Number of people

11 am train

100
90
80
70
60
50
40
30
20
10

People don't get off the train between stations

People don't get off the train between stations

N   Cf   S   C

Station

Joining up the plotted points of this bar-line graph can be useful when comparing data or looking for trends:

- Most people get off at Cardiff.
- More people travel at 9 a.m. than 11 a.m. generally.
- More people got off at Carmarthen at 11 a.m. than 9 a.m.

However, the line segments between the plotted points do *not* represent actual data – people don't get off the train between stations!

(b) This shows the maximum temperature during one week in Leeds and Manchester:

	Sa	S	M	T	W	Th	F
Leeds (°F)	73	72	74	70	68	72	75
Manchester (°F)	70	71	70	69	68	71	72

Key	
Saturday	Sa
Sunday	S
Monday	M
Tuesday	T
Wednesday	W
Thursday	Th
Friday	F

This data is **continuous**. It is useful to plot the points and draw a graph:

Temperature (°F)

75
74
73
72
71
70
69
68
67
66
65
64

Leeds

Manchester

Remember: your axes don't need to begin at zero.

Sa   S   M   T   W   Th   F

Day

These graphs are useful when comparing data:

- Manchester was generally colder than Leeds during this week.
- Leeds had a greater range of maximum temperatures during this week.
- Wednesday was the coldest day in both cities, when they both had a maximum temperature of 68°F.

Because this data is continuous, the line segments between the plotted points can also give useful information:

- Between Sunday and Monday, the temperature rose in Leeds and fell in Manchester.
- The maximum temperature in Leeds fell more sharply between Monday and Tuesday than between Tuesday and Wednesday.

Exercise 9D

1   State whether the following are discrete or continuous data.
   (a) The number of ice creams sold yesterday at a cricket match.
   (b) The number of runs scored in the match.
   (c) The temperature during the day at the match.
   (d) The number of spectators at the match.
   (e) The ages of the spectators.
   (f) The height of the flagpole.
   (g) The length of the pitch.
   (h) The weight of the ball.
   (i) The area of the ground.

2   The graph shows the cost of silver, in pounds per ounce, last year.

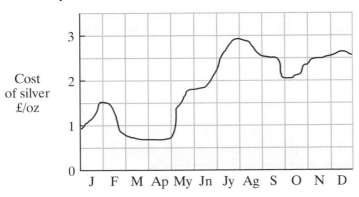

(a) By how much did the price rise during the year?
(b) What was the highest price reached?
(c) In which month was the biggest fall in price?
(d) When could you buy the silver for less than 75p an ounce?
(e) In which months was the price between £1.50 and £2 an ounce?

3 Draw line graphs to represent each of the following:

(a) The number of phone calls Sheila made last week, as shown in the table:

	Mon	Tues	Wed	Thurs	Fri	Sat	Sun
No. of calls	5	3	8	6	4	7	10

(b) The maximum temperature, in °C, last week as shown in the table:

	Mon	Tues	Wed	Thurs	Fri	Sat	Sun
Temperature	9	10	8	8	11	9	7

(c) The weight, in kilograms, of a baby in its first seven months:

	Jan	Feb	Mar	Apr	May	June	July
Weight	3.6	4.0	4.6	5.6	6.4	7.0	7.7

(d) The number of litres of petrol in a car's tank:

	Mon	Tues	Wed	Thurs	Fri	Sat	Sun
No. of litres	61	58	32	29	60	38	33

9.5 Histograms

A histogram is often used to represent continuous data. It is very similar to a bar chart, but because the data is continuous, there must not be any gaps between the bars.

Example 5

For homework, 20 pupils were asked to design a symmetrical pattern for the front of their DT folder.

This table shows how many minutes the class spent on their homework:

Time in minutes	Frequency
10 to less than 20	1
20 to less than 30	2
30 to less than 40	4
40 to less than 50	7
50 to less than 60	6

Draw a histogram for this data.

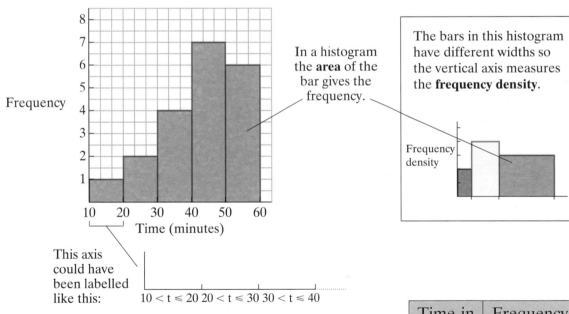

In a histogram the **area** of the bar gives the frequency.

The bars in this histogram have different widths so the vertical axis measures the **frequency density**.

This axis could have been labelled like this: $10 < t \leq 20$ $20 < t \leq 30$ $30 < t \leq 40$

When drawing a histogram using continuous data, it is important to think of sensible **class boundaries**.

This table is confusing. Where would you put a value of 20? Or 30?

The class boundaries have overlapping values.

Each of these is called a **class** or **interval**.

Time in minutes	Frequency
10–20	?
20–30	?
30–40	?

Exercise 9E

1   The lengths of 30 runner beans were recorded to the nearest cm.

Length (cm)	1–5	6–10	11–15	16–20	21–25
Number of beans	3	7	10	8	2

(a) Draw a histogram to represent this data using
the class boundaries in the table.

(b) Which interval would you use for a bean of
length (i) 10.8 cm, (ii) 15.1 cm.

Hint: remember to round the lengths to the nearest cm first.

2   Michael noted the number of cars arriving and leaving
a supermarket over 24 minutes.

Time (mins)	1–4	5–8	9–12	13–16	17–20	21–24
Cars arriving	5	12	8	10	7	9
Cars leaving	6	9	11	4	14	7

(a) Draw a bar chart to represent both sets of data.

(b) Draw a histogram for each set of data.

3   Forty people entered a crossword competition. This
table shows how long it took them to complete the
crossword, to the nearest minute.

Time taken to nearest minute	5–8	9–12	13–16	17–20	21–24	25–28
Number of people	2	4	12	10	8	4

(a) Draw a histogram to illustrate this data.

(b) Did most people take a long time to finish the
crossword, or did they all finish quickly? Comment
on anything else you notice.

(c) In which interval is the median?

(d) Which is the modal interval?

4   Rain measured the heights of 11 plants for her school
project, to the nearest cm:

   3 cm, 10 cm, 27 cm, 14 cm, 7 cm, 4 cm, 15 cm, 8 cm, 19 cm, 7 cm, 21 cm.

(a) Using the intervals 1–4, 5–8, 9–12, and so on,
create a frequency table.

(b) Using the information from your frequency table,
draw a histogram to represent the data.

(c) In which interval is the median?

(d) Which is the modal interval?

9.6 Pie charts

A pie chart uses a circle to represent data.

This pie chart shows the different ways that pupils come to school.

The sections clearly show the proportion of pupils using each method.

It is easy to see that

- a lot of pupils walk to school
- only a few pupils come by train
- a similar number of pupils come by car or bus, and so on.

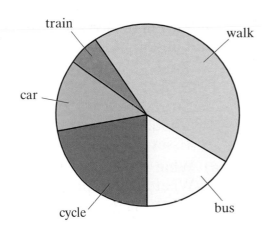

To draw a pie chart, you need to work out what size to draw the sections, by using angles.

If you draw a line from the centre of the circle to the edge and, starting at the line, go all the way around until you are back at the line, you will go through 360°.

When dividing the circle into sections, you have to divide this 360° in the correct proportions.

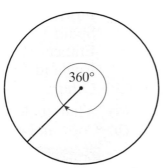

Example 6

12 pupils were asked what their favourite colour was. Use the table of results to draw a pie chart to represent this data.

Colour	Frequency
Blue	3
Red	6
Green	2
Yellow	1

There are 12 pupils altogether, which will be represented by the pie chart (360°).

Each pupil will be represented by $360° \div 12 = 30°$

If 1 pupil (yellow) is 30°

$$3 \text{ pupils (blue)} = 3 \times 30° = 90°$$
$$6 \text{ pupils (red)} = 6 \times 30° = 180°$$
$$\text{and } 2 \text{ pupils (green)} = 2 \times 30° = 60°$$

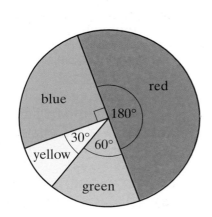

Exercise 9F

1   The pie chart shows where the 18 members
    of a London office live:

    Kent   6
    Sussex   2
    Surrey   5
    Middlesex   4
    Essex   1

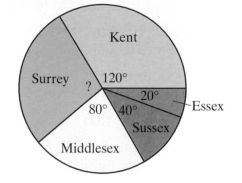

    (a) What is the size of the missing angle?
    (b) What angle represents one member?
    (c) What fraction of members come from
        (i) Kent, **(ii)** Middlesex?

2   The pie chart shows where 24 pupils went for
    their holiday last year.

    Florida, USA   3
    Spain   6
    France   5
    England   8
    Other   2

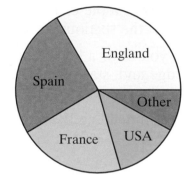

    (a) What angle represents one pupil?
    (b) Copy and complete the table:

Country	Number of pupils	Angle on pie chart
USA		
Spain		
France		
England		
Other		

3   The table shows the number of birds seen on a bird table one morning:

    (a) On a pie chart, what angle
        would represent one bird?
    (b) What angle would
        represent starlings?
    (c) Draw a pie chart to
        represent this data.

Type of bird	Number
Sparrow	6
Blackbird	4
Thrush	2
Robin	1
Starling	5

4 The musical instruments played by members of a music club are shown in the table:

Instrument	Violin	Flute	Piano	Drums	Clarinet	Cello	Trumpet
Number	6	3	8	4	5	1	3

(a) On a pie chart, what angle would represent one instrument?
(b) What angle would represent (i) the clarinet, (ii) the drums?
(c) Draw a pie chart to represent this data.

5 The table shows the sport played by pupils last Saturday:

Sport	Hockey	Tennis	Swimming	Rugby	Soccer	Netball	Squash
Number	7	5	3	9	6	4	2

(a) Represent this data by drawing (i) a pie chart, (ii) a bar chart.
(b) What proportion of pupils played (i) soccer, (ii) rugby?

6 The flavour of ice cream chosen by a group of tourists was:

Flavour	Vanilla	Cherry	Raspberry	Coffee	Mint	Chocolate
Number	15	8	10	12	6	9

(a) Represent this data by drawing (i) a pie chart, (ii) a bar chart.
(b) What proportion of tourists chose (i) raspberry, (ii) coffee?
(c) What percentage chose (i) vanilla, (ii) mint?

7 Lee bought presents for the family. He spent on each:

    Mother   £6.00
    Father   £3.50
    Sister   £4.00
    Brother   £4.50

(a) Draw a pie chart to represent this data.
(b) If he started with £20 what percentage did he spend (i) on his mother, (ii) altogether?

8 Anne did some baby-sitting and was paid the following amounts:
    £8, £10, £6.50, £4.50, £7.00.

(a) Draw a pie chart to represent this data.
(b) What was the average amount she was paid?

9.7 Scatter graphs

Another useful way of comparing data is by drawing a scatter diagram.

Example 7

Here are the exam results for 10 pupils:

Paper 1	41	52	67	55	37	78	43	59	53	66
Paper 2	52	63	71	65	48	75	56	66	58	68

If these pairs of marks, (41, 52), (52, 63), and so on are plotted, the result is:

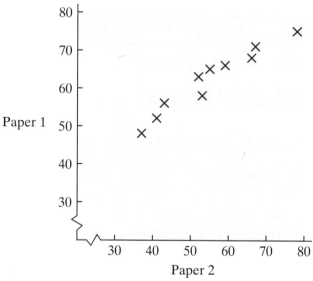

There seems to be a relationship between the marks. Pupils who got high marks on paper 1 also got high marks on paper 2.

The relationship between two sets of data is called **correlation**. Here are two types of correlation:

If there is no correlation the points will be randomly distributed.

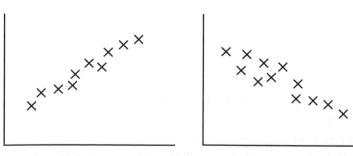

Positive correlation   Negative correlation

Example 8

The table shows the amount of petrol left in a car's tank on a journey:

Number of litres	Miles travelled
44	15
40	34
38	50
36	64
34	78

Number of litres	Miles travelled
31	102
24	146
20	175
17	206
12	240

(a) Draw a scatter graph.
(b) What type of correlation does it show?
(c) Estimate the mileage travelled when the tank is empty.

(a)

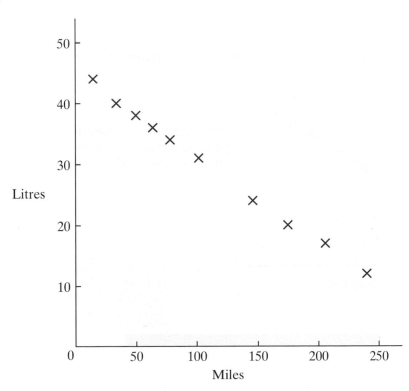

(b) There is negative or inverse correlation. The longer the journeys, the less petrol there is in the tank.

(c) When the tank is empty, the car will have travelled approximately 300 miles.

Example 9

The scatter graph shows the marks in an Art exam and a French exam:

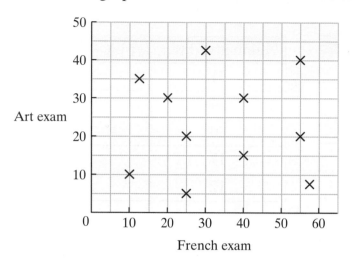

The scatter graph shows no obvious relationship, so there is no correlation.

Example 10

The scatter diagram shows the number of ice-creams sold each day over the last fortnight in Brighton and the number of people who went each day to the British Museum. (Each cross represents a single day during the fortnight.)

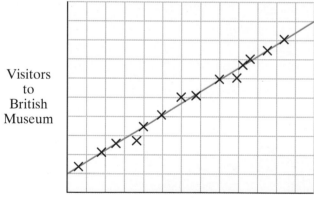

Although it would appear that there is good correlation, the two items have no connection, so it is unlikely there is any correlation.

Exercise 9G

1   Draw simple diagrams to illustrate:
   (a) no correlation
   (b) perfect positive correlation
   (c) low inverse correlation
   (d) high negative correlation.

2   What type of correlation would you expect between the
    following?
    (a) hand span and height
    (b) reaction time and alcohol
    (c) speed and braking distance
    (d) accidents and cinema attendance.

3   The table shows the marks for two science papers:

Paper 1	30	45	18	32	28	15	40	24	35	20
Paper 2	28	42	12	34	30	14	38	20	32	18

    (a) Show this data on a scatter diagram.
    (b) What type of correlation is there?
    (c) Which paper do you think was the easier? Give
       your reason.

4   The runs scored by two teams in a one-innings match
    are given in the table:

Batsman	No. 1	No. 2	No. 3	No. 4	No. 5	No. 6	No. 7	No. 8	No. 9	No. 10	No. 11
Surrey	2	1	96	25	40	14	19	4	11	2	0
Sussex	1	17	26	17	18	3	8	22	11	3	1

    (a) Show this data on a scatter diagram.
    (b) What type of correlation is there?
    (c) How many more runs did Surrey score than
       Sussex?

5   The table shows pupils' marks in a series of tests:

Mathematics	34	18	46	28	49	23	40	16	24	38
Physics	30	16	42	30	45	18	38	16	22	33
German	26	40	30	37	17	32	45	15	41	20
History	28	32	22	25	24	30	25	34	23	22

    (a) Draw scatter graphs to compare:
       (i)   Mathematics and Physics
       (ii) Mathematics and German
       (iii) Mathematics and History
       (iv) German and History.
    (b) What type of correlation does each have?
    (c) Comment on your findings.

6 The number of cars sold by two branches of a garage is given in the table:

	Jan	Feb	Mar	Apr	May	Jun	Jul	Aug	Sept	Oct	Nov	Dec
North Street	5	55	40	15	33	45	12	58	50	25	20	10
Hatton Row	25	45	42	35	11	25	45	44	12	40	10	15

(a) Represent this data by drawing **(i)** a dual bar chart,
   (ii) a scatter diagram.
(b) Comment on your results.

Summary of key points

1 Data which can be counted is called **discrete** data.

2 Data which cannot take exact values and must be weighed or measured is called **continuous** data.

10 Number patterns

Number patterns are everywhere.

The number of spirals in this sunflower are from a very famous number pattern called the Fibonacci sequence.

10.1 Patterns from shapes

Look at this pattern made from squares.

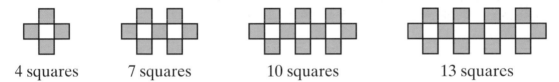

4 squares   7 squares   10 squares   13 squares

In numbers the pattern is:

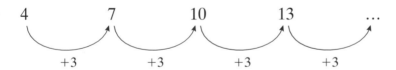

The rule to go from one shape to the next is **+3** squares.

Exercise 10A

1   For these shape patterns:
    • Draw the next two shapes.
    • Write down the number pattern.
    • Write down the rule to go from one shape to the next.

    (a)

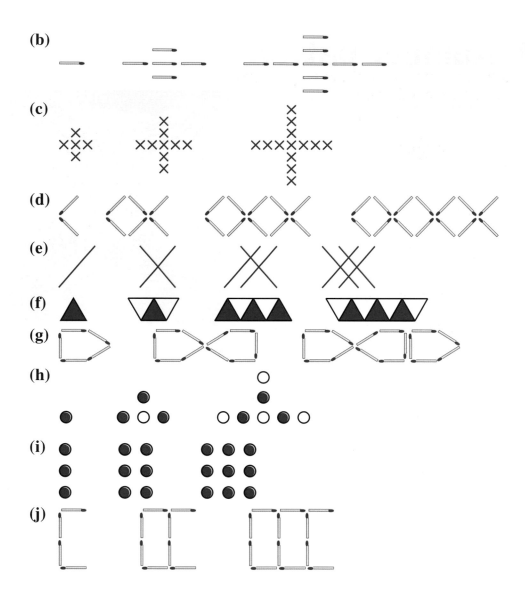

10.2 Number machines

You can use number machines to make number patterns.

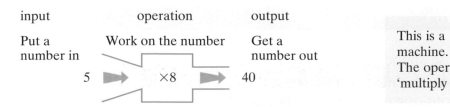

This is a ×8 number machine.
The operation is 'multiply by 8'.

You can **input** a sequence of numbers.
Then you will get a sequence of numbers as **output**.

You can show this in a table.

Example 1

Find the output when you input the number pattern
1, 2, 3, 4 into a '×6' number machine.

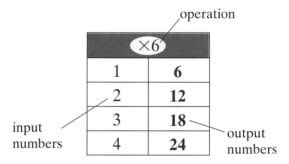

operation

×6	
1	**6**
2	**12**
3	**18**
4	**24**

input numbers

output numbers

When you put a
pattern into a
number machine the
output numbers
make a pattern too.
Input: 1, 2, 3, 4
Rule is **×6**
Output: 6, 12, 18, 24

Two-step number machines

You can show two-step number machines in a table too.

Example 2

Find the output from a '×3 −2' number machine if you
input the pattern 2, 4, 6, 8.

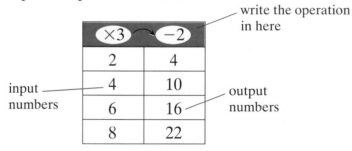

write the operation
in here

×3	−2
2	4
4	10
6	16
8	22

input numbers

output numbers

input   output

$2 \times 3 = 6 \Rightarrow 6 - 2 = 4$

$4 \times 3 = 12 \Rightarrow 12 - 2 = 10$

$6 \times 3 = 18 \Rightarrow 18 - 2 = 16$

$8 \times 3 = 24 \Rightarrow 24 - 2 = 22$

Exercise 10B

1 Write down the output numbers for these number machines:

(a)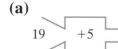

19   +5

(b)

17   −4

(c)

4   ×6

(d)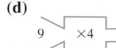

9   ×4

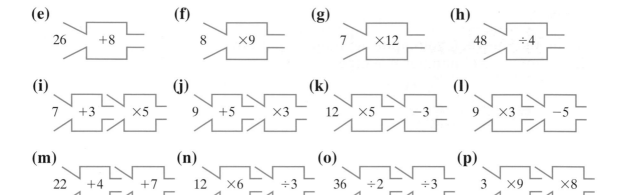

(e) 26 +8

(f) 8 ×9

(g) 7 ×12

(h) 48 ÷4

(i) 7 +3 ×5

(j) 9 +5 ×3

(k) 12 ×5 −3

(l) 9 ×3 −5

(m) 22 +4 +7

(n) 12 ×6 ÷3

(o) 36 ÷2 ÷3

(p) 3 ×9 ×8

2   Copy and complete the tables to show the output numbers.

(a)

×4	
1	
2	
3	
4	
5	

(b)

+19	
1	
2	
3	
4	
5	

(c)

×7	
1	
2	
3	
4	
5	

(d)

÷2	
2	
4	
6	
8	
10	

(e)

×3	
5	
10	
15	
20	
25	

(f)

÷3	
3	
6	
9	
12	
15	

(g)

×10	
10	
20	
30	
40	
50	

(h)

×3	
1	
3	
5	
7	
9	

(i)

+3	×2
1	
2	
3	
4	
5	

(j)

×5 → −4	
1	
2	
3	
4	
5	

(k)

×10 → ÷2	
1	
2	
3	
4	
5	

(l)

+6 → +7	
1	
2	
3	
4	
5	

(m)

×5 → ÷2	
2	
4	
6	
8	
10	

(n)

+4 → +9	
0	
2	
4	
6	
8	

(o)

÷5 → +6	
5	
10	
15	
20	
25	

(p)

×10 → −6	
10	
20	
30	
40	
50	

(q)

×9 → ÷3	
1	
3	
5	
7	
9	

(r)

÷2 → −3	
8	
16	
24	
32	
40	

10.3 Inverses

An inverse operation 'undoes' the original operation.

Operation	Inverse
+	−
−	+
×	÷
÷	×

Example 3

Copy and complete the table:

×5	
2	10
	15
4	20
	25
	30

The inverse of ×5 is ÷5

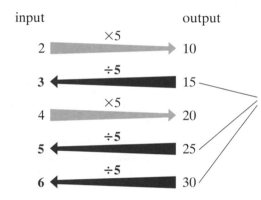

Use the inverse operation on these to find the missing input numbers.

Exercise 10C

1 Write the inverse operations:

(a) ×6   (b) ÷9   (c) −100 (d) ×52   (e) ÷$\frac{1}{2}$

(f) ×$\frac{1}{4}$ (g) +62   (h) −74   (i) ×212   (j) ÷169

2 Copy and complete these tables:

(a)

+7	
4	
	12
	13
7	14
	15

(b)

−3	
9	
	7
	8
	9
13	

(c)

×4	
	16
5	
	24
7	
	32

(d)

÷5	
	5
	10
	15
	20
	25

(e)

×9	
	27
	36
	45
	54
	63

(f)

−8	
6	−2
	−1
8	
	1
	2

(g)

+4	
21	
	26
	27
24	
	29

(h)

÷3	
	3
18	6
	9
	12
	15

(i)

÷9	
54	
	7
72	
	9
	10

(j)

×10	
	1000
	2000
	3000
	4000
	5000

(k)

×7	
6	
	49
	56
	63
10	

(l)

×11	
	77
	88
	99
	110
	121

10.4 Number sequences

Each number in a sequence is called a **term**.

9, 18, 27, 36, 45, . . . , . . . , . . .

This is the **first term** or term number 1.

This is the **fifth term** or term number 5.

An unknown number in the sequence is the **nth term** or term number n.

When exploring number sequences you look for:

■ **a rule to find the next term**

■ **a rule to find *any* term – the nth term.**

Finding the next term

To find the next term in this sequence, add 9:

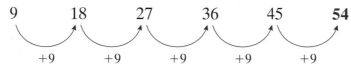

The next term is **54** and the rule is **+9**.

Exercise 10D

For each sequence write down:
- the next 3 terms
- the rule you used.

(a) 2, 5, 8, ... **(b)** 4, 8, 12, 16, ... **(c)** 50, 45, 40, ...
(d) 100, 110, 120, ... **(e)** 1, 4, 7, 10, ... **(f)** 3, 6, 9, 12, ...
(g) 60, 50, 40, ... **(h)** 64, 32, 16, ... **(i)** 2, 4, 8, 16, ...
(j) 10 000, 1000, 100, ... **(k)** 11, 61, 111, ... **(l)** $1\frac{1}{2}$, 3, $4\frac{1}{2}$, ...

Finding the nth term

You can show number sequences in a table.
This can help you spot the **general rule** or the **nth term rule**.

Example 4

Find the general rule for this sequence:

2, 4, 6, 8, 10, ...

Write the sequence and the term numbers in a table:

The 7th term will be $7 \times 2 = 14$
The general rule for this sequence is:
the **nth term** is $n \times 2 = 2n$.

> Look for the term number and the sequence number.
> Here the rule is ×2.

Term number	Sequence
1 ——×2—→	2
2 ——×2—→	4
3 ——×2—→	6
4 ——×2—→	8
5 ——×2—→	10
6 ——×2—→	12
⋮	⋮
n ——×2—→	$2n$

Exercise 10E

1   Find the general rule for each sequence.

(a)

Term number	Sequence
1 —— +5 —→ 6	
2 —— +5 —→ 7	
3 —— +5 —→ 8	
4 —— +5 —→ 9	
5 —— +5 —→ 10	
⋮	⋮
n —— +5 —→	

(b)

Term number	Sequence
1 —— ×3 —→ 3	
2 —— ×3 —→ 6	
3 —— ×3 —→ 9	
4 —— ×3 —→ 12	
5 —— ×3 —→ 15	
⋮	⋮
n —— ×3 —→	

(c)

Term number	Sequence
1 —— + —→ 12	
2 —— + —→ 13	
3 —— + —→ 14	
4 —— + —→ 15	
5 —— + —→ 16	
⋮	⋮
n —— + —→	

(d)

Term number	Sequence
1 —— − —→ 0	
2 —— − —→ 1	
3 —— − —→ 2	
4 —— − —→ 3	
5 —— − —→ 4	
⋮	⋮
n —— − —→	

(e)

Term number	Sequence
1 —— × —→ 10	
2 —— × —→ 20	
3 —— × —→ 30	
4 —— × —→ 40	
5 —— × —→ 50	
⋮	⋮
n —— × —→	

(f)

Term number	Sequence
1 —————→ 5	
2 —————→ 10	
3 —————→ 15	
4 —————→ 20	
5 —————→ 25	
⋮	⋮
n —————→	

(g)

Term number	Sequence
1	18
2	19
3	20
4	21
5	22
⋮	⋮
n	

(h)

Term number	Sequence
1	1000
2	2000
3	3000
4	4000
5	5000
⋮	⋮
n	

(i)

Term number	Sequence
1	−1
2	0
3	1
4	2
5	3
⋮	⋮
n	

(j)

Term number	Sequence
1	7
2	14
3	21
4	28
5	35
⋮	⋮
n	

2   For each sequence:
- put the information into a table
- find the general rule.

(a) 8, 9, 10, 11, 12, ...   (b) 6, 12, 18, 24, 30, ...
(c) 8, 16, 24, 32, 40, ...   (d) 23, 24, 25, 26, 27, ...
(e) 25, 50, 75, 100, 125, ...   (f) −1, −2, −3, −4, −5, ...
(g) 14, 15, 16, 17, 18, ...   (h) $\frac{1}{2}$, 1, $1\frac{1}{2}$, 2, $2\frac{1}{2}$, ...

Hint
×

Hint
÷

Finding terms

When you know the general rule you can find any term in a sequence.

Example 5

Find the 10th, 12th and 100th terms if the general rule is:

   nth term $= 4n$

$4n = 4 \times n$

If nth term is $4n$:

   10th term is $4 \times 10 = 40$
   12th term is $4 \times 12 = 48$
   100th term is $4 \times 100 = 400$

Exercise 10F

1 (a) Find the 5th term if the nth term is $6n$
   (b) Find the 8th term if the nth term is $8n$
   (c) Find the 12th term if the nth term is $n + 5$
   (d) Find the 20th term if the nth term is $3n - 1$
   (e) Find the 3rd term if the nth term is $5n - 2$
   (f) Find the 50th term if the nth term is $6n + 1$
   (g) Find the 100th term if the nth term is $n \div 2$
   (h) Find the 7th term if the nth term is $3n + 4$
   (i) Find the 11th term if the nth term is $11n$
   (j) Find the 18th term if the nth term is $n \div 3$

10.5 Using the difference to find the general rule

The sequence

$4, 7, 10, 13, 16, \ldots$

can be written in a table:

Term number	Sequence
1	4
2	7
3	10
4	13
5	16
6	19
$\vdots$	$\vdots$
10	31
$\vdots$	$\vdots$
100	301
$\vdots$	$\vdots$
n	$3n + 1$

+3
+3
+3
+3

The difference
between terms is +3

The first part of the
general rule is $3n$

The difference between consecutive terms gives you the *first part* of the general rule.

To find the *second part* of the general rule you need to try a few values:

Term number	$3n$	Sequence
1	3	4
2	6	7
3	9	10

Each time $3n$ is 1 less than the sequence.

You need to add 1 to $3n$.

The general rule is $3n + 1$.

■ **The difference between terms in a sequence gives the number to multiply n by in the general rule.**
You may need to add or subtract a number to complete the general rule.

Example 6

Find the nth term of the sequence

$$3, 8, 13, 18, 23, \ldots$$

Write the sequence in a table:

Term number	Sequence
1	3
2	8
3	13
4	18
5	23
⋮	⋮
n	

+5
+5
+5
+5

The rule must start with $5n$

Try a few values:

Term number	5n	Sequence
1	5	3
2	10	8
3	15	13

Each time $5n$ is 2 more than the sequence.
You need to subtract 2 from $5n$.

The general term is $5n - 2$

Example 7

Find the general term of the sequence

20, 16, 12, 8, 4, ...

Write the information in a table:

Term number	Sequence
1	20
2	16
3	12
4	8
5	4
⋮	⋮
n	

−4
−4
−4
−4

Rule starts
$-4 \times n$

Try a few values:

Term number	−4n	Sequence
1	−4	20
2	−8	16
3	−12	8

Each time $-4n$ is 24 less than the sequence. You have to add 24.

The general term is $-4n + 24$.

Exercise 10G

For each sequence use differences to find the 10th, 100th and nth terms.

(a)

Term number	Sequence
1	3
2	6
3	9
4	12
5	15
⋮	⋮
10	
⋮	⋮
100	
⋮	⋮
n	

+3
+3
+3
+3

(*Hint*: nth term = ☐n)

(b)

Term number	Sequence
1	5
2	10
3	15
4	20
5	25
⋮	⋮
10	
⋮	⋮
100	
⋮	⋮
n	

+5
+5
+5
+5

(*Hint*: nth term = ☐n)

(c)

Term number	Sequence
1	4
2	7
3	10
4	13
5	16
⋮	⋮
10	
⋮	⋮
100	
⋮	⋮
n	

+3

(*Hint*: nth term = ☐n + ☐)

(d)

Term number	Sequence
1	5
2	7
3	9
4	11
5	13
⋮	⋮
10	
⋮	⋮
100	
⋮	⋮
n	

+2

(*Hint*: nth term = ☐n + ☐)

(e)

Term number	Sequence
1	13
2	14
3	15
4	16
5	17
⋮	⋮
10	
⋮	⋮
100	
⋮	⋮
n	

$+1$

(*Hint*: nth term = ☐n + ☐)

(f)

Term number	Sequence
1	7
2	11
3	15
4	19
5	23
⋮	⋮
10	
⋮	⋮
100	
⋮	⋮
n	

$+4$

(*Hint*: nth term = ☐n + ☐)

(g)

Term number	Sequence
1	0
2	1
3	2
4	3
5	4
⋮	⋮
10	
⋮	⋮
100	
⋮	⋮
n	

(*Hint*: ☐n − ☐)

(h)

Term number	Sequence
1	27
2	24
3	21
4	18
5	15
⋮	⋮
10	
⋮	⋮
100	
⋮	⋮
n	

-3

(*Hint*: $-3n$ + ☐)

(i)

Term number	Sequence
1	9
2	14
3	19
4	24
5	29
$\vdots$	$\vdots$
10	
$\vdots$	$\vdots$
100	
$\vdots$	$\vdots$
n	

(j)

Term number	Sequence
1	-1
2	-2
3	-3
4	-4
5	-5
$\vdots$	$\vdots$
10	
$\vdots$	$\vdots$
100	
$\vdots$	$\vdots$
n	

-1

Summary of key points

1 When exploring number sequences you look for:
   - a rule to find the next term
   - a rule to find *any* term – **the nth term**

2 The difference between terms in a sequence gives the number to multiply n by in the general rule. You may need to add or subtract a number to complete the general rule.

11 Decimals

11.1 Writing decimal numbers in size order

Sometimes you need to sort decimal numbers in order of size.

Five pupils took part in a long jump competition. The lengths (in metres) of their jumps were:
    3.24,   3.7,   5.1,   3.53,   4.03

Write these lengths in order of size, starting with the largest.

First look at the whole number part:

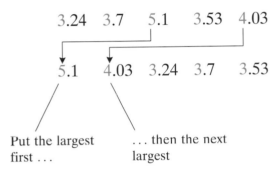

Put the largest first . . .   . . . then the next largest

3.24, 3.7 and 3.53 all have 3 units.
Sort them using the tenths digit.

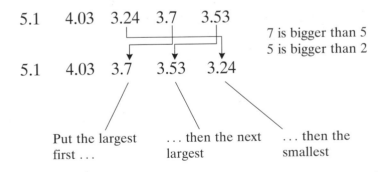

7 is bigger than 5
5 is bigger than 2

Put the largest first . . .   . . . then the next largest   . . . then the smallest

Now the lengths are in size order: 5.1, 4.03, 3.7, 3.53, 3.24

■   **To sort decimal numbers in order of size:**
- **first compare the whole numbers**
- **next compare the tenths**
- **then compare the hundredths and so on.**

Example 1

Put these decimals in order, smallest first:

    0.381   0.452   0.486   0.38   0.484

There are no units so sort them by tenths first:

    0.381   0.452   0.486   0.38   0.484

    0.381   0.38   0.486   0.452   0.484

Next sort the hundredths into order:

    0.381   0.38   0.486   0.452   0.484

    0.381   0.38   0.452   0.486   0.484

And finally the thousandths:

    0.381   0.38   0.452   0.486   0.484

    0.38   0.381   0.452   0.484   0.486

Hint:
Think of 0.38 as 0.380

Exercise 11A

1   Rearrange these decimal numbers in order of size, starting with the largest:

    (a) 4.5, 4.23, 4.82, 3.24, 3.06   (b) 3.08, 5.6, 5.09, 3.52, 3.7
    (c) 6.3, 4.8, 6.02, 6.17, 4.56   (d) 0.43, 0.06, 0.41, 0.8, 0.09
    (e) 0.31, 0.42, 0.37, 0.48, 0.6   (f) 5.08, 4.09, 5.3, 3.5, 3.17

2   Put these numbers in order of size, smallest first.

    (a) 4.85, 5.9, 5.26, 4.09, 5.33
    (b) 5, 7.23, 5.01, 7.07, 5.008
    (c) 2.009, 0.3, 2.04, 2.16, 0.06
    (d) 0.45, 0.09, 0.48, 0.032, 0.5
    (e) 3.4, 1.2, 0.48, 1.25, 1.256
    (f) 2.354, 2.362, 2.402, 2.4, 2.368, 2.524

11.2 Adding and subtracting decimal numbers

George bought a birthday cake that
weighed 1.74 kg and a bun that weighed 60 g.
Work out the total weight, in kg, of the
cake and the bun.

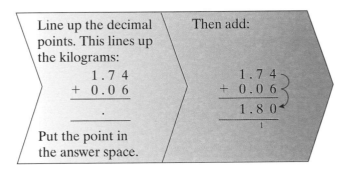

First change 60 g to 0.06 kg.

Line up the decimal points. This lines up the kilograms:	Then add:
$\begin{array}{r} 1.74 \\ +\ 0.06 \\ \hline \quad . \end{array}$	$\begin{array}{r} 1.74 \\ +\ 0.06 \\ \hline 1.80 \\ \scriptstyle 1 \end{array}$
Put the point in the answer space.	

1.80 and 1.8 have
the same value. The
answer is a number,
not an amount of
money, so the zero
in the hundredths
place can be
omitted.

The total weight is 1.8 kg.

■ **To add or subtract decimals:**
- **line up the decimal points**
- **put the point in the answer**
- **add or subtract.**

Example 2

Work out 58.7 − 15.42. Show all your working.

Line up the decimal points.	Put a zero in the hundredths place.	You need to change 7 tenths into 6 tenths and 10 hundredths.	Complete the subtraction:
$\begin{array}{r} 58.70 \\ -\ 15.42 \\ \hline \end{array}$		$\begin{array}{r} 58.\overset{6}{\cancel{7}}\overset{1}{0} \\ -\ 15.\ 4\ 2 \\ \hline .\qquad 8 \end{array}$	$\begin{array}{r} 58.\overset{6}{\cancel{7}}\overset{1}{0} \\ -\ 15.\ 4\ 2 \\ \hline 43.28 \end{array}$
Put the decimal point in the answer space.		Take away the hundredths: 10 − 2 = 8	

The answer is 43.28.

Example 3

Add 5.6, 3.204 and 14.63.
Write out the addition ...

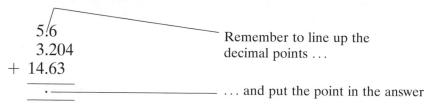

$$\begin{array}{r} 5.6 \\ 3.204 \\ + \ 14.63 \\ \hline . \\ \hline \end{array}$$

Remember to line up the decimal points ...

... and put the point in the answer

... and add

$$\begin{array}{r} 5.6 \\ 3.204 \\ + \ 14.63 \\ \hline 23.434 \\ \hline {\scriptstyle 1\ 1} \end{array}$$

Count any empty spaces as zero

The answer is 23.434

Example 4

Without doing any working on paper, write down the number that should go in the box to make these true:

(a) $1.3 + \boxed{} = 2$ **(b)** $7 - 6.8 = \boxed{}$

(a) $1.3 + \boxed{} = 2$

     The answer is 0.7

The number in the box must be less than 1
You can work out mentally that $0.3 + 0.7 = 1$
so $1.3 + 0.7 = 2$

(b) $7 - 6.8 = \boxed{}$

$7 - 6.8 = 7 - 6 - 0.8$
$ = 1 - 0.8$
$ = 0.2$

The answer is 0.2.

The number in the box must be less than 1
You can work out mentally that $1 = 0.8 + 0.2$
so $1 - 0.8 = 0.2$

Exercise 11B

1 Work out:
     (a) £42.38 + £23.46   **(b)** 4.86 kg + 3.72 kg
     (c) 126.4 + 0.83   **(d)** 4.23 + 13 + 0.529

2 Find:
(a) £5.73 − £2.48   (b) £14.30 − £7.76
(c) 7.4 − 4.6   (d) 12.9 − 7.23

3 Without doing any working on paper, write down the number that should go in the box to make these true:
(a) $2.4 + \boxed{} = 3$
(b) $4.7 + \boxed{} = 5$
(c) $5 - 4.2 = \boxed{}$
(d) $4 - 3.6 = \boxed{}$
(e) $2.8 + \boxed{} = 3$
(f) $5 - 4.1 = \boxed{}$
(g) $7.9 + \boxed{} = 8$
(h) $6 - 5.3 = \boxed{}$

4 Karla cut a length of 0.74 m from a three metre length of ribbon. Work out the length of ribbon left over.

5 Joe put 350 g of chopped tomatoes into a saucepan weighing 1.18 kg. Work out the total weight, in kg, of the saucepan and the tomatoes.

11.3 Changing decimals to fractions and fractions to decimals

■ **You can write decimal numbers as fractions by using a place value diagram.**

Example 5

Change 0.35 into a fraction in its simplest form.

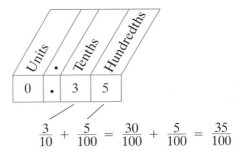

$$\frac{3}{10} + \frac{5}{100} = \frac{30}{100} + \frac{5}{100} = \frac{35}{100}$$

So 0.35 is the same as 35 hundredths.

To find the simplest form, divide top and bottom by 5:

$$0.35 = \frac{35}{100} = \frac{7}{20}$$

$\div 5$

$\div 5$

So 0.35 is equal to $\frac{7}{20}$.

■ **To change fractions to decimal numbers divide the numerator (top) by the denominator (bottom).**

Example 6

Change these fractions into decimal numbers

(a) $\frac{2}{5}$ **(b)** $\frac{3}{8}$ **(c)** $\frac{6}{25}$

(a) $\frac{2}{5}$ means $2 \div 5 = 0.4$

(b) $\frac{3}{8}$ means $3 \div 8 = 0.375$

(c) $\frac{6}{25}$ means $6 \div 25 = 0.24$

Use these calculator keys:

Exercise 11C

1 Change these decimals to fractions in their simplest form:

     (a) 0.7   **(b)** 0.4   **(c)** 0.15
     (d) 0.16   **(e)** 0.25   **(f)** 0.8
     (g) 0.31   **(h)** 0.05   **(i)** 0.75
     (j) 0.36   **(k)** 0.14   **(l)** 0.025
     (m) 0.28   **(n)** 0.06   **(o)** 0.84
     (p) 0.625   **(q)** 0.2   **(r)** 0.18

2 Change these fractions to decimal numbers:

     (a) $\frac{3}{10}$ **(b)** $\frac{23}{100}$ **(c)** $\frac{7}{100}$
     (d) $\frac{413}{1000}$ **(e)** $\frac{4}{5}$ **(f)** $\frac{1}{8}$
     (g) $\frac{9}{20}$ **(h)** $\frac{6}{25}$ **(i)** $\frac{3}{5}$
     (j) $\frac{7}{8}$ **(k)** $\frac{1}{40}$ **(l)** $\frac{3}{16}$
     (m) $\frac{2}{25}$ **(n)** $\frac{17}{20}$ **(o)** $\frac{34}{125}$

11.4 Rounding to the nearest whole number

It is sometimes useful to give your answer to the nearest whole number. This can help you check answers.

■ **To round to the nearest whole number, look at the digit in the first decimal place.**
  ● **If it is 5 or more round the whole number up to the next whole number.**
  ● **If it is less than 5 do not change the whole number.**

23.**6**

More than 5 so round up to 24

Example 7

Round these decimals to the nearest whole number.
(a) 45.3   (b) 56.5
(c) 0.73   (d) 19.81

(a) 45.3 is between 45 and 46.
The digit in the first decimal place is 3 so round to 45.
(b) 56.5 is between 56 and 57.
The digit in the first decimal place is 5 so round up to 57.
(c) 0.73 is between 0 and 1.
The digit in the first decimal place is 7 so round up to 1.
(d) 19.81 is between 19 and 20.
The digit in the first decimal place is 8 so round up to 20.

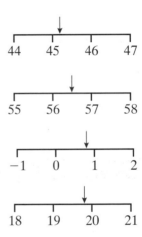

Exercise 11D

Round the decimals to the nearest whole number.

	(a)	(b)	(c)	(d)
1	3.9	4.1	7.5	5.83
2	5.281	6.723	20.38	19.7
3	0.8	15.399	28.35	100.08
4	69.81	12.07	4.99	19.53
5	3.298	49.8	399.7	26.19
6	68.47	0.74	59.5	2619.48

11.5 Rounding to a number of decimal places

You sometimes need to be more accurate than just using whole numbers.

■ **To round numbers to a given number of decimal places look at the digit in the next decimal place.**

'Decimal place' is sometimes written as **dp**.

Example 8

Write 6.2374 correct to 2 decimal places.

Look at the digit in the third decimal place.

    6.2374

6.2374 is between 6.23 and 6.24. The digit in the third decimal place is 7 so you round up to 6.24.

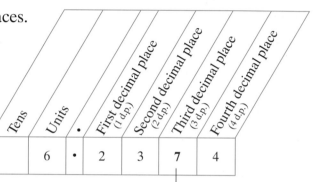

So 6.2374 = 6.24 (correct to 2 decimal places).

You can write this as 6.24 (to 2 dp).

Remember: less than 5, round down 5 or more, round up

Example 9

Round 7.3495
(a) to 1 dp   (b) to 2 dp   (c) to 3 dp

(a) To round to 1 dp look at the digit in the second decimal place. The digit is 4 so round down.
    7.3495 = 7.3 (to 1 dp)

7.3|495

(b) To round to 2 dp look at the digit in the third decimal place. The digit is 9 so round up.
    7.3495 = 7.35 (to 2 dp)

7.34|95

(c) To round to 3 dp look at the digit in the fourth decimal place. The digit is 5 so round up.
    7.3495 = 7.350 (to 3 dp)

7.349|5

You must include the final zero, as '3 dp' means that three decimal places must be shown.

Rounding money answers to the nearest penny

Rounding money answers is the same as rounding to 2 dp.

Example 10

Twelve people share equally the £86.50 cost of a small party. How much does each person pay?
Give your answer to the nearest penny.

Work out £86.50 ÷ 12

Using a calculator, the result is £7.208333333.

This is between £7.20 and £7.21.
The digit in the third decimal place is 8 so round up.

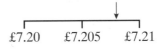

£7.20   £7.205   £7.21

Each person pays £7.21.

■ **To round an answer in pounds to the nearest penny, look at the digit in the third decimal place.**

- **If it is 5 or more round up the whole number of pence.**
- **If it is less than 5 do not change the whole number of pence.**

6.53**5**18

5 so round up to £6.54

Example 11

The answer to a calculation is £38.46253. Write this answer to the nearest penny.

£38.46**2**53 is between £38.46 and £38.47
The digit in the third decimal place is 2 so you round down.

The answer is £38.46 (to the nearest penny).

Recurring decimals

When you work out answers on your calculator you will sometimes find the pattern of digits repeats.

0.222222 . . . . . is called **0.2 recurring**. It is written **0.2̇** (with a dot over the 2) for short.

5.24242424 . . . . . is written **5.2̇4̇** (with dots over the 2 and 4).

0.222 . . . .

The dots show that the number repeats forever.

Use one recurring dot to show that one digit repeats forever.

Use two recurring dots to show that two digits repeat forever.

Example 12

Change these fractions to decimals. Write your answers as recurring decimals and to 2 decimal places:

(a) $\frac{1}{3}$ (b) $\frac{2}{3}$ (c) $\frac{2}{11}$

(a) $\frac{1}{3}$ means $1 \div 3$, which equals $0.33333\ldots$ $0.33\!\mid\!333\ldots$
    This is $0.\dot{3}$ as a recurring decimal or 0.33 to 2 dp.

(b) $\frac{2}{3}$ means $2 \div 3$, which equals $0.66666\ldots$ $0.66\!\mid\!666\ldots$
    This is $0.\dot{6}$ as a recurring decimal or 0.67 to 2 dp.

(c) $\frac{2}{11}$ means $2 \div 11$, which equals $0.181818\ldots$ $0.18\!\mid\!181\ldots$
    This is $0.\dot{1}\dot{8}$ as a recurring decimal or 0.18 to 2 dp.

Exercise 11E

1   Round each number to 1 dp.
    (a) 12.78   (b) 46.82   (c) 9.461   (d) 0.835

2   Round each number to 2 dp.
    (a) 6.349   (b) 46.222   (c) 5.625   (d) 0.0528

3   Round each number to 3 dp.
    (a) 3.7524   (b) 4.5635   (c) 3.0007   (d) 0.1498

4   Write these recurring decimals using recurring dots.
    (a) 0.111111...   (b) 3.62222...
    (c) 19.323232...   (d) 7.6191919...

5   Change these fractions to decimals. Write your answers as recurring decimals and to 2 decimal places.
    (a) $\frac{2}{9}$ (b) $\frac{5}{12}$ (c) $\frac{1}{24}$
    (d) $\frac{5}{6}$ (e) $\frac{7}{15}$ (f) $\frac{11}{30}$
    (g) $\frac{3}{11}$ (h) $\frac{6}{11}$

Questions **6** to **9** are the answers to calculations. Write the answers to the nearest penny.

6   (a) £5.291   (b) £7.839   (c) £13.238

7   (a) £8.635   (b) £0.9463   (c) £32.6372

8   (a) £128.62813   (b) £7642.6518   (c) £24.387423

9   (a) £158.29416   (b) £3128.9246   (c) £321.1973

In questions **10** and **11** give your answers to the nearest penny.

10 The price of a Hi-Fi system is £145. Ross pays for the Hi-Fi system in six equal instalments. Work out the amount of one instalment.

11 Aisleen buys a camera. The cash price is £141.27. Aisleen pays a deposit of one fifth of the cash price. How much is the deposit?

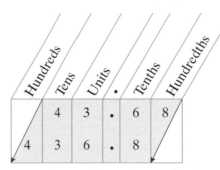

11.6 Multiplying decimals

Multiplying by 10, 100 and 1000

You can multiply decimal numbers by 10, 100 and 1000 in the same way that you multiply whole numbers by 10, 100 and 1000.

■ **To multiply decimal numbers by 10 move the digits one place to the left.**

So $43.68 \times 10 = 436.8$

■ **To multiply decimal numbers by 100 move the digits two places to the left.**

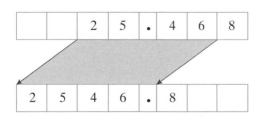

So $25.468 \times 100 = 2546.8$

■ **To multiply decimal numbers by 1000 move the digits three places to the left.**

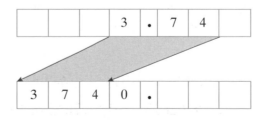

So $3.74 \times 1000 = 3740$

Example 13

Without using a calculator write down the answers to:

(a) 3.62×10

(b) 0.47×1000

(a) $3.62 \times 10 = 36.2$ Move the digits 1 place to the left.

(b) $0.47 \times 1000 = 470$ Move the digits 3 places to the left.

Multiplying by whole numbers

You need to know how to multiply decimal numbers by small whole numbers without using a calculator.

Example 14

Find the cost of 3 sandwiches at £1.65 each.

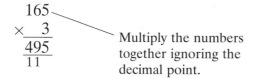

Multiply the numbers together ignoring the decimal point.

£1.65 × 3 is approximately £2 × 3 = £6.

The number 165 is 100 times 1.65, so 495 is 100 times the actual answer. To find the actual answer divide 495 by 100.

The cost of the sandwiches is £4.95.

Notice that the answer and the original number have the same number of digits after the decimal point:

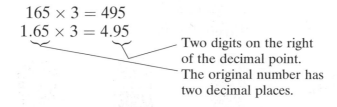

$$165 \times 3 = 495$$
$$1.65 \times 3 = 4.95$$

Two digits on the right of the decimal point.
The original number has two decimal places.

- ■ **When you multiply a decimal number by a whole number the answer has the same number of digits after the decimal point as the original decimal number.**

Example 15

Work out 7.23×4

7.23×4 is approximately $7 \times 4 = 28$

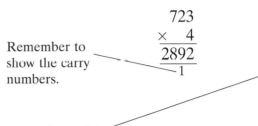

Remember to show the carry numbers.

$$\begin{array}{r} 723 \\ \times\ \ 4 \\ \hline 2892 \\ {}^{1} \end{array}$$

7.23

Two digits on the right of the decimal point, so the answer has two digits on the right of the decimal point.

The answer is 28.92.

Exercise 11F

Write down the answers in questions **1** and **2**:

1. **(a)** 5.26×100 **(b)** 23.7×10 **(c)** 0.452×10
    (d) 0.028×10 **(e)** 9.34×1000 **(f)** 0.09×100

2. **(a)** 6.34×100 **(b)** 26.52×10 **(c)** 3.468×1000
    (d) 3.83×10 **(e)** 56.8×100 **(f)** 0.05×1000

3. Find the cost of:
    (a) 3 melons at £1.45 each.
    (b) 2 kg of apples at £0.82 per kg.
    (c) 6 pencils at £0.34 each.
    (d) 4 shirts at £14.26 each.

Work out the answers in questions **4** and **5** showing all your working.

4. **(a)** 7.3×2 **(b)** 5.3×3 **(c)** 5.4×5
    (d) 6.23×4 **(e)** 13.2×8 **(f)** 5.14×7

5. **(a)** 32.24×6 **(b)** 3.7×5 **(c)** 35.43×7
    (d) 6.38×5 **(e)** 7.35×4 **(f)** 13.26×8

6. Calculate the total cost, in pounds (£), of three pies at £1.55 each and three drinks which cost 42 pence each.

7. Find the total weight, in kg, of five loaves which weigh 0.49 kg each and two cakes which weigh 1.28 kg each.

11.7 Dividing decimals

Dividing by 10, 100 and 1000

You can divide decimal numbers by 10, 100 and 1000 in the same way that you divide whole numbers by 10, 100 and 1000.

■ **To divide decimal numbers by 10 move the digits one place to the right.**

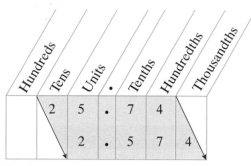

So $25.74 \div 10 = 2.574$

■ **To divide decimal numbers by 100 move the digits two places to the right.**

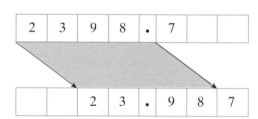

So $2398.7 \div 100 = 23.987$

■ **To divide decimal numbers by 1000 move the digits three places to the right.**

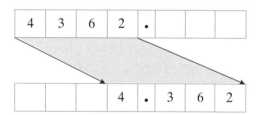

So $4362 \div 1000 = 4.362$

Example 16

Without using a calculator write down the answers to:

(a) $53.26 \div 100$ **(b)** $2.8 \div 1000$

(a) $53.26 \div 100 = 0.5326$ Move the digits 2 places to the right.

(b) $2.8 \div 1000 = 0.0028$

Move the digits 3 places to the right. Put in two zeros to show there are no tenths or hundredths.

Dividing by small whole numbers

You also need to know how to divide decimal numbers by small whole numbers without using a calculator.

■ **To divide a decimal number by a whole number:**
  ● **line up the decimal point in the answer**
  ● **divide as normal.**

Example 17

Work out:

(a) $19.2 \div 6$ **(b)** $0.28 \div 8$

(a) $19.2 \div 6$ is approximately $20 \div 6 =$ approximately 3.

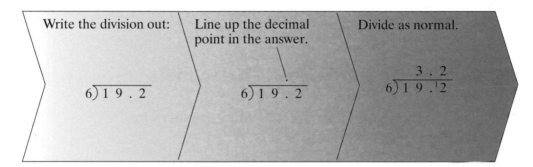

Write the division out: Line up the decimal point in the answer.   Divide as normal.

The answer is 3.2.

(b) $0.28 \div 8$

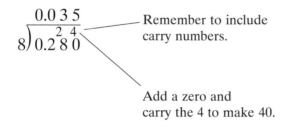

Remember to include carry numbers.

Add a zero and carry the 4 to make 40.

The answer is 0.035.

Exercise 11G

Write down the answers in question **1**.

1   **(a)** $562 \div 10$ **(b)** $93.4 \div 100$ **(c)** $285.6 \div 10$
     (d) $873.5 \div 1000$ **(e)** $4.6 \div 100$ **(f)** $23.9 \div 1000$
     (g) $2.8 \div 100$ **(h)** $0.07 \div 10$ **(i)** $3.6 \div 1000$

2 Find one share if
  (a) three people share £3.96 equally,
  (b) four people share £174.40 equally,
  (c) six people share £10.32 equally,
  (d) seven people share £94.71 equally.

Work out the answers in questions **3** and **4**, showing all your working:

3 **(a)** $7.6 \div 2$ **(b)** $9.6 \div 4$ **(c)** $162.5 \div 5$
    (d) $25.26 \div 6$ **(e)** $0.816 \div 8$ **(f)** $0.378 \div 7$
    (g) $0.0056 \div 4$ **(h)** $9.036 \div 9$ **(i)** $2.205 \div 3$

4 25.5 kg of rice is packed into 6 bags each containing an equal weight. Work out the weight of rice in each bag.

5 Sharon had an 8.6 metre ball of string. She divided the string into five pieces of equal length. What was the length, in metres, of each piece of string?

11.8 Using mental methods with decimals

■ **You can multiply and divide some decimal numbers by whole numbers using mental methods.**

You can multiply and divide some decimal numbers by small whole numbers without using a calculator or doing any working on paper.

Example 18

Work these out mentally:

(a) 3.2×4 **(b)** $27.6 \div 3$

(a) 3.2×4 is approximately $3 \times 4 = 12$
$3.2 = 3 + 0.2$ so
$3.2 \times 4 = (3 \times 4) + (0.2 \times 4)$
$$= \quad 12 \quad + \quad 0.8$$
So the answer is 12.8

(b) $27.6 \div 3$ is approximately $30 \div 3 = 10$
write $27.6 \div 3$ as
$(27 \div 3) + (0.6 \div 3)$
$$= 9 \quad + \quad 0.2$$
So the answer is 9.2

You can do mental calculations with larger numbers by using factors.

Example 19

Work these out, using the factors of the whole number:
(a) 4.2×21 **(b)** $74.16 \div 18$

(a) 4.2×21 is approximately $4 \times 20 = 80$
$4.2 \times 21 = 4.2 \times 3 \times 7$
$4.2 \times 3 = 12.6$
$12.6 \times 7 = 88.2$

So $12.6 \times 21 = 88.2$

Remember: the results will have 1 decimal place.

$$
\begin{array}{r}
126 \\
\times\ \ \ 7 \\
\hline
882 \\
1\ 4 \\
\end{array}
$$

(b) $74.16 \div 18$ is approximately $70 \div 20 = 7 \div 2 = 3.5$
$74.16 \div 18 = (74.16 \div 3) \div 6$
$74.16 \div 3 = 24.72$
$24.72 \div 6 = 4.12$

So $74.16 \div 18 = 4.12$

$$
\begin{array}{r}
2\,4.7\,2 \\
{}^{1\ 2} \\
3)\overline{7\,4.1\,6} \\
\end{array}
$$

$$
\begin{array}{r}
4.1\,2 \\
{}^{1} \\
6)\overline{2\,4.7\,2} \\
\end{array}
$$

Do these calculations on paper to help you.

Exercise 11H

1 Work these out without writing down any working:
    (a) 3.4×2 **(b)** 5.3×3 **(c)** 6.2×4
    (d) 9.3×2 **(e)** $8.4 \div 4$ **(f)** $18.9 \div 3$
    (g) $24.6 \div 6$ **(h)** $21.7 \div 7$

2 Use the factors of the whole number to work out:
    (a) 4.2×15 **(b)** 3.1×14 **(c)** 2.3×24
    (d) $34.5 \div 15$ **(e)** $93.6 \div 18$ **(f)** $71.4 \div 21$

3 Use any of the methods shown in this section to find:
    (a) 4.1×6 **(b)** 6.2×7 **(c)** $24.8 \div 8$
    (d) 5.2×16 **(e)** $99.2 \div 32$ **(f)** $249.6 \div 24$

11.9 Finding approximate answers

You can check your answers by making an **estimation**.

■ **To estimate an answer to a calculation, round all the numbers and do the calculation with the rounded numbers.**

Example 20

Estimate the answer to:

(a) 4.86×3.2 **(b)** $37.92 \div 4.8$ **(c)** $\dfrac{92.36 - 63.25}{4.1}$

(a) Round to whole numbers:

4.86×3.2

$\approx 5 \times 3 = 15$ (Actual answer 15.552)

$\approx$ means nearly equal to

(b) Round to whole numbers:

$37.92 \div 4.8$

$\approx 38 \div 5$

This is still not easy, so round 38 to the nearest 10:

$38 \div 5$

$\approx 40 \div 5 = 8$ (Actual answer 7.9)

(c) Round to whole numbers:

$\dfrac{92.36 - 63.25}{4.1}$

$\approx \dfrac{92 - 63}{4}$

Then round 92 and 63 to the nearest 10:

$\dfrac{92 - 63}{4}$

$\approx \dfrac{90 - 60}{4} = \dfrac{30}{4} = \dfrac{15}{2} = 7.5$ (Actual answer 7.1)

Exercise 11I

1 For each question:
- estimate the answer using approximate values,
- work out the exact answer using a calculator.

(a) 7.92×3 **(b)** 6.18×5

(c) 20.4×3.9 **(d)** 28.7×3.1

(e) $12.81 \div 4.2$ **(f)** $80.18 \div 1.9$

(g) 196.5×4.2 **(h)** $62.35 \div 5.8$

(i) $42.38 \div 5.2$ **(j)** $3.1 \times (4.3 + 5.9)$

(k) $\dfrac{80.6 + 42.36}{5.8}$ **(l)** $\dfrac{19.645 - 4.73}{1.9}$

Summary of key points

1 To sort decimal numbers in order of size:
   - first compare the whole numbers
   - next compare the tenths
   - then compare the hundredths and so on.

2 To add or subtract decimals:
   - line up the decimal points
   - put the point in the answer
   - add or subtract.

3 You can write decimal numbers as fractions by using a place value diagram.

4 To change fractions to decimal numbers divide the numerator (top) by the denominator (bottom).

5 To round to the nearest whole number, look at the digit in the first decimal place.
   - If it is five or more round the whole number up.
   - If it is less than 5 do not change the whole number.

23.**6**

More than 5
so round up
to 24

6 To round numbers to a given number of decimal places (dp) look at the digit in the next decimal place.

7 To round an answer in pounds to the nearest penny, look at the digit in the third decimal place.
   - If it is 5 or more round up the whole number of pence.
   - If it is less than 5 do not change the whole number of pence.

6.53**5**18

5 so round
up to £6.54

8 To multiply decimals:
   - by 10 move the digits one place to the left.
   - by 100 move the digits two places to the left.
   - by 1000 move the digits three places to the left.

$43.68 \times 10 = 436.8$
$25.46 \times 100 = 2546$
$3.74 \times 1000 = 3740$

9 When you multiply a decimal number by a whole number the answer has the same number of digits after the decimal point as the original decimal number.

10 To divide decimals:
- by 10 move the digits one place to the right.
- by 100 move the digits two places to the right.
- by 1000 move the digits three places to the right.

$5.742 \div 10 = 0.5742$
$239.87 \div 100 = 2.3987$
$4362 \div 1000 = 4.362$

11 To divide a decimal number by a whole number:
- line up the decimal point in the answer
- divide as normal.

12 You can multiply and divide some decimal numbers by whole numbers using mental methods.

13 To estimate an answer to a calculation, round all the numbers and do the calculation with the rounded numbers.

12 Percentages

12.1 Percentages, fractions and decimals

Percentages, fractions and decimals can be used to write amounts which are not whole numbers.

19% means 19 out of 100.

As a fraction this is $\frac{19}{100}$.

19% and $\frac{19}{100}$ represent the same amount.

- **You can write any percentage as a fraction with a denominator of 100.**
  For example, $7\% = \frac{7}{100}$

Example 1

Write 15% as a fraction in its simplest form.

$$15\% \text{ means } \quad \frac{15}{100} \overset{\div 5}{\underset{\div 5}{=}} \frac{3}{20}$$

Divide the numerator and denominator by the highest common factor 5.

Remember:
The simplest form means there is no equivalent fraction with smaller numerator and denominator.

So $15\% = \frac{3}{20}$.

You can also write a percentage as a decimal:

8% means $\frac{8}{100}$ which means $8 \div 100 = 0.08$

Remember:
To divide by 100 move the digits two places to the right.

- **To change a percentage to a decimal divide by 100.**
  For example: 25% means $25 \div 100 = 0.25$

Example 2

Change to decimals:
(a) 5%
(b) 12%

(a) $5\% = \frac{5}{100} = 5 \div 100 = 0.05$

(b) $12\% = \frac{12}{100} = 12 \div 100 = 0.12$

You can write decimals and fractions as percentages.

- **To change a decimal to a percentage multiply the decimal by 100%.**

- **To change a fraction to a percentage, first change the fraction to a decimal then multiply by 100%.**

Example 3

Change these to percentages:

(a) 0.24

(b) $\frac{3}{4}$

(c) $\frac{1}{3}$

33.333 ... is a recurring decimal and is written as 33.$\dot{3}$

(a) $0.24 = 0.24 \times 100\% = 24\%$

(b) $\frac{3}{4} = 3 \div 4 = 0.75 = 0.75 \times 100\% = 75\%$

(c) $\frac{1}{3} = 1 \div 3 = 0.3333\ldots = 0.3333\ldots \times 100\% = 33.\dot{3}\%$
  (or $33\frac{1}{3}\%$)

You can read more about recurring decimals on page 207.

Here are some common percentages and their equivalent fractions and decimals. It is useful to be able to recognise them.

$25\% = \frac{1}{4} = 0.25$ $50\% = \frac{1}{2} = 0.5$ $75\% = \frac{3}{4} = 0.75$

$10\% = \frac{1}{10} = 0.1$ $20\% = \frac{1}{5} = 0.2$ $70\% = \frac{7}{10} = 0.7$

$33\frac{1}{3}\% = \frac{1}{3} = 0.\dot{3}$ $66\frac{2}{3}\% = \frac{2}{3} = 0.\dot{6}$ $1\% = \frac{1}{100} = 0.01$

Exercise 12A

1   Change these percentages to fractions:
    (a) 17%   (b) 37%   (c) 3%   (d) 23%
    (e) 1%   (f) 99%   (g) 31%   (h) 43%

2   Change these percentages to fractions in their simplest form:
    (a) 70%   (b) 25%   (c) 45%   (d) 8%
    (e) 14%   (f) 35%   (g) 60%   (h) 20%

3   Change these percentages to decimals:

(**a**) 7%   (**b**) 52%   (**c**) 35%   (**d**) 80%

(**e**) 6%   (**f**) 60%   (**g**) 16%   (**h**) 17.5%

4   Change these decimals and fractions to percentages:

(**a**) 0.36   (**b**) 0.9   (**c**) 0.04   (**d**) 0.125

(**e**) $\frac{3}{10}$ (**f**) $\frac{2}{5}$ (**g**) $\frac{3}{25}$ (**h**) $\frac{11}{20}$

5   Copy and complete this table of equivalent percentages, fractions and decimals.

Percentage	Fraction	Decimal
80%	$\frac{4}{5}$	0.8
29%		
	$\frac{3}{4}$	
		0.03
35%		
		0.36
6%		
	$\frac{2}{3}$	

80%, $\frac{4}{5}$ and 0.8 are equivalent. They are three different ways of writing the same number.

12.2 Finding a percentage of an amount

Sometimes you can find percentages of an amount without using a calculator. This method uses fractions.

Example 4

Work out 20% of £45.

First convert 20% to a fraction in its simplest form:
$\frac{20}{100} = \frac{2}{10} = \frac{1}{5}$

Then work out $\frac{1}{5}$ of £45 by dividing £45 by 5

$£45 \div 5 = £9$

So 20% of £45 is £9.

Some percentages cannot be written as simple fractions. You will need to use a calculator.

$20\% = \frac{1}{5}$
So I must divide £45 by 5.

Example 5

Work out 19% of 25 kg.

$19\% = \frac{19}{100} = 19 \div 100 = 0.19$ ——— First change 19% to a decimal

$0.19 \times 25 \,\text{kg} = 4.75 \,\text{kg}$ ——— Then multiply the decimal by the amount.

So 19% of 25 kg is 4.75 kg.

Your calculator may have a short way of doing this with the ▣ % key. Find out how to do this.

■ **To find a percentage of an amount change the percentage to a fraction or decimal and multiply the fraction or decimal by the amount.**

VAT

Value Added Tax (VAT) is the amount that is added to bills for services and purchases. The rate for VAT in the UK for most goods and services is $17\frac{1}{2}\%$.

Example 6

VAT at $17\frac{1}{2}\%$ is added to a plumber's bill of £28.34.
Work out the total amount to be paid.

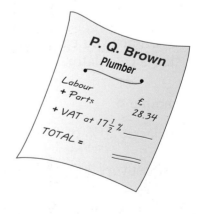

$$17\frac{1}{2}\% = 17.5\% = 17.5 \div 100 = 0.175$$

So VAT $= 17\frac{1}{2}\%$ of £28.34 $= 0.175 \times £28.34$

$\qquad = £4.9595$

$\qquad = £4.96$ (to the nearest penny)

Total cost $= £28.34 + £4.96 = £33.30$ (to the nearest penny)

You should also know a non-calculator method to work out VAT at $17\frac{1}{2}\%$.

Example 7

Without using a calculator, work out the VAT at $17\frac{1}{2}\%$ on a telephone bill of £26.

$$17\tfrac{1}{2}\% = 17.5\% = 10\% + 5\% + 2.5\%$$

10% of £26 $= \frac{1}{10} \times £26 = £26 \div 10 = £2.60$

5% is half of 10%, so 5% of £26 $= £1.30$ (halving)

2.5% is half of 5%, so 2.5% of £26 $= £0.65$ (halving)

Adding, 17.5% of £26 $= £4.55$

So the VAT $= £4.55$

$$
\begin{array}{r}
10\% \\
\text{half of } 10\% = 5\% \\
\text{half of } 5\% \;= 2.5\% \\
\hline
\text{Total} \qquad = 17.5\%
\end{array}
$$

$$
2\,)\,\overline{1.\overset{1}{3}\overset{1}{0}} \\
0.65
$$

Exercise 12B

In this exercise take the VAT rate to be $17\frac{1}{2}\%$.

1 There are 32 people on the bus and 25% of those got on at the last stop. How many of them got on at the last stop?

2 In a sale all the marked prices were reduced by 10%. Work out the reduction for a shirt with a marked price of £16.

3 20% of the 250 pupils in Year 9 chose swimming as their favourite sport. How many of the pupils chose swimming?

4 Work out:
  (a) 10% of £9
  (b) 50% of £14
  (c) 20% of £15
  (d) 25% of 36 kg
  (e) 75% of 28 m
  (f) 30% of 20 kg
  (g) 1% of £234
  (h) 5% of £70
  (i) $33\frac{1}{3}\%$ of 24 kg

5 Work out the VAT on these prices:
  (a) £40
  (b) £60
  (c) £240
  (d) £28
  (e) £720
  (f) £34
  (g) £26
  (h) £62.40

6 Work out:
  (a) 17% of £80
  (b) 41% of £250
  (c) 3% of £28
  (d) 8% of 45 m
  (e) 5% of 64 kg
  (f) 12.5% of £22

10 Add VAT to these prices:
   (a) £56
   (b) £14.80
   (c) £279.99

12.4 Making comparisons using percentages

You can compare two amounts by writing one amount as a percentage of the other.

Example 10

Write 350 g as a percentage of 2 kg.

To compare the amounts the units must be the same. Here we will change 2 kg to 2000 g.

Step 1: Write the amounts as a fraction: $\frac{350}{2000}$

Step 2: Change the fraction to a decimal:
   $350 \div 2000 = 0.175$

Step 3: Change the decimal to a percentage:
   $0.175 \times 100\% = 17.5\%$

So 350 g is 17.5% of 2 kg.

■ **To write one amount as a percentage of another:**

  ● **Write one amount as a fraction of the other.**
  ● **Change the fraction to a decimal.**
  ● **Multiply the decimal by 100%.**

You can also use percentages to compare results of surveys and other statistics.

Example 11

A year 9 survey asked pupils to choose their favourite sport to watch. Use percentages to compare the results for tennis, football and snooker.

63 out of 180 pupils like watching Tennis best

$\frac{4}{9}$ of the pupils like watching Football best

15% of the pupils like watching Snooker best

Change the results to percentages:

Tennis: 63 out of 180 $= \frac{63}{180} = 0.35 = 0.35 \times 100\% = 35\%$

Football: $\frac{4}{9} = 4 \div 9 = 0.4444\ldots = 44.44\ldots\% = 44.4\%$ (to 1 dp)

Snooker: 15%

The percentages show that football is the most popular to watch, then tennis, then snooker.

■ **You can use percentages to compare numerical data.**

Exercise 12D

1 Write:
   (a) 4 kg as a percentage of 80 kg
   (b) 36 pence as a percentage of £2.25
   (c) 70 cm as a percentage of 4 m
   (d) 870 g as a percentage of 3 kg

2 Out of 125 new light bulbs inspected, 5 did not work. What percentage of the light bulbs did not work?

3 Goran sowed 60 flower seeds and 57 of them produced plants. What percentage of the seeds produced plants?

4 900 pupils took part in a sponsored walk and 594 of them finished within 3 hours. What percentage of the pupils is this?

5 In a class of 30 pupils, 18 of them are girls. What percentage of the class are girls?

6 There are 32 cars in the staff car park and 12 of them are red. What percentage of the cars are red?

7 Abigail gained 46 marks out of 50 for the first Maths test and 54 marks out of 60 for the second Maths test.
   (a) Change the results to percentages.
   (b) In which test did Abigail do best?

8 81.25% of the Group 9M pupils entered the Year 9 competition, 27 of the 30 pupils in Group 9F entered and $\frac{7}{8}$ of Group 9R entered.
   (a) Write the entries of Group 9F and Group 9R as percentages.
   (b) Which Group had the biggest percentage entry?

13 Probability

The probability that a newborn baby will be a girl is $\frac{1}{2}$. You can also write this as 50% or 0.5.

Probability uses numbers to say how likely something is to happen.

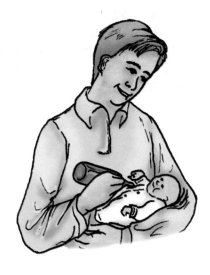

13.1 The probability scale

You can mark probabilities on a scale from 0 to 1.

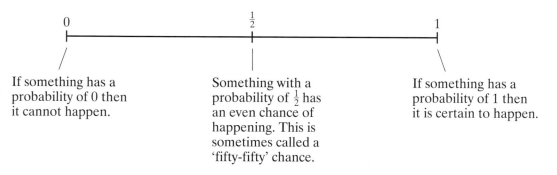

If something has a probability of 0 then it cannot happen.

Something with a probability of $\frac{1}{2}$ has an even chance of happening. This is sometimes called a 'fifty-fifty' chance.

If something has a probability of 1 then it is certain to happen.

■ **All probabilities have a value from 0 to 1.**

■ **You can write probabilities as fractions, decimals or percentages.**

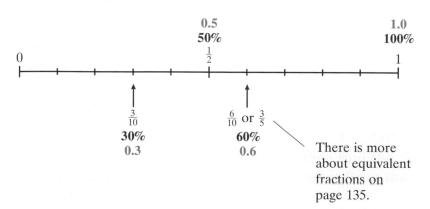

There is more about converting to decimals and percentages on page 219.

There is more about equivalent fractions on page 135.

Example 1

Mark these on a probability scale. Give reasons for your answers.

(a) You will win the lottery on Saturday.
(b) It will snow in London this winter.
(c) Christmas will be on December 25th this year.

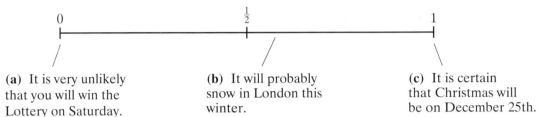

(a) It is very unlikely that you will win the Lottery on Saturday.

(b) It will probably snow in London this winter.

(c) It is certain that Christmas will be on December 25th.

Example 2

Write these probabilities as fractions, decimals and percentages.

(a) $\frac{1}{10}$, 0.1, 10%
(b) $\frac{3}{4}$, 0.75, 75%

Exercise 13A

1   Draw a probability scale from 0 to 1. Mark each of these probabilities on it and give a reason for your answer.

   (a) Your hair will turn purple overnight.
   (b) Manchester United will win the Premiership.
   (c) The next person you talk to will be a girl.
   (d) You will eat shepherd's pie sometime next year.
   (e) Horse number 4 will win the race.
   (f) The white horse will come last.

$$P(\text{red}) = \tfrac{5}{9}$$
$$P(\text{green}) = \tfrac{1}{9}$$

The denominator tells us the number of possible outcomes.

$$\tfrac{9}{9} = 1$$

All the probabilities must add up to 1, or $\tfrac{9}{9}$.

$$P(\text{red}) + P(\text{green}) + P(\text{yellow}) = \tfrac{9}{9}$$
$$\tfrac{5}{9} + \tfrac{1}{9} + P(\text{yellow}) = \tfrac{9}{9}$$

So
$$P(\text{yellow}) = \tfrac{9}{9} - \tfrac{5}{9} - \tfrac{1}{9}$$
$$= \tfrac{3}{9} = \tfrac{1}{3}$$

The probability something will not happen

In Example 6, the probability of choosing a red cube was $\tfrac{5}{9}$.

The probability of choosing a colour other than red was $\tfrac{4}{9}$.

$$P(\text{red}) + P(\text{not red}) = 1$$
$$P(\text{not red}) = 1 - P(\text{red})$$

■ **P(event not happening) = 1 − P(event happening)**

Example 7

The probability of the roulette ball landing on black is $\tfrac{18}{37}$. Find the probability of the ball not landing on black.

$$P(\text{not black}) = 1 - P(\text{black})$$
$$= 1 - \tfrac{18}{37}$$
$$= \tfrac{37}{37} - \tfrac{18}{37} = \tfrac{19}{37}$$

Example 8

On a given day in Cyprus, there is a 3% chance of rain. What is the probability it will not rain that day?

$$P(\text{rain}) = 3\% \text{ or } \tfrac{3}{100}$$
$$P(\text{not rain}) = 1 - P(\text{rain})$$
$$= 1 - \tfrac{3}{100}$$
$$= \tfrac{97}{100} \text{ or } 97\%$$

You can use a simpler method when working with percentages.

What do I do if the probability is given as a percentage?

- Change the probability to a fraction
- Do your calculations
- Write your answers as a fraction and a percentage

■ **P(event not happening) = 100% − P(event happening)**

Exercise 13D

1   David, Uchenna, Ali and Sara are running in
    a 100 m race. David has a $\frac{2}{11}$ chance of
    winning, Ali has a $\frac{5}{11}$ chance of winning, and
    Sara has a $\frac{1}{11}$ chance of winning.

   (a) Write down all the possible outcomes.
   (b) What is the probability Uchenna will win
        the race?

2   Chocolates are available in bags, boxes or tins. There
    are four types of chocolate. Copy and complete this
    table showing the probabilities of picking each type of
    chocolate.

	Bag	Box	Tin
Strawberry cream	$\frac{2}{7}$	$\frac{3}{13}$	
Hazel whip	$\frac{1}{7}$		$\frac{3}{26}$
Rum crunch		$\frac{9}{13}$	$\frac{8}{13}$
Choco fudge	$\frac{1}{7}$	0	$\frac{1}{26}$

Hint: When adding
and subtracting
fractions, make sure
all your fractions
have the same
denominator. There
is more about this
on page 137.

3   A bag contains red, blue and green counters. A counter
    is chosen at random from the bag. The probability of
    choosing a red counter is 20%. The probability of
    choosing a green counter is 30%.

   (a) Write these probabilities as fractions with the same
        denominator.
   (b) Find the probability of choosing a blue counter.
        Give your answer as a fraction and a percentage.

(b) She chooses one combination at random. What is the probability that it will involve swimming?

(c) What is the probability that it will include quadbiking?

(d) What is the probability that it will involve neither windsurfing nor mountain biking?

(e) What is the probability that Mrs Archer will choose a combination that you would enjoy?

6 Two ordinary dice are rolled. Use your sample space diagram from question **1** to find the answers.

(a) How many outcomes are there?

(b) What is the chance of rolling a double 6?

(c) What is the chance of rolling any double?

(d) What is the chance of not rolling a double?

(e) What is the chance of rolling a pair of even numbers?

(f) What is the chance of rolling a pair of prime numbers?

Summary of key points

1 All probabilities have a value from 0 to 1.

2 You can write probabilities as fractions, decimals or percentages.

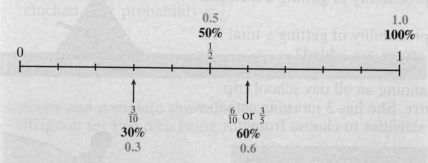

3 The probability that an event will happen is:

$$P(event) = \frac{\text{the number of successful outcomes}}{\text{total number of possible outcomes}}$$

4 The probabilities of all the possible outcomes of an event add up to one.

5 P(event not happening) = 1 − P(event happening)

6 P(event not happening) = 100%
                           −P(event happening)

7 When two events happen at the same time you can show all the possible outcomes on a sample space diagram.

14 Formulae and equations

Formulae are used everywhere.

When swimming through coral reefs, a diver needs to know how long she has before the oxygen in her tanks runs out. Scientists use formulae to estimate this time.

14.1 Substituting into word formulae

You can use word formulae to help you solve problems.

Example 1

The formula for the distance travelled is

distance travelled = speed × time taken

John rides his bike for 3 hours at 10 miles per hour. Work out the distance travelled.

Distance travelled = speed × time taken
$$= \quad 10 \quad \times \quad 3$$
$$= 30 \text{ miles}$$

Always write the formula first.

Example 2

Pay = hours worked × rate of pay − deductions

Natalie works for 20 hours at £3 per hour and has deductions of £2.50.

Pay = hours worked × rate of pay − deductions
$$= 20 \times 3 - 2.50$$
$$= 60 - 2.50$$
$$= £57.50$$

Deductions are taken away from people's pay for Income Tax and National Insurance.

Exercise 14A

1 Pay = rate of pay × hours worked + overtime
Henry works for £4 per hour for 15 hours with £5 overtime. Work out Henry's pay.

2 Use the formula to work out the cost of 5 books at £4 each.

Cost of books = cost of 1 book × number bought

3 The cost in pence of hiring a car is worked out using the formula

cost = 500 + 20 × number of miles travelled

Work out the cost of hiring a car and travelling

(a) 600 miles
(b) 50 miles
(c) 250 miles.

4 The cost in pounds of hiring a bike is worked out using the formula

cost = 5 + 4 × number of days

Work out the cost of hiring a bike for

(a) 5 days   **(b)** 1 day   **(c)** 7 days.

5 Tim and Louise's ages add up to 50.
This can be written as the formula

Tim's age + Louise's age = 50

Work out Louise's age if Tim is 26 years old.

6 The perimeter of an isosceles triangle is given by the formula

perimeter = 2 × length of equal side + length of other side

Use the formula to work out the perimeter when the equal side is 10 cm and the other side is 8 cm.

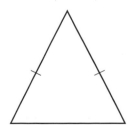

7   Natasha uses the formula

cakes left $= 24 -$ cakes eaten

to see how many cakes are left after her
brother Sergei came home from school.
How many cakes were left if Sergei ate:

(a) 1 cake

(b) 20 cakes

(c) 5 cakes

(d) no cakes

(e) n cakes?

8   The cooking time in minutes for a chicken can be
worked out using the formula

time $=$ weight of chicken in kg $\times 40 + 20$

How long will it take to cook a chicken weighing

(a) 2 kg   **(b)** 1 kg   **(c)** 2.5 kg

(d) 1.5 kg   **(e)** 500 g   **(f)** n kg?

14.2 Order of operations

In maths the order in which you do things matters.
You have to carry out the operations $+$, $-$, $\times$
and $\div$ in the correct order to get the correct answer.

■   **You can use the word BIDMAS to remind you
of the order of operations:**

Brackets   You work out the brackets first
Indices
Division
Multiplication
Addition
Subtraction   then work down the list

Example 3

Work out:

(a) $5 \times 6 - 4$ **(b)** $5(6 - 4)$

(a) Multiply first
$= 30 - 4$
Now subtract 4
$= 26$

(b) Work out the bracket first
$= 5(2)$
Now multiply
$= 10$

Exercise 14B

Work out

1 $2 \times 5 + 2$	**2** $2 \times (5 + 2)$	**3** $4(2 + 3)$
4 4×3^2	**5** $5(3 + 2)$	**6** $2 \times 2 + 3 \times 3$
7 $2^2 + 3^2$	**8** $3 + 4 - 5$	**9** $2(7 - 3)$
10 $5 \times 4 - 2$	**11** $3 - 2 \times 1$	**12** $10 + 3 \times 5$
13 $8 + 2 \times 3$	**14** $8 - 2 \times 3$	**15** $12 - 3 \times 4$
16 $5(14 - 9)$	**17** $(5 + 4) \div 3$	**18** $(17 - 5) \div 3$
19 $(15 - 5) \times 10$	**20** $(15 - 5) \div 10$	**21** $3(3^2 + 4^2) \div 5$

Remember:
$4(2 + 3)$ means
$4 \times (2 + 3)$

14.3 Substituting into formulae

Using algebra you can write letters in place of numbers.
You can then give the letters numerical values.

Example 4

$a = 2, b = 3, c = 1$

Find the value of s when

(a) $s = a + b$ **(b)** $s = 3a$ **(c)** $s = 2(2b - c)$

$s = a + b$
$= 2 + 3$
$= 5$

$s = 3a$
$= 3 \times a$
$= 3 \times 2$
$= 6$

$s = 2(2b - c)$
$= 2 \times (2 \times b - c)$
$= 2 \times (2 \times 3 - 1)$
$= 2 \times (6 - 1)$
$= 2 \times 5$
$= 10$

Exercise 14C

1 $a = 2, b = 3, c = 1, d = 0$
Find the value of p when

(a) $p = a + c$ (b) $p = 2b$
(c) $p = 5c$ (d) $p = 2a + b$
(e) $p = 3c - a$ (f) $p = 2(a + b)$
(g) $p = 4b - 2a$ (h) $p = a \times b$
(i) $p = a \times d$ (j) $p = ab$
(k) $p = b + c$ (l) $p = bc$
(m) $p = b^2$ (n) $p = a^3$
(o) $p = 2b - a$ (p) $p = a(b + c)$

> Don't forget:
> ab means $a \times b$

2 $p = 5, q = 2, r = 3, s = 1$
Find the value of m when

(a) $m = p + q$ (b) $m = q + r$ (c) $m = 3r$
(d) $m = 2p - r$ (e) $m = 3q - p$ (f) $m = 3(p + q)$
(g) $m = 2(p - r)$ (h) $m = 4(2r - p)$ (i) $m = 4r - 6q$
(j) $m = pq$ (k) $m = rs$ (l) $m = p^2$
(m) $m = r^2$ (n) $m = q^3$ (o) $m = 3p + 2r - q$

14.4 Substituting into harder formulae

You can use algebra to write formulae with letters instead of words.

Example 5

Remember the formula from Example 1:

    $Distance = speed \times time$

We can write this as

    $D = s \times t$

the formula for the distance travelled D at speed s in time t.

Work out the distance travelled in 3 hours at 30 miles per hour.

$t = 3$ hours
$s = 30$ miles per hour

So $D = s \times t$
          $= 30 \times 3$
          $= 90$ miles

Example 6

$P = H \times R + O - d$

This formula gives a persons pay £P who works for H hours at a rate of pay of £R per hour with £O overtime and £d deductions.

Compare this to the word formula in Example 2.

Work out Jayne's pay if she works for 10 hours at £4 per hour with overtime of £3 and deductions of £8.

$H = 10, R = 4, O = 3, d = 8$

$$P = 10 \times 4 + 3 - 8$$
$$= 40 + 3 - 8$$
$$= 43 - 8 = £35$$

Don't forget
BIDMAS
$\times$ comes before $+$ and $-$

Exercise 14D

1   The perimeter P of a square is given by the formula $P = 4 \times l$. Work out the perimeter of these squares:

   (a) $l = 2$ **(b)** $l = 5$ **(c)** $l = 10$
   (d) $l = 4$ **(e)** $l = 2.5$ **(f)** $l = 1.2$

2   The perimeter P of a rectangle is given by the formula $P = 2(l + w)$. Work out the perimeter of rectangles with these measurements:

   (a) $l = 3, w = 2$ **(b)** $l = 4, w = 3$
   (c) $l = 5, w = 3$ **(d)** $l = 6, w = 3$

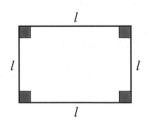

3   Mary works her pay P out using the formula $P = H \times W - d$. Work out Mary's pay if

   (a) $H = 10, W = 3, d = 4$
   (b) $H = 20, W = 4, d = 10$
   (c) $H = 40, W = 3, d = 20$
   (d) $H = 12, W = 2.50, d = 1$

4   Simon uses this formula $C = 2a - b$.
   Work out the value of C when

   (a) $a = 2, b = 1$ **(b)** $a = 6, b = 3$
   (c) $a = 10, b = 4$ **(d)** $a = 7, b = 5$
   (e) $a = 12, b = 24$ **(f)** $a = 20, b = 10$

5 Ruth uses this formula to work out the value of y:

$$y = 3(x - 2)$$

Work out the value of y when

(a) $x = 4$ (b) $x = 3$ (c) $x = 2$
(d) $x = 10$ (e) $x = 5$ (f) $x = 12$

6 Danielle uses the formula $A = 3r^2$ to work out an estimate for the area of some circles. Find the value of A when

Don't forget
$3r^2$ means $3 \times r \times r$

(a) $r = 4$ (b) $r = 3$ (c) $r = 1$
(d) $r = 2$ (e) $r = 10$ (f) $r = 5$

7 Anadeep uses the formula $v = u + at$ to work out the value of v.
Find the value of v when

(a) $u = 0, a = 2, t = 4$ (b) $u = 10, a = 3, t = 2$
(c) $u = 20, a = 5, t = 2$ (d) $u = 0, a = 10, t = 2$
(e) $u = 20, a = 10, t = 5$ (f) $u = 30, a = 5, t = 4$

8 Sue uses the formula $g = t^2 - 5t$ to work out the value of g. Find the value of g when

(a) $t = 5$ (b) $t = 10$ (c) $t = 6$
(d) $t = 8$ (e) $t = 12$ (f) $t = 0$

14.5 Solving equations with one operation

■ **An equation is a number sentence where one side of the equals sign exactly balances the other side.**

Remember:
A formula is true
for many values.
An equation is true
for only one value.

$$\frac{x + 5 \quad = \quad 9}{\blacktriangle}$$

■ **To solve an equation you have to find the number value of the letter.**

Sometimes you can do this by using your basic number facts. In this case you know that $4 + 5 = 9$ so x must equal 4.

Example 7

Solve the equation:

$$p - 4 = 3$$

Since $7 - 4 = 3$ then $p = 7$

Example 8

Solve the equation:

$$3q = 12$$

Since $\quad 3 \times 4 = 12$ then $q = 4$

Don't forget
$3q$ means $3 \times q$

Exercise 14E

Solve these questions using your basic number facts:

(a) $a + 2 = 5$
(b) $b - 3 = 2$
(c) $5c = 10$
(d) $d \div 2 = 5$
(e) $e + 3 = 6$
(f) $4f = 12$
(g) $\dfrac{g}{3} = 2$
(h) $4 + h = 5$
(i) $6 - i = 2$
(j) $3j = 15$
(k) $\dfrac{k}{5} = 2$
(l) $l + 4 = 8$
(m) $5 - m = 2$
(n) $2n = 8$
(o) $p \div 2 = 3$

You also need to be able to solve equations in a mathematical way so that you can solve more difficult equations.

Example 9

Solve the equation:

$$x + 19 = 35$$

To get x on its own you must get rid of $+19$.

The inverse of $+19$ is -19, so you take 19 from each side.

$$x = 35 - 19$$
$$x = 16$$

Example 10

Solve $\dfrac{x}{4} = 18$

The inverse of $\div 4$ is $\times 4$ so you multiply each side by 4:

$x = 18 \times 4$

$x = 72$

> **Remember**
>
> $\dfrac{x}{4}$ means $x \div 4$

Exercise 14F

1   Solve these equations. You should be able to check your answers by doing them in your head.

    (a) $x + 5 = 9$ **(b)** $x - 4 = 2$ **(c)** $3x = 12$ **(d)** $5p = 20$

    (e) $\dfrac{b}{4} = 3$ **(f)** $q \div 2 = 6$ **(g)** $r + 7 = 10$ **(h)** $s - 5 = 5$

    (i) $5j = 10$ **(j)** $\dfrac{k}{5} = 4$ **(k)** $3t = 18$ **(l)** $y + 5 = 5$

2   Solve these equations:

    (a) $a + 15 = 29$ **(b)** $b + 17 = 32$ **(c)** $c - 15 = 23$ **(d)** $c - 26 = 2$

    (e) $3c = 39$ **(f)** $4g = 56$ **(g)** $\dfrac{h}{3} = 51$ **(h)** $\dfrac{k}{5} = 75$

    (i) $p + 17 = 83$ **(j)** $q + 24 = 72$ **(k)** $r - 23 = 49$ **(l)** $s - 24 = 1$

    (m) $7q = 91$ **(n)** $6x = 144$ **(o)** $\dfrac{x}{8} = 17$ **(p)** $\dfrac{y}{7} = 25$

14.6 Solving equations with two operations

Sometimes you have to solve equations with two operations.

Example 11

Solve the equation:

$2x + 3 = 11$

The inverse of $+3$ is -3, so take 3 from each side:

$2x = 11 - 3$

$2x = 8$

The inverse of $\times 2$ is $\div 2$, so divide both sides by 2:

$x = 8 \div 2$

$x = 4$

> For this type of equation you get rid of the $+3$ first.

Exercise 14G

1   Solve these equations:

(a) $2a + 1 = 5$ (b) $3a + 2 = 11$

(c) $4p + 5 = 13$ (d) $5p - 1 = 4$

(e) $4q - 3 = 5$ (f) $3r - 5 = 7$

(g) $4p + 7 = 19$ (h) $3x - 2 = 13$

(i) $7y - 2 = 19$ (j) $10x + 5 = 45$

(k) $7q - 15 = 20$ (l) $3t + 5 = 35$

(m) $2p + 3 = 9$ (n) $3x - 17 = 13$

(o) $5p + 7 = 32$ (p) $3q + 5 = 32$

Don't forget deal with the + or − first.

2   Solve these equations:

(a) $3a + 2 = 17$ (b) $2p - 3 = 11$ (c) $5x + 2 = 17$

(d) $2r + 7 = 23$ (e) $5r + 6 = 31$ (f) $2t - 5 = 37$

(g) $10p + 7 = 77$ (h) $8q - 5 = 27$ (i) $2r + 7 = 35$

(j) $2t + 1 = 75$ (k) $3r - 1 = 44$ (l) $2t + 1 = 6$

14.7 Solving equations with brackets

You will need to be able to solve equations with brackets.

■ **To solve equations there are 3 steps:**

Step 1 Multiply out the brackets.

Step 2 Deal with + or −

Step 3 Deal with the number in front of the letter.

Example 12

Solve the equation $2(x + 3) = 12$

Step 1 Multiply out the bracket:

Multiply $x + 3$ by 2. $2 \times x + 2 \times 3 = 12$

$2 \times x = 2x$, $2 \times 3 = 6$. $2x + 6 = 12$

Step 2 Deal with $+6$:

$$2x = 12 - 6$$
$$2x = 6$$

Step 3 Deal with $2x$.

$$x = 6 \div 2$$
$$x = 3$$

Exercise 14H

1 Solve these equations:
- **(a)** $2(x + 1) = 8$
- **(b)** $3(x + 1) = 12$
- **(c)** $2(x - 2) = 8$
- **(d)** $5(a + 2) = 20$
- **(e)** $3(p - 2) = 15$
- **(f)** $4(r + 1) = 16$
- **(g)** $2(p + 5) = 14$
- **(h)** $3(q - 2) = 18$
- **(i)** $2(t + 5) = 18$
- **(j)** $5(s - 4) = 25$
- **(k)** $2(y + 3) = 20$
- **(l)** $10(v - 2) = 100$

2 Solve the equations:
- **(a)** $2(3x + 4) = 20$
- **(b)** $2(3x + 4) = 14$
- **(c)** $2(2x + 1) = 14$
- **(d)** $2(3p + 1) = 26$
- **(e)** $5(2p - 6) = 30$
- **(f)** $10(2p - 1) = 90$
- **(g)** $3(2x - 1) = 15$
- **(h)** $3(2q + 5) = 21$
- **(i)** $3(2q - 5) = 15$
- **(j)** $6(3r - 1) = 84$

Remember:
$2 \times 3x = 6x$ and
$2 \times 4 = 8$
so
$2(3x + 4) = 6x + 8$

14.8 Solving equations with letters on both sides

Sometimes you have to solve equations with letters on both sides of the equals sign.

■ **To solve equations with letters on both sides of the equals sign there are 3 steps:**

Step 1 Move the letters to one side of the equals sign: always keep the letters on the side with the bigger number of letters.

Step 2 Deal with + or −

Step 3 Deal with the number in front of the letter.

Example 13

Solve the equation $3x + 1 = x + 7$

Step 1 $3x$ is bigger than x so keep the xs on the left hand side.

$$3x + 1 - x = 7$$
$$2x + 1 = 7$$

Step 2 Deal with $+1$:

$$2x = 7 - 1$$
$$2x = 6$$

Step 3 Deal with $2x$:

$$x = 6 \div 2$$
$$x = 3$$

Example 14

$4x + 2 = 5x - 3$

Step 1 $5x$ is bigger than $4x$ so keep the xs on the right hand side.

$2 = 5x - 3 - 4x$

$2 = x - 3$

Step 2 Deal with -3

$2 + 3 = x$

Step 3 Only $1x$ so OK.

$5 = x$

or $x = 5$

Solve the equations:

1 $2x + 1 = x + 5$ **2** $3x + 4 = 2x + 7$

3 $3x + 2 = x + 8$ **4** $5x + 3 = 3x + 9$

5 $4x - 3 = 2x + 5$ **6** $2x + 5 = 3x - 2$

7 $3x + 7 = 5x - 7$ **8** $4x + 12 = 7x - 3$

9 $4x - 7 = x + 14$ **10** $5x - 8 = 2x + 10$

14.9 Inequalities

Helen has one tooth missing.
Sam has five teeth missing.

Helen is missing fewer teeth than Sam. You know this because 1 is less than 5.
You can write this: $1 < 5$

You also know 5 is greater than 1.
You can write this: $5 > 1$

■ **Expressions and numbers that are not equal are called inequalities.**

■ **> means *greater than*
< means *less than***

The thinner end points towards the smaller number. The thicker end points towards the larger number.

Example 15

Put the correct sign between these numbers.

(a) 5, 3   **(b)** 4, 10

   5 is more than 3 so you use >   4 is less than 10 so you use <
   5 > 3   4 < 10

Example 16

Write down the whole numbers n where

   $n > 2$ and $n < 7$

This means that n must be more than 2 and less than 7
n could be 3, 4, 5 or 6.

Exercise 14J

1 Put the correct sign between these numbers to make
    them correct inequalities:

   (a) 5, 2   **(b)** 3, 7   **(c)** 2, 8
   (d) 5, 10   **(e)** 10, 6   **(f)** 2, 20
   (g) 1.5, 1.6   **(h)** 2.1, 2.0   **(i)** 7, 6.9
   (j) 6.9, 6.99   **(k)** 0, 7   **(l)** 4, 0
   (m) 0.9, 1   **(n)** 1, 0.95   **(o)** 2.3, 2.29

2 Write down whether these statements are true or
    false.
    If they are false then put the correct sign between them.

   (a) $5 > 2$ **(b)** $2 < 7$
   (c) $3 > 1$ **(d)** $5 < 4$
   (e) $3 > 2.5$ **(f)** $2.5 < 2.4$
   (g) $3.9 > 4$ **(h)** $5.6 < 6$
   (i) $6.9 > 7$ **(j)** $7 > 6.9$

3 Write down all the whole numbers n that are true when

   (a) $n > 2$ and $n < 5$ **(b)** $n > 5$ and $n < 8$
   (c) $n > 1$ and $n < 4$ **(d)** $n > 3$ and $n < 10$
   (e) $n > 20$ and $n < 25$ **(f)** $n > 0$ and $n < 6$
   (g) $n > 30$ and $n < 36$ **(h)** $n > 2$ and $n < 4$
   (i) $n > 10$ and $n < 12$ **(j)** $n > 5$ and $n < 9$

14.10 Writing your own equations

Sometimes you will have to solve problems and a
good way of doing this is to write the problem as
an equation. Once you have done this you can
solve the equation.

Example 17

Stephanie thinks of a number.
She doubles it and adds 3.
Her answer is 15.
What number does Stephanie think of?

Let the number be n
Double the number will be $2n$.
Add 3 means the answer is $2n + 3$

So $\quad 2n + 3 = 15$

$$2n = 15 - 3 = 12$$

$$n = 12 \div 2$$

$$n = 6$$

so the number is 6.

Example 18

The perimeter of this triangle is 21.
Find the value of x.

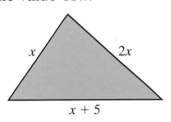

$$x + 2x + x + 5 = 21$$

$$4x + 5 = 21$$

$(-5) \quad 4x = 21 - 5 = 16$

$$4x = 16$$

$(\div 4) \quad\quad\quad x = 4$

$x + 2x + x = 4x$

The lengths of the sides of the triangle are 4, 8 and 9.

Exercise 14K

Write an equation for each of these problems.
Use your equation to solve the problem.

1 Jim thought of a number n. He added 5. His answer
was 9. What number did Jim think of?

2 Pat thought of a number. She took away 5. Her answer
was 9. What number did Pat think of?

3 Mike thought of a number. He doubled it. His answer
was 10. What number did Mike think of?

4 Tom thought of a number. He divided it by 4. His
answer was 6. What number did Tom think of?

5 Sue thought of a number. She doubled it and added 3.
Her answer was 9. What number did Sue think of?

6 Caroline thought of a number. She doubled it and took
away 7. Her answer was 15. What number did Caroline
think of?

7 The perimeter of this triangle is 22.
Work out the length of each side.

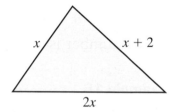

8 The perimeter of this square is 12.
Work out the length of each side.

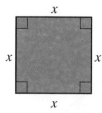

9 The perimeter of this rectangle is 30 cm.
Work out the length of each side.

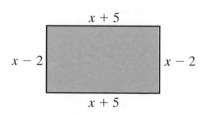

10 Jimmy is y years old.
His sister Natasha is 5 years older.
The total of their ages is 33.
How old are Jimmy and Natasha?

Summary of key points

1 You can use BIDMAS to remind you of the order of operations.

Brackets
Indices
Division
Multiplication
Addition
Subtraction

2 An equation is a number sentence where one side of the equals sign exactly balances the other side.

3 To solve an equation you have to find the value of the letter.

4 To solve equations with brackets there are 3 steps:

Step 1 Multiply out the brackets.
Step 2 Deal with + or −.
Step 3 Deal with the number in front of the letter.

STEP 1 $2(x + 2) = 10$
STEP 2 $2x + 4 = 10$
STEP 3 $2x = 6$
$x = 3$

5 To solve equations with letters on both sides of the equals sign there are 3 steps:

Step 1 Move the letters to one side of the equals sign: always keep the letters on the side with the bigger number of letters.
Step 2 Deal with + or −
Step 3 Deal with the number in front of the letter.

STEP 1 $5x + 1 = 2x + 7$
STEP 2 $3x + 1 = 7$
STEP 3 $3x = 6$
$x = 2$

6 Expressions and numbers that are not equal are called inequalities.

7 > means greater than.
< means less than.

15 Perimeter, area and volume

15.1 Perimeter and area

Ron has built a base for a garden shed
He has used square slabs.
The length of a side of each slab is one metre.

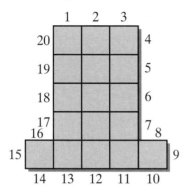

Each slab is one square metre.
You write 1 m²

The distance around the base is 20 metres.

There are 17 slabs. So the area of the base is 17 square metres.

- **The distance around a flat shape is called the perimeter**
- **The amount of space covered by a flat shape is called the area.**

Example 1

This patio is made from metre square slabs.

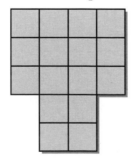

Work out the perimeter and area of the patio.

There are 18 one metre edges.
The perimeter of the patio is 18 metres (or 18 m).

There are 16 metre square slabs.
The area of the patio is 16 square metres (or 16 m²).

Exercise 15A

1 This patio has been made from metre square slabs.

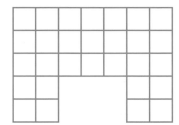

Work out:

(a) the perimeter of the patio
(b) the area of the patio.

2 These shapes have been drawn on cm² paper.
Work out the perimeter and area of each shape.

(a)   **(b)**   **(c)**

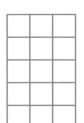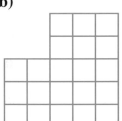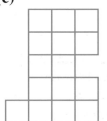

3 This rectangle has been made from centimetre square tiles.

(a) Work out the perimeter and area of the rectangle.
(b) What do you notice about the answers in part (a)?
(c) Rearrange all of the tiles to form another rectangle.
(d) Work out the perimeter of the new rectangle.

Remember:
Always give the units
in your answers.

Example 2

Work out the perimeter of this sports field.

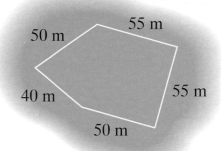

The perimeter is the distance around a flat shape.
To find the perimeter, add the lengths of all the sides:

$$40 + 50 + 55 + 55 + 50 = 250$$

The perimeter of the sports field is 250 m.

Exercise 15B

1   Work out the perimeters of each of these shapes.
    (Make sure you give the units with each answer.)

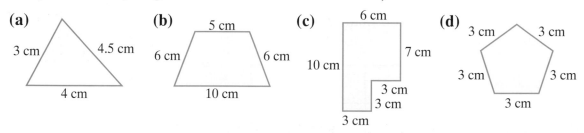

2   The diagram represents the plan of a floor space.

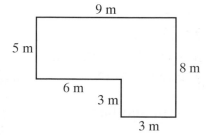

Work out the perimeter of the floor space.

3 The perimeter of this quadrilateral is 55 cm.

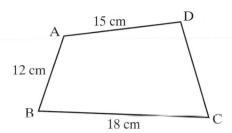

Work out the length of the side CD.

4 Which of the two shapes, **A** or **B**, has the greatest perimeter and by how much?

A

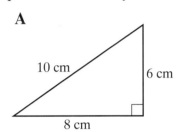

B

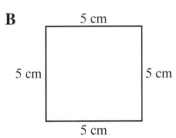

15.2 Formulae for perimeter and area of a rectangle

The perimeter of this rectangle is:

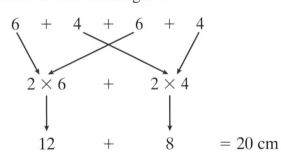

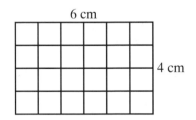

■ **The perimeter of a rectangle is given by the formula:**
   perimeter = 2 × length + 2 × width

or

   perimeter = 2 × (length + width)

Using letters for numbers this formula can be written as

$$\text{perimeter} = 2 \times (\text{length} + \text{width})$$
$$p = 2 \times (l + w)$$
$$p = 2(l + w)$$

Remember:
Always work the
brackets out first.
There is more about
this on page 255.

■ **The formula for the perimeter of a rectangle is:**
   perimeter $= 2(l + w)$

The area of a rectangle can be worked out ...

... by counting squares   ... by using a formula.

1	2	3	4	5	6
7	8	9	10	11	12
13	14	15	16	17	18
19	20	21	22	23	24

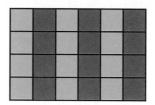

There are 24 squares, so the area of this rectangle is 24 cm²

The rectangle has 6 columns of 4 squares. The area is the total number of squares:
$6 \times 4 = 24$ cm²

■ **The area of a rectangle is:**
   area = length × width   or   area $= l \times w$

Example 3

Use the formulae to work out the perimeter and area of this rectangular flag.

$$\text{Perimeter} = 2 \times (l + w)$$
$$= 2 \times (5 + 3) = 2 \times 8$$
$$= 16 \, \text{m}$$

$$\text{Area} = l \times w$$
$$= 5 \times 3$$
$$= 15 \, \text{m}^2$$

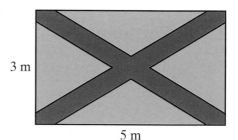

3 m

5 m

Exercise 15C

1   Work out the perimeter and area of each of these rectangles.

(a)   5 cm

4 cm

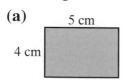

(b)   3 cm

7 cm

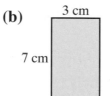

(c)   10 cm

6 cm

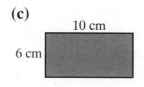

(d)   4 cm

15 cm

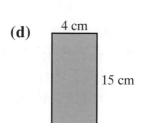

2 The diagram represents an architects plan of a new football pitch.

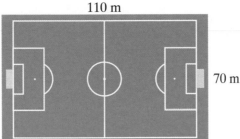

110 m

70 m

Work out:

(a) the perimeter of the pitch (b) the area of the pitch.

3 Sue's bedroom floor is in the shape of the letter T:

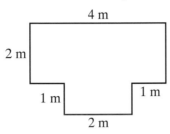

4 m

2 m

1 m 1 m

2 m

Hint:

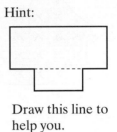

Draw this line to help you.

Work out the perimeter and the area of the floor.

4 The perimeter of a rectangle is 26 cm.
The length of the rectangle is 8 cm.
Work out:

(a) the width of the rectangle (b) the area of the rectangle.

5 Work out the perimeter and area of this floor.

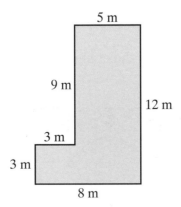

5 m

9 m

12 m

3 m

3 m

8 m

6 A rectangle measures 4 cm by 25 cm.

(a) Work out the perimeter and area of the rectangle.

A square has the same area as the rectangle.

(b) How long is each side of the square?

15.3 Estimating areas

To find the area of a curved shape you can estimate how many squares it covers.

Example 4

Estimate the area of this shape:

Put a cross in each whole square and a dot in each part square:

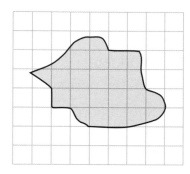

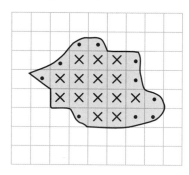

There are 14 crosses and 10 dots.

Each cross is $1\,cm^2$: $14 \times 1 = 14\,cm^2$
Each dot is $\frac{1}{2}\,cm^2$: $10 \times \frac{1}{2} = 5\,cm^2$

So a good estimate for the area is $19\,cm^2$.

Exercise 15D

1   Work out an estimate for the area of these shapes drawn on cm^2 paper.

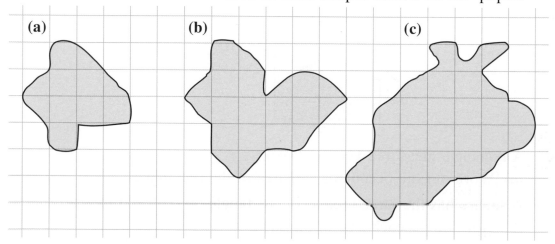

(a)   (b)   (c)

2   This map of an island has been drawn on squared paper.

The length of a side of each square represents 1 km.

Work out an estimate for the area of the island.

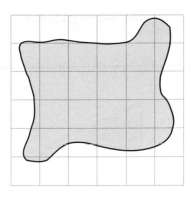

15.4 Area of a triangle

The area of any triangle is half the area of its surrounding rectangle.

To find the area of this triangle . . .   . . . draw it as half a rectangle.

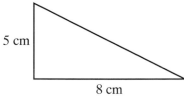   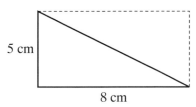

Area of surrounding rectangle is $8 \times 5 = 40 \, \text{cm}^2$

So the area of the triangle is $\frac{1}{2}$ of $40 = 20 \, \text{cm}^2$

The area of any triangle is $\frac{1}{2}$ area of the surrounding rectangle.

■   **The area of a triangle is:**
area of a triangle $= \frac{1}{2} \times$ base $\times$ height

Example 5

Work out the area of this triangle:

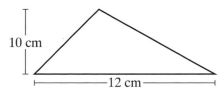

Use the formula:

$$\text{Area} = \frac{1}{2} \times \text{base} \times \text{height}$$
$$= \frac{1}{2} \times 12 \times 10$$
$$= \frac{1}{2} \times 120$$
$$= 60 \, \text{cm}^2$$

Exercise 15E

1   Work out the area of each of these triangles.

(a)   3 cm, 8 cm

(b)   6 cm, 4 cm

(c)   10 cm, 3 cm

(d)   8 cm, 5 cm

(e)   8 cm, 8 cm

(f)   12 cm, 6 cm

(g)   8 cm, 10 cm

(h)   8 cm, 15 cm

2   Here are three shapes labelled A, B and C.

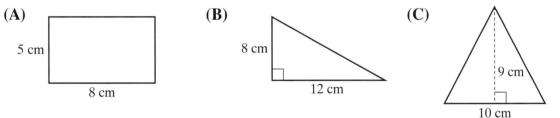

(A)   5 cm, 8 cm

(B)   8 cm, 12 cm

(C)   9 cm, 10 cm

   (a) Starting with the smallest, list the shapes in order
   of the sizes of their areas.
   (b) Work out the difference between the largest and
   smallest area.

3   The diagram shows the plan of Three Corner Park:

   Work out the area of the park.

   60 m, 150 m

4   Work out the area of the shaded region:

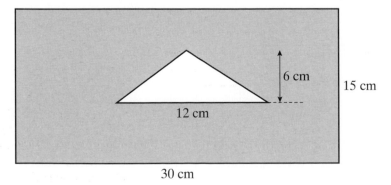

   6 cm, 15 cm, 12 cm, 30 cm

5 The perimeter of this triangle is 40 cm.
Work out:

(a) the length of AB
(b) the area of the triangle ABC.

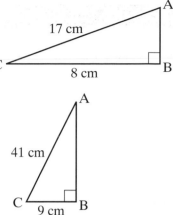

6 The area of this triangle is 180 cm².
Work out the perimeter of the triangle.

7 A square has a perimeter of 40 cm.
A triangle has an area equal to the area of this square.
Work out possible values for the base and height of the triangle.

15.5 Composite shapes

To find the area of a composite shape, split it up into simpler shapes:

Method 1

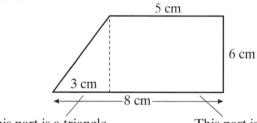

This part is a triangle
with area = $\frac{1}{2} \times 3 \times 6 = 9$ cm²

This part is a rectangle
with area = $5 \times 6 = 30$ cm²

Hint:
Draw in this line
to help you:

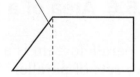

So the area of the shape is $9 + 30 = 39$ cm²

Method 2

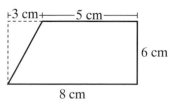

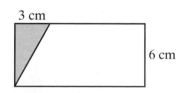

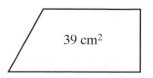

Complete the rectangle
and work out the area:
$8 \times 6 = 48$ cm²

Work out the area of the
shaded triangle:
$\frac{3}{4} \times 3 \times 6 = 9$ cm²

The area of the original
shape is the area of the
rectangle minus the area
of the triangle:
$48 - 9 = 39$ cm²

Exercise 15F

1   Use each method to work out the area of this shape.
    Make sure you get the same answer on both occasions.

    Decide which method you like best.

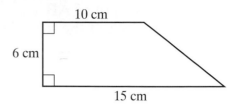

2   Work out the area of these shapes.
    Use the method you find easiest.

(a)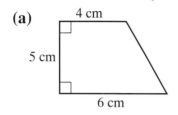

(b)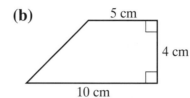

(c)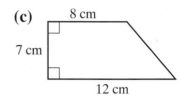

(d)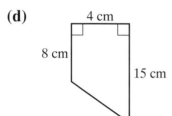

(e)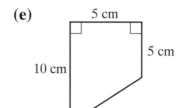

(f)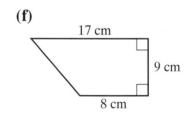

15.6 Area of a parallelogram

A parallelogram is a four-sided shape with two sets of parallel sides.

To find its area, imagine making it into a rectangle like this:

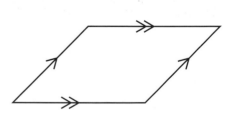

Cut out the triangle…

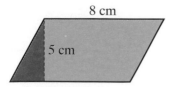

…move it to the other end like this:

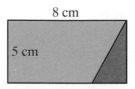

This rectangle has the same area as the parallelogram.

The height is 5 cm.
The length is 8 cm.

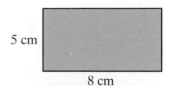

The area is:
length $\times$ width $= 8 \times 5$
$= 40 \text{ cm}^2$

■ **The area of a parallelogram is:**

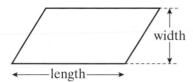

width

←———length———→

area of a parallelogram = length × width

Example 6

Work out the area of this parallelogram:

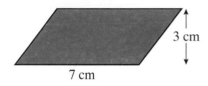

3 cm

7 cm

Length $= 7\,\text{cm}$ Width $= 3\,\text{cm}$

So, using the formula:

$$\begin{aligned}\text{Area} &= \text{length} \times \text{width} \\ &= 7 \times 3 \\ &= 21\,\text{cm}^2\end{aligned}$$

Exercise 15G

1   Work out the area of each of these parallelograms

(a)

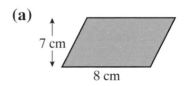

7 cm

8 cm

(b)

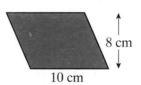

8 cm

10 cm

(c)

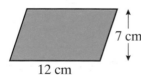

7 cm

12 cm

2   Work out the shaded area.

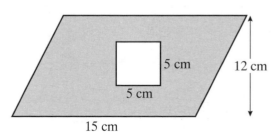

5 cm

5 cm

12 cm

15 cm

15.7 Circumference of a circle

■   **The perimeter of a circle is called its *circumference*.**

The circumference of a circle is related to its diameter.

The circumference is **less** than
4 diameters:

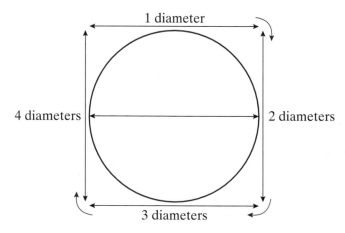

Each half of the circumference
is **greater** than 1 diameter …

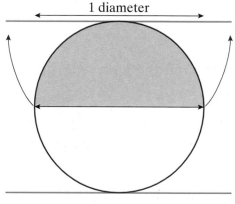

… so the whole circumference
is greater than 2 diameters.

The circumference is less than 4 diameters but it is also
greater than 2 diameters.
So a reasonable estimate for the circumference is 3
diameters.

Example 7

Draw a circle with diameter 3 cm and check that it has a
circumference of approximately 9 cm.

Draw the circle on cm² paper
and mark points 1 cm apart
around it.

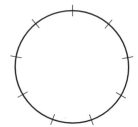

Join the points to form a
shape with a perimeter just less
than the circumference of the circle.

The perimeter of the shape is just over 9 cm.
So the estimate $3 \times \text{diameter} = 3 \times 3 = 9$ cm is a
reasonable estimation for the circumference.

Exercise 15H

1 Repeat the process in Example 7 for circles with a diameter of:

(a) 4 cm   (b) 5 cm

2 Work out an estimate for the circumference of a circle of radius 10 metres.

15.8 Introducing π

In the last section you saw that a good estimate for the circumference of a circle is $3 \times$ diameter.

The exact value of the circumference is given by the formula:

circumference $= \pi \times$ diameter

π is the number you get if you divide the circumference of any circle by its diameter. It is the same value for every circle.

π is a Greek letter and it is pronounced 'pie'.

The value of π is 3.14 correct to two places of decimals.

■ **The circumference of a circle is:**

circumference $= \pi \times$ diameter
$= \pi \times 2 \times$ radius
$= 2 \times \pi \times$ radius

You might see this formula shortened to $2\pi r$.

Example 8

Work out the circumference of a circle of radius 3 cm.

Circumference $= 2 \times \pi \times$ radius
$= 2 \times \pi \times 3$
$= 2 \times 3.14 \times 3$

So circumference $= 18.84$ cm

Note: When you get to the stage

circumference $= 2 \times \pi \times 3$

then it can be written

circumference $= 2 \times 3 \times \pi$
$= 6\pi$ cm

In some test questions you might be able to leave this as your answer. But only if the question says: *leave your answers in terms of* π.

Exercise 15I

1 Work out the circumference of a circle of radius:
   (a) 5 cm   **(b)** 4 cm   **(c)** 8 cm   **(d)** 10 cm
   In each case give your answer
   • correct to 2 decimal places
   • in terms of π.

2 Work out the circumference of each circle.

   (a) 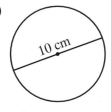   **(b)** 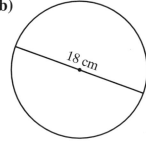   **(c)**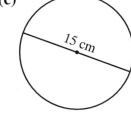

3 The centre-circle on a soccer pitch has a radius of 9 metres.
   Work out the circumference of the centre-circle.

4 Work out the circumference of this circle. Give your answer:
   (a) in centimetres, correct to 2 decimal places
   (b) in terms of π.

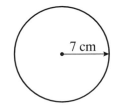

5 Work out the perimeter of this semicircle.
   Give your answer in centimetres, correct to two decimal places.

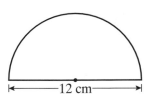

6 The diagram represents a running track.

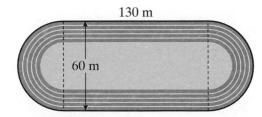

   The track has two straight edges and two semicircular ends.
   Work out the total distance around the track.

7 The wheels on Jon's bike have a radius of 33 cm.

Work out the circumference of his wheels.

8 This door is in the shape of a rectangle with a semicircle at the top.

Work out the perimeter of the door.

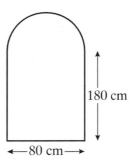

180 cm

←—80 cm—→

9 Work out the circumference of this circle.

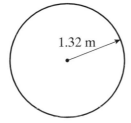

1.32 m

Give your answer:

(a) in metres, correct to two decimal places
(b) in centimetres, correct to the nearest centimetre
(c) in terms of π for both metres and centimetres.

Hint:
convert the units
before you do the
calculation.

15.9 Estimating the area of a circle

The area of a circle can be estimated like this:

This square is
made from 8
equal triangles:

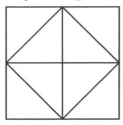

The area of the
circle is greater
than 4 triangles …

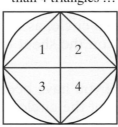

… but less than 8
triangles.

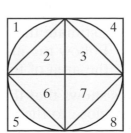

So the area of the circle is **greater** than half of the square but **less** than the whole square.

A good estimate for the area of the circle is about $\frac{3}{4}$ of the area of the square.

Example 9

Work out an estimate for the area of a circle with a radius of 4 cm.

Draw the surrounding square. Its sides are of length 8 cm.

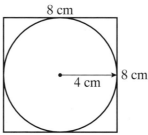

Each side of the square is the same length as 2 × radius.

The area of the square is $8 \times 8 = 64 \, \text{cm}^2$
So an estimate for the area of the circle is:

$$\frac{3}{4} \times 64 = 48 \, \text{cm}^2$$

Exercise 15J

1   Estimate the area of each circle.

(a)   (b)   (c)   (d)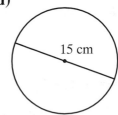

2   **Activity**   You will need **Activity Sheet 16**.

  ● Estimate the area of each circle, as in question 1.
  ● Follow the instructions on the sheet to work out the area of the circle.

  This shows that the estimate you have been using is very close to the actual area of the circle.

15.10 The exact area of a circle

A circle can be divided into a large number of sectors.

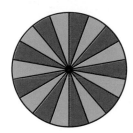

You can rearrange the sectors to make a rectangle like this:

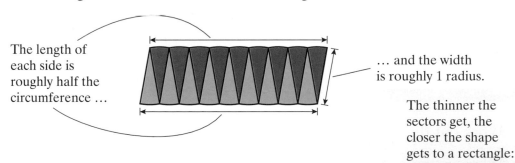

The length of each side is roughly half the circumference …

… and the width is roughly 1 radius.

The thinner the sectors get, the closer the shape gets to a rectangle:

The area of this rectangle is:

area = half the circumference (length) × radius (width)
    = π × radius   × radius
    = π × radius^2

■ **The area of a circle is:**
    area = π × radius^2

Hint:
The circumference of a circle is:
    $2 \times \pi \times$ radius
so half the circumference is:
    $\pi \times$ radius

Example 10

Work out the area of this circle.

4 cm

Use the formula
    area = π × radius^2
        = $\pi \times 4^2$
        = $\pi \times 16$ (area = 16π cm^2 if the answer is left in terms of π)
        = 3.14×16
        = 50.24 cm^2

Example 11

Work out the area of this table mat:

Split the mat into a rectangle and a semicircle.

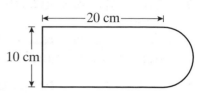

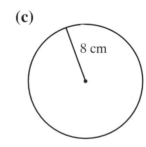

The area of the semicircle is:
$\frac{1}{2}$ of $\pi \times 5^2 = \frac{1}{2} \times \pi \times 25 = 39.25$ cm^2

The area of the rectangle is:
$10 \times 20 = 200$ cm^2

So the total area is $200 + 39.25 = 239.25$ cm^2

Exercise 15K

1 Work out the area of each of these circles.

(a)　　　　　(b)　　　　　(c)　　　　　(d)

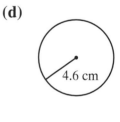

5 cm　　12 cm　　8 cm　　4.6 cm

2 Work out the area of a circle of radius

(a) 6 cm　　(b) 10 cm　　(c) 7 cm　　(d) 15 cm
(e) 2.8 cm　　(f) 5.4 cm　　(g) 9.3 cm　　(h) 12.7 cm

Give all your answers in cm^2, correct to two places of decimals.

3 Work out the area of this circle.

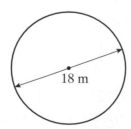

18 m

Give your answer in:
(a) m^2, correct to 2 dp　　(b) units of π.

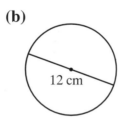

4 Mrs Coles has a circular rug with a diameter of 5 metres.
Work out the area of the rug giving your answer to the nearest whole number of square metres.

5 Work out the area of each of these semicircles.

(a)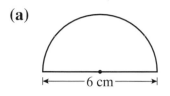

(b)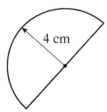
4 cm

(c)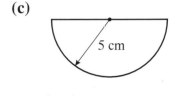
5 cm

6 cm

6 This is an architect's plan of a new swimming pool:
Work out the area of the pool floor, giving your answer in square metres, correct to two places of decimals.

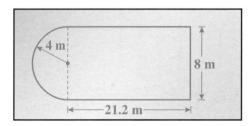
4 m
8 m
21.2 m

7 Work out the shaded area in each case.

(a)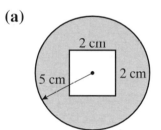
2 cm
2 cm
5 cm

(b)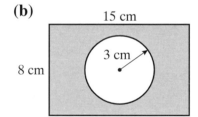
15 cm
3 cm
8 cm

(c)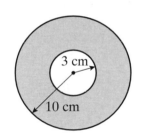
3 cm
10 cm

15.11 Volume and surface area of a cuboid

Solid and hollow shapes take up space in three dimensions.
They are called 3-dimensional shapes.

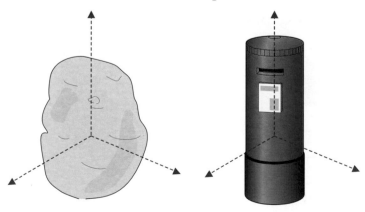

■ **The volume is the amount of space taken up by a 3-dimensional shape.**

You can find the volume of a cuboid by counting cubes:

This cuboid is made from centimetre cubes:

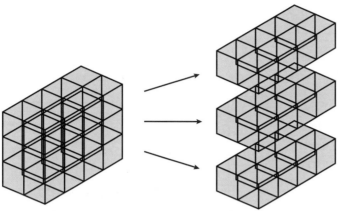

Each cube has a volume of 1 cm³ or 1 cubic centimetre.

There are 3 layers of 8 cubes each.

There are 3 layers of 2×4 cubes $= 3 \times 8$
$$= 24 \text{ cubes}$$

So the volume of the cuboid is 24 cm³

Remember:
You write cubic centimetres as cm³

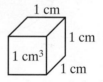

■ **For any cuboid:**

volume of a cuboid = length × width × height

Surface area of a cuboid

This cuboid has six faces:

Two like this ...   ... two like this   ... and two like this.

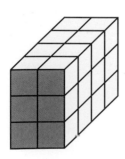

$3 \times 2 = 6 \text{ cm}^2$

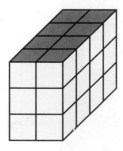

$4 \times 2 = 8 \text{ cm}^2$

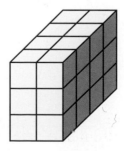

$4 \times 3 = 12 \text{ cm}^2$

The **surface area** of the cuboid is the total area of all six faces:

2 lots of $3 \times 2 \longrightarrow 2 \times 6 = 12$ (2 × height × width)

2 lots of $4 \times 2 \longrightarrow 2 \times 8 = 16$ (2 × length × width)

2 lots of $4 \times 3 \longrightarrow 2 \times 12 = 24$ (2 × length × height)

The surface area is $12 + 16 + 24 = 52 \, \text{cm}^2$

■   **For any cuboid the surface area is:**
   surface area = 2 × (length × width)
                      + 2 × (length × height) + 2 × (width × height)

Example 12

Work out:

(a) the volume

(b) the surface area of this cuboid.

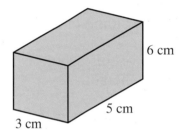

Volume = length × width × height

Volume = $5 \times 3 \times 6 = 90 \, \text{cm}^3$

Surface area =
(2 × length × width) + (2 × length × height) + (2 × width × height)

$2 \times 5 \times 3$ + $2 \times 5 \times 6$ + $2 \times 3 \times 6$

30   +   60   +   36 $= 126 \, \text{cm}^2$

Exercise 15L

1   Work out the volume and surface area of each of these cuboids.

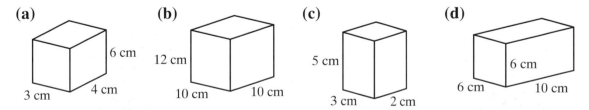

(a) 6 cm, 3 cm, 4 cm

(b) 12 cm, 10 cm, 10 cm

(c) 5 cm, 3 cm, 2 cm

(d) 6 cm, 6 cm, 10 cm

2   A block of metal is a cuboid with length = 14 cm, width = 10 cm and height = 15 cm.
   Work out the volume of the block of metal.

3 Work out:

(a) the volume
(b) the surface area

of a cube with sides of length 5 cm.

4 Shani's filing cabinet is a cuboid. The base is a square of side 30 cm.
Work out:

(a) the surface area of the filing cabinet
(b) the volume of the filing cabinet.

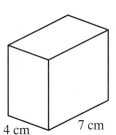

5 Ron and David have dug out a fishpond.
The pond is in the shape of a cuboid 2.5 m long, 3.4 m wide and 0.3 m deep.
What is the volume of the pond?

6 The volume of this cuboid is 280 cm³:
Work out its height.

7 The volume of a cube is 216 cm³.
Work out:

(a) the length of a side of the cube
(b) the surface area of the cube.

15.12 Volume of a prism

A cuboid is a special case of a prism.
It is a prism with a rectangular base.

Here are some other prisms:

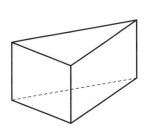
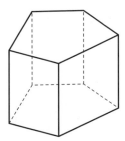
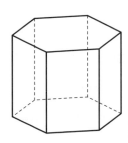

In each case the **base** and the **top** face are identical and they are joined by straight edges.

Remember:
A prism is a solid with a constant cross-section.

The formula for the volume of a cuboid is:

$$\text{volume} = \underbrace{\text{length} \times \text{width}} \times \text{height}$$

$$\downarrow$$

$$= \quad \text{area of base} \times \text{height}$$

and this is truc for any prism.

■   **The volume of a prism is:**

   volume = area of base × height

Exercise 15M

1   Work out the volume for each of these prisms.

(a)

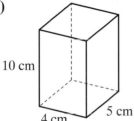

(b)

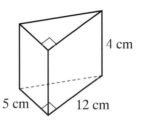

(c)

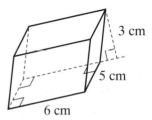

2   Work out the volume of each of these prisms.

(a)

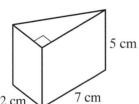

(b)

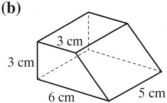

(c)

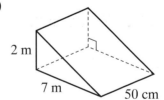

3   The diagram represents the end face of a prism:

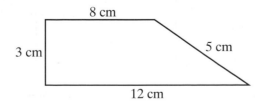

   If the prism is 7 cm wide, work out:
   (a) the area of the end face
   (b) the volume of the prism.

4 The diagram represents a door stop in the shape of a wedge.
Work out the volume of the wedge.

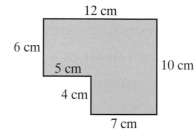

16 cm

4 cm

9 cm

5 The diagram represents the base of a prism.
The height of the prism is 15 cm.
Work out the volume of the prism.

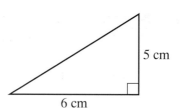

12 cm

6 cm

5 cm

4 cm

7 cm

10 cm

6 The diagram represents the base of a prism.
The volume of the prism is 180 cm³.
Work out the height of the prism.

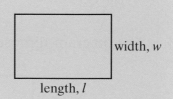

5 cm

6 cm

Summary of key points

1 The distance around a flat shape is called the perimeter.

2 The amount of space covered by a flat shape is called the area.

3 The perimeter of a rectangle is given by the formula:
perimeter $= 2 \times$ length $+ 2 \times$ width
or
perimeter $= 2 \times$ (length $+$ width)

4 The formula for the perimeter of a rectangle is:
perimeter $= 2(l + w)$

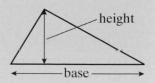

width, w

length, l

5 The area of a rectangle is:
area $=$ length $\times$ width   or   area $= l \times w$

6 The area of a triangle is:
area $= \frac{1}{2} \times$ base $\times$ height

height

base

7 The area of a parallelogram is:
area = length × width

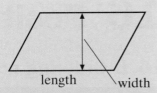

length   width

8 The perimeter of a circle is called its circumference.

9 The circumference of a circle is:
circumference = π × diameter
    = π × 2 × radius
    = 2 × π × radius

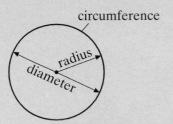

circumference

radius

diameter

10 The area of a circle is:
area = π × radius^2

11 The volume is the amount of space taken up by a 3-dimensional shape.

12 The volume of a cuboid is:
volume = length × width × height

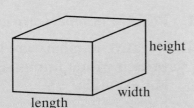

height

length   width

13 The surface area of a cuboid is:
surface area = 2 × (length × width) + 2 × (length × height)
    + 2 × (width × height)

14 The volume of a prism is:
volume = area of base × height

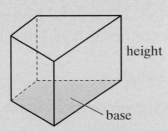

height

base

16 Positive and negative numbers

16.1 Ordering numbers

Mount Everest is the highest mountain in the world. Its summit is 8848 m above sea level.

The Dead Sea is the lowest place on Earth. It is 396 m below sea level. You can write this as −396 m.

- ■ **Positive numbers are greater than zero.**

- ■ **Negative numbers are less than zero. They are written with a minus sign in front of the number. For example, −6**

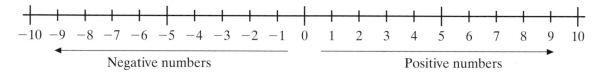

You can use a horizontal number line to answer questions about positive and negative numbers.

Example 1

Write down these numbers in order of size, starting with the smallest:

−4, 5, 0, −7, −1, 2, −9, −3.

Mark the positions of the numbers on a number line.

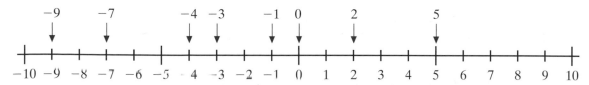

The order is −9, −7, −4, −3, −1, 0, 2, 5.

Example 2

Write down all the whole numbers that are greater than −8, less than 5 and are even.

The numbers are *greater than* −8, so −8 is not included.

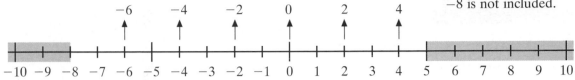

The numbers are −6, −4, −2, 0, 2 and 4.

Exercise 16A

Use a number line to answer these questions.

1 Write these numbers in order of size, starting with the smallest:
   (a) 3, −7, −4, −9, 5, −1.
   (b) 6, −3, 3, −5, 2, −8.
   (c) 4, −6, −8, 3, −1, −5.
   (d) 4, −7, 1, −3, −2, −8.

2 Write these numbers in order of size, starting with the largest:
   (a) −8, 4, −10, −6, 5, −3.
   (b) −5, 3, −9, 7, −4, −1.
   (c) 2, −8, 3, −5, −7, −3.
   (d) −9, 2, −6, −1, 5, −5.

3 Write down all the whole numbers that are greater than −6 and less than 5.

Hint: −6 and 5 are not included.

4 Write down all the whole numbers that are greater than −9, less than 6 and are even.

5 Write down all the whole numbers that are greater than −7, less than 4 and are odd.

6 Ali chooses a whole number that is less than −3, greater than −6 and is even. What number does Ali choose?

7 Write down all the whole numbers that are less than 10, greater than −8 and are multiples of 3.

16.2 Using the number line

You can answer questions by moving up or down the number line.

Example 3

Use a number line to find the number that is:

(a) 3 more than -7 　　　　　　**(b)** 5 less than 2.

(a) You have 3 more so the number gets bigger.

Start at -7 and move
3 spaces to the right.

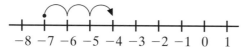

The answer is -4.

3 more than -7 is the same as $-7 + 3$.
5 less than 2 is the same as $2 - 5$.

(b) You have 5 less so the number gets smaller.

Start at 2 and move
5 spaces to the left.

The answer is -3.

$-7 + 3 = -4$.
$2 - 5 = -3$.

Example 4

Use a number line to find the answers:

(a) $1 - 5$ 　　　　　　**(b)** $-3 + 6$

(a) You start at 1 and *take away* 5.

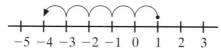

The answer is -4.

(b) You start at -3 and *add* 6.

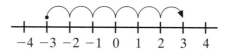

The answer is 3.

Exercise 16B

Use a number line to answer these questions.

1   Find the number that is:

(a) 4 more than 3	**(b)** 5 more than -2	**(c)** 2 less than -3
(d) 7 less than 3	**(e)** 6 more than -2	**(f)** 4 less than 0
(g) 7 more than -6	**(h)** 5 less than -3	**(i)** 8 more than -8
(j) 3 less than 1	**(k)** 5 more than -7	**(l)** 6 less than -3

2   **(a)** Find the number that is 6 more than −1.

   (b) Work out −1 + 6.

3   Work out:

   (a) 4 − 9   **(b)** −3 + 5
   (c) 1 − 2   **(d)** 2 − 6
   (e) −3 + 3   **(f)** 1 − 7
   (g) −4 + 5   **(h)** 5 − 8
   (i) −2 + 5   **(j)** −1 + 8
   (k) 0 − 3   **(l)** −6 + 6

16.3 Number patterns

Sometimes you need to continue patterns of numbers.

Example 5

Write down the next two numbers in this pattern:

   11, 8, 5, 2, . . .

The numbers go down by 3 each time.

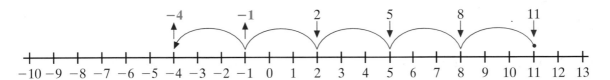

The next two numbers in the pattern are −1 and −4.

Exercise 16C

Use a number line to answer these questions.

1   Write down the next two numbers in each pattern:

   (a) 9, 7, 5, 3, . . .   **(b)** 8, 6, 4, 2, . . .
   (c) 10, 7, 4, 1, . . .   **(d)** 4, 2, 0, −2, . . .
   (e) −9, −7, −5, −3, . . .   **(f)** −11, −8, −5, −2, . . .
   (g) −10, −6, −2, 2, . . .   **(h)** −10, −8, −6, −4, . . .
   (i) 2, −1, −4, −7, . . .   **(j)** 13, 9, 5, 1, . . .

2 This number line shows a number pattern:

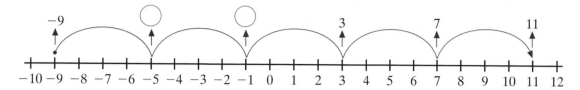

Write down the missing numbers.

3 Work out the two missing numbers in each number pattern:

(a) 7, 5, 3, 1, ☐, ☐, −5.

(b) −8, −6, −4, −2, ☐, ☐, 4.

(c) 13, 10, 7, 4, ☐, ☐, −5.

(d) −11, −8, −5, −2, ☐, ☐, 7.

(e) 15, 11, 7, 3, ☐, ☐, −9.

(f) −11, −9, −7, −5, ☐, ☐, 1.

16.4 Using number tables

You can use number tables to add and subtract positive and negative numbers. You use different tables for add and subtract.

Example 6

Use number tables to find the answers:

(a) $1 + -3$

(b) $3 - -1$

(a)

First number

+	3	2	1	0	−1	−2	−3
3	6	5	4	3	2	1	0
2	5	4	3	2	1	0	−1
1	4	3	2	1	0	−1	−2
0	3	2	1	0	−1	−2	−3
−1	2	1	0	−1	−2	−3	−4
−2	1	0	−1	−2	−3	−4	−5
−3	0	−1	−2	−3	−4	−5	−6

Second number

$1 + -3 = -2$

(b)

First number

−	3	2	1	0	−1	−2	−3
3	0	−1	−2	−3	−4	−5	−6
2	1	0	−1	−2	−3	−4	−5
1	2	1	0	−1	−2	−3	−4
0	3	2	1	0	−1	−2	−3
−1	4	3	2	1	0	−1	−2
−2	5	4	3	2	1	0	−1
−3	6	5	4	3	2	1	0

Second number

$3 - -1 = 4$

Exercise 16D

Use the tables in Example 6 to find the answers:

1 $2 + -3$	**2** $-2 + -3$	**3** $-1 + 2$
4 $-3 - -2$	**5** $-2 - 3$	**6** $1 - -3$
7 $-2 - 1$	**8** $-3 + -3$	**9** $3 - 1$
10 $3 + -2$	**11** $1 - 2$	**12** $1 + -3$
13 $-1 - 3$	**14** $-1 + -2$	**15** $2 + -2$

16.5 Adding and subtracting positive and negative numbers

You already know the rules for adding and subtracting positive numbers:

■ **If you add a positive number the result is bigger.**

answer goes up

■ **If you subtract a positive number the result is smaller.**

answer goes down

The temperature of this ice is $-2°C$.

If you add ice to a warm drink the temperature of the drink goes down.

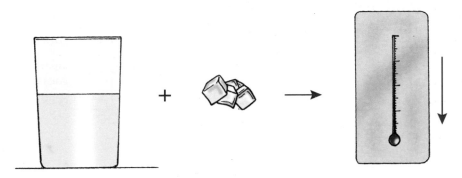

■ **If you add a negative number the result is smaller.**  **answer** goes down

Example 6(a) also shows this rule.

$$1 + -3 = -2$$

Adding the negative number -3 to 1 gives the result -2, which is smaller than 1.

Example 6(b) shows what happens when you subtract a negative number.

$$3 - -1 = 4$$

Subtracting the negative number -1 from 3 gives the result 4, which is bigger than 3.

■ **If you subtract a negative number the result is bigger.**  **answer** goes up

Example 7

Use the rules of addition and subtraction to find the answers:

(a) $3 + -5$ **(b)** $-2 - -7$

(a) Start at 3

 **answer** goes down

So $3 + -5 = 3 - 5 = -2$

(b) Start at -2

 **answer** goes up

So $-2 - -7 = -2 + 7 = 5$

Exercise 16E

Use the rules shown to find the answers:

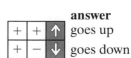
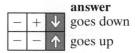

1
  (a) $-7 - 1$ **(b)** $-4 + -3$ **(c)** $3 - 6$
  (d) $-8 - -3$ **(e)** $7 - -3$ **(f)** $-8 + 1$
  (g) $6 + -2$ **(h)** $-3 - -5$ **(i)** $-5 + -4$
  (j) $-7 - -2$ **(k)** $-2 - -4$ **(l)** $9 - -4$

2
  (a) $-9 - 6$ **(b)** $11 + -3$ **(c)** $-2 - -16$
  (d) $3 + -1$ **(e)** $-4 + 16$ **(f)** $8 - -2$
  (g) $3 - 17$ **(h)** $-4 + -1$ **(i)** $-4 + 1$
  (j) $-16 - -3$ **(k)** $-2 + -4$ **(l)** $-8 + 12$

3   Work out:

(a) $2 + +7$ (b) $-4 + 6$

(c) $-9 + 2$ (d) $3 + -4$

(e) $2 + -5$ (f) $1 + -7$

(g) $-2 + -4$ (h) $-1 + -3$

(i) $-6 + -3$ (j) $-8 + 3$

(k) $4 + -7$ (l) $-4 + -2$

Summary of key points

1   Positive numbers are greater than zero.

2   Negative numbers are less than zero. They are written with a minus sign in front of the number. For example, -6.

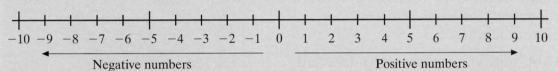

3   If you add a positive number the result is bigger.
If you subtract a positive number the result is smaller.

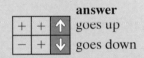

4   If you add a negative number the result is smaller.
If you subtract a negative number the result is bigger.

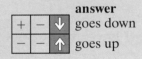

17 Using and applying mathematics

Introduction

This chapter is about the **problem-solving process**. In the chapter you will learn more about how to use and apply mathematics to **investigate** a problem-solving situation.

17.1 The problem

This problem is about making kerbs of various lengths from kerbstones of different lengths.

At the start we just have two different kerbstones:

white kerbstones

which are of length 1 unit

red kerbstones

which are of length 2 units.

Suppose that we wanted to make a kerb of length 10 units using these white and red kerbstones. Some of the different ways of doing this are:

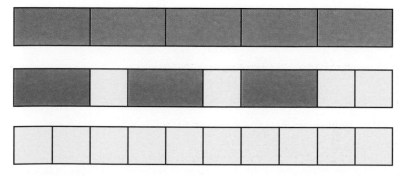

There are a lot of different ways and we would probably get mixed up if we tried to list them all.

Solving the problem means that if you need a kerb of a particular length, you can state how many different ways there are of making that length of kerb. You should also be able to explain why your answer is true.

Understand the problem

The first thing you need to do is make sure that you understand the problem.

In this problem you have a selection of:

white kerbstones ▢ of length 1 unit

and red kerbstones ▬ of length 2 units

You are going to investigate the **number of different ways** of making a kerb of any length.

For instance, if the kerb is of length 5 units then some of the different ways of making it are:

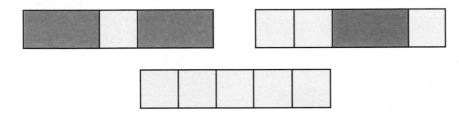

Have you seen the problem or something like it before?

Before starting to tackle any problem you should always ask yourself if you have seen the problem or something like it before. If you have then you may be able to benefit from that experience.

This chapter will assume that the kerbstone problem is new to you.

Exercise 17A

Here are four different ways of making a kerb of length five units using the white and red kerbstones:

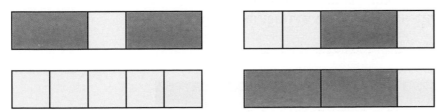

Find at least **two other ways** of making a kerb of length five units.

17.2 Simplify the problem

The first stage of the problem-solving process is to make the problem as simple as you can.

Start by looking at some kerbs of very short lengths, such as 1, 2 and 3 units.

The simplest case is when the kerb is of length 1 unit.

A very simple case is called a **trivial** case.

It can be made in only **one way**. by using a single white kerbstone:

When the length of the kerb is two units it can be made in two ways:

and

When the length of the kerb is three units it can be made as:

or as . . .

So when the length of the kerb is three units, it can be made in three ways.

Now you have three simple results:

Length of kerb	Number of ways
1	1
2	2
3	3

At this stage you might start to think that the number of different ways of making a kerb is always equal to the length of the kerb – but you would be wrong, as the next exercise shows.

Exercise 17B

Show that there are five different ways of making a kerb of length four units.

17.3 Developing strategies

One of the most important parts of the problem-solving and investigation process is developing a strategy.

For the kerbs problem it might look nice to have lots of pictures of white and red kerbstones but it is much more efficient to use letters:

w to represent white 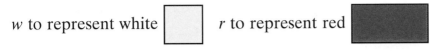 *r* to represent red

You can now represent your kerbs using the letters *r* and *w* in different orders. The five different kerbs of length 4 units look like this:

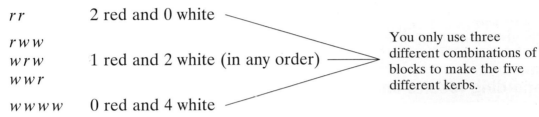

r r   2 red and 0 white

r w w
w r w   1 red and 2 white (in any order)
w w r

w w w w   0 red and 4 white

You only use three different combinations of blocks to make the five different kerbs.

There are three different kerbs that use one red block and two white blocks.

There is a pattern where it seems as if the red (or *r*) *slides* down a diagonal

r w w
w r w
w w r

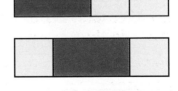

You now have three strategies that are helpful in solving the problem:

1   using letters to represent the kerbstones

2   separating the different combinations of blocks such as 1 red and 2 white, etc.

3   the *sliding* of a single letter down a diagonal.

Strategy 3 is an example of writing your results in a **systematic** way.
If you had written:

w w r
r w w
w r w

you might not have spotted a pattern.

Example 1

Use the strategies to find all eight ways of making a kerb of length five units.

A kerb of length 5 units can be made as:

2 red and 1 white	*r r* w *r* w *r* w *r r*	3 ways
1 red and 3 white	*r* w w w w *r* w w w w *r* w w w w *r*	4 ways
0 red and 5 white	w w w w w	1 way

This gives a total of $3 + 4 + 1 = 8$ ways.

Recording results and making observations

You now have five results. It is a good idea to record your results in a table:

Length of kerb	Number of different ways of making the kerb
1	1
2	2
3	3
4	5
5	8

You need to be able to make observations based on your results.

For instance, quite simply you might see that:

As the length of the kerb increases then the number of ways of making it also increases.

At a slightly higher level of difficulty and awareness you might notice that:

The pattern for the number of ways of making a kerb goes

odd	even	odd	odd	even
1	2	3	5	8

Then at an even higher level you might notice that:

The pattern for the number of ways of making a kerb, that is, the numbers:

1,   2,   3,   5,   8

is generated by the following rule.

The next number is the sum of the previous two numbers

$$3 + 5 = 8$$

1,   2,   3,   5,   8

$$2 + 3 = 5$$

Making and testing a prediction

You now have a possible rule for finding the next number in the sequence. This is called a **conjecture**. It is a statement about **what you think is happening**. The conjecture is:

The next number is the sum of the previous two numbers.

You can use your conjecture to make a **prediction**. You can add your prediction to your table of results:

Length of kerb	Number of different ways of making the kerb
1	1
2	2
3	$2 + 1 = 3$
4	$3 + 2 = 5$
5	$5 + 3 = 8$
6	$8 + 5 = 13$

Using your conjecture, you can predict that there are 13 different ways of making a kerb of length 6 units.

You now need to **test your prediction**. You can use your strategies to find the number of different kerbs of length 6 units:

3 red and 0 white	*r r r*	1 way

2 red and 2 white

r r w w
r w r w
r w w r
w r r w
w r w r
w w r r

6 ways

1 red and 4 white

r w w w w
w r w w w
w w r w w
w w w r w
w w w w r

5 ways

0 red and 6 white	*w w w w w w*	1 way

There are $1 + 6 + 5 + 1 = 13$ ways to make a kerb of length 6.

You now have 6 definite results:

Length of kerb	Number of different ways of making the kerb
1	1
2	2
3	3
4	5
5	+ 8
6	= 13

You have made a prediction, tested it and found it to be true. You can be **very confident** that the general rule is true.

However, there is far more to establishing the truth in mathematics than the confidence that comes from predicting and testing.

Exercise 17C

Use the general rule:

1 (a) make a prediction for the number of different ways
       of making a kerb of length 7 units.
   (b) test that prediction.

2 make predictions for the number of different ways of
   making a kerb of length:
   (a) 8 units   (b) 9 units   (c) 10 units

17.4 Using symbols

In section 17.3 you used letters to represent the kerbstones.
It will be useful to be able to write the general rule using
letters and symbols.

The general rule for the kerbstones problem is:

  The next number in the sequence is the
  sum of the previous two numbers.

One way to write this in symbols would be to call the
next number the nth number. Then you could write
the rule as:

  $n\text{th} = (n-1)\text{th} + (n-2)\text{th}$

This is a better way of writing the rule, but it
is still not very elegant. You could use the
symbol U_n to mean the nth term of the sequence.

You couldn't just write

$n = (n-1) + (n-2)$

This is an equation which
can be solved to give
$n = 3$.

Example 2

Write down U_5 for the sequence given by the kerbstones
problem.

The sequence is:

  1, 2, 3, 5, 8, 13, ...
                  ↑
            The 5th term is 8

$U_5 = 8$

Example 3

Write down the general rule for the kerbstone problem using U_n to represent the nth term of the sequence.

The rule is:

$$n\text{th} = (n-1)\text{th} + (n-2)\text{th}$$

You can write this:

$$U_n = U_{n-1} + U_{n-2}$$

Exercise 17D

1   For the kerbstone sequence:

$$1, \quad 2, \quad 3, \quad 5, \quad 8, \quad 13, \quad \ldots$$

write down the values of:
(a) U_1 (b) U_4 (c) U_7 (d) $U_8 + U_9$

2   Write these rules using U_n to represent the nth term of the sequence.
(a) The next number in the sequence is twice the previous number.
(b) The next number in the sequence is the previous number plus three.
(c) The next number in the sequence is the product of the previous two numbers.

Remember:
the product of a and b is $a \times b$ or ab.

17.5 Have you seen it before?

At any stage in the problem-solving or investigative process you should ask yourself, *'Have I seen this or something like this before?'*

You might have seen the sequence

$$1, \quad 2, \quad 3, \quad 5, \quad 8, \quad 13, \quad \ldots$$

before.

The sequence is known as the **Fibonacci sequence**. It was first developed by an Italian mathematician called Leonardo of Pisa in the thirteenth century.

Example 4

For the Fibonacci sequence:

$$1, \quad 2, \quad 3, \quad 5, \quad 8, \quad 13, \quad 21, \quad \ldots$$

Work out the value of $\dfrac{U_5}{U_4}$

$U_5 = 8, U_4 = 5$

So $\dfrac{U_5}{U_4} = \dfrac{8}{5} = 1.6$

Exercise 17E

For the Fibonacci sequence, work out these values:

1 $\dfrac{U_6}{U_5}$

2 $\dfrac{U_{n+1}}{U_n}$ for values of n from 1 to 9

3 Draw axes on graph paper. Put n along the horizontal axis from 0 to 9. Put $\dfrac{U_{n+1}}{U_n}$ on the vertical axis from 0 to 3, using a scale of 1 cm to 0.25.
Plot your values from question **2**. What do you notice?

4 Without working out any values, write down what you think $\dfrac{U_{100}}{U_{99}}$ might be to one decimal place.

Summary of key points

In any problem-solving or investigative situation you should

1 Make sure that you understand the problem.

2 Ask yourself if you have seen the problem or something like it before. You may be able to benefit from that experience.

3   Simplify the problem.

4   Develop strategies to deal with the problem.

5   Record results and make observations.

6   Make and test predictions.

7   Make a generalisation.

8   Use symbols wherever appropriate.

18 Calculators and computers

This unit shows you ways of using scientific calculators, graphical calculators and computer software to help build on and extend the work you have been studying in the other units of this book.

The examples will work on *Casio* calculators, the spreadsheet examples are based on *Microsoft Excel* and the examples for drawing bearings with *WinLogo*.

18.1 Reflex angles

You can draw reflex angles on a computer using the program *WinLogo*.

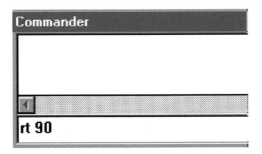

Example 1

Draw on screen:

(a) an angle of 230°

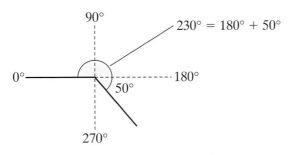

(a) Type rt 90 fd 100 rt 50 fd 100

In *WinLogo* you must provide instructions to move the 'turtle' around the screen.

The turtle begins this way round

rt 90

will turn it 90° clockwise

fd 100

will move it forward '100' places and draw a line '100' units long

Now turn right through the required angle
rt 50

(b) an angle of 340°

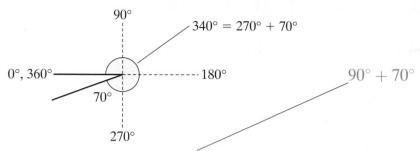

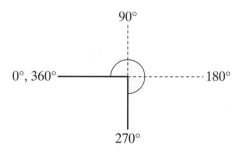

(b) Type cs rt 90 fd 100 rt 160 fd 100

Exercise 18A

Use *WinLogo* to draw:

1 An angle of 270°

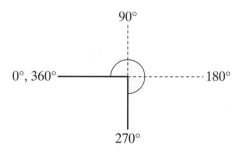

2 An angle of 200°

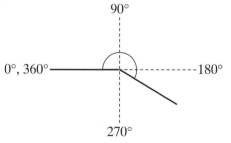

It is a good idea to plan your drawings on paper first, as you need to work out the angles to turn through!

Remember to clear the screen between each question.

3 An angle of 290°

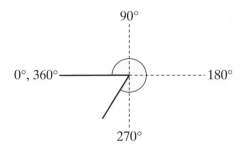

4   An angle of 350°

5   An angle of 190°

6   An angle of 215°

18.2 Straight lines

You can draw lines on a graphical calculator. After you have switched on the calculator select the GRAPH icon using the arrow keys and then press the EXE key to display a window similar to

```
G-Func :Y =
Y1:
Y2:
Y3:
Y4:
SEL DEL    DRAW
```

Press SHIFT F3 to bring up the V-Window

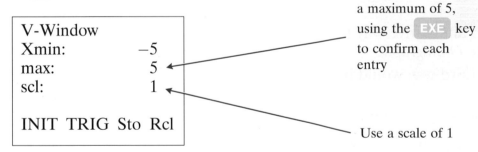

```
V-Window
Xmin:           −5
max:             5
scl:             1

INIT TRIG Sto Rcl
```

Change the size of the *x*-axis to a minimum of −5 and a maximum of 5, using the EXE key to confirm each entry

Use a scale of 1

Press the down arrow key to produce a similar window for *y* and change the *y*-axis from −5 to 5, using a scale of 1, again.

When finished press EXE to bring up the G-Func menu again.

Exercise 18B

1 Draw four different lines parallel to $y = x + 2$
(*Hint*: Enter each line as $y = x + a$ or $y = x - a$,
where a is any positive number not equal to 2.)

2 Draw four different lines parallel to $y = 2x + 1$
(*Hint*: Enter each line as $y = 2x + b$, where b is
any positive or negative number not equal to 2.)

3 Draw four different non-parallel lines but all
passing through the point $(0, 1)$
(*Hint*: Enter each line as $y = cx + 1$, and choose
four *different* values for c, a positive number.)

4 Draw four different lines with a steeper gradient
than $y = x$ and all passing through the origin.

5 Draw four different lines with a shallower
gradient than $y = x$.
(*Hint*: One line could be $y = 0.3x$.)

To begin question 1, press

to store the equation
Y1=X+3.
Now type similar
equations for Y2, Y3 and
Y4.

Finally press
F4 to produce your four
lines.

Press
SHIFT F3 EXE to
return to the GRAPH
Mode and delete your
equations one by one by
using the arrow keys to
select the equations and
then the F2 key

followed by F1

An alternative way to do this exercise is to use a computer software package
like *Omnigraph*.

A third way would be to use a spreadsheet. You will have to create the
points in the columns on your spreadsheet.

Example 1(d) on page 101 could be produced as follows:

	A	B
1	x	y
2	-4	-16
3	-3	-13
4	-2	-10
5	-1	-7
6	0	-4
7	1	-1
8	2	2
9	3	5
10	4	8

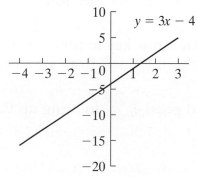

- -4 was entered in cell A2.
- =A2+1 was entered in cell A3 and was
  copied down to cell A10
- =3*A2-4 was entered in cell B2 and was
  copied down to cell B10

18.3 Fractions

You can use the fraction key on your calculator to answer the type of questions you met in Unit 8.

Your fraction key may look like this $\boxed{a^{b/c}}$

Example 2

(a) Find $\frac{2}{3} + 3\frac{1}{4}$

(b) Find $7\frac{1}{2} \div 2\frac{2}{3}$

(c) Find $\frac{3}{4}$ of £9624

(a) Press

$\boxed{2}\ \boxed{a^{b/c}}\ \boxed{3}\ \boxed{+}\ \boxed{3}\ \boxed{a^{b/c}}\ \boxed{1}\ \boxed{a^{b/c}}\ \boxed{4}\ \boxed{=}$

Answer $= 3\frac{11}{12}$

(b) Press

$\boxed{7}\ \boxed{a^{b/c}}\ \boxed{1}\ \boxed{a^{b/c}}\ \boxed{2}\ \boxed{\div}\ \boxed{2}\ \boxed{a^{b/c}}\ \boxed{2}\ \boxed{a^{b/c}}\ \boxed{3}\ \boxed{=}$

Answer $= 2\frac{13}{16}$

(c) Press

$\boxed{3}\ \boxed{a^{b/c}}\ \boxed{4}\ \boxed{\times}\ \boxed{9}\ \boxed{6}\ \boxed{2}\ \boxed{4}\ \boxed{=}$

Answer $= £7218$

Press the multiplication key for 'of' in $\frac{3}{4}$ of £9624

Exercise 18C

1   Calculate:
   (a) $9\frac{11}{12} \times 3\frac{3}{4}$
   (b) $12\frac{1}{2} \div 7\frac{3}{4}$
   (c) $11\frac{1}{5} - 5\frac{12}{13}$
   (d) $\frac{5}{6}$ of £2137.74
   (e) $\frac{5}{17} + 4\frac{5}{9} \times \frac{3}{5}$
   (f) $42 \div \frac{6}{7}$
   (g) $\frac{6}{7} \div 42$

2   (a) There are 105 passengers on a bus and $\frac{7}{15}$ of them are students. How many students are on the bus?
   (b) At the next bus stop $\frac{5}{7}$ of the students get off. How many students get off the bus?
   (c) How many passengers are left on the bus?
   (d) At the next stop $\frac{3}{10}$ of the passengers get off and 15 people get on. How many passengers are on the bus now?
   (e) If $\frac{5}{8}$ of the remaining passengers are female, how many are male?
   (f) At the next stop $\frac{7}{12}$ of the male passengers and $\frac{2}{5}$ of the female passengers get off the bus. How many passengers are left on the bus?

18.4 Handling data

You can use a spreadsheet to create bar charts, pie charts and scatter graphs.

Exercise 18D

1   The average number of words per minute typed by a group of eleven Year 8 students is shown in the frequency table below:

Student	Ali	Emma	Jill	Serge	Mario	Shaheen
Words per minute	23	35	16	32	36	11

Student	Errol	Bob	Sara	Andre	Aurore
Words per minute	19	15	22	13	27

Enter all the data into rows 1 and 2 of a spreadsheet.

	A	B	C	D	
1	Student	Ali	Emma	Jill	
2	Words per minute	23	35	16	

Highlight all the data and use the chart wizard to create a bar chart. Make sure you add appropriate labels to your chart at stage 3 of the wizard.

In Excel a bar chart is called a column chart!

At the last stage of the wizard choose the option to place the chart as a new sheet

2 The number of ice creams sold by Henry in his shop during one week in July are shown in the following frequency table:

Day of the week	Monday	Tuesday	Wednesday	Thursday
Number of ice creams sold	62	65	78	36

Day of the week	Friday	Saturday	Sunday
Number of ice creams sold	58	91	70

- Enter the data into cells A4 to H4 and A5 to H5 of your spreadsheet.
- Use the chart wizard to create a pie chart of your data and again place the chart as a new sheet at the last stage of the wizard.
- Give two reasons why you think the sales were so low on the Thursday.
- Enter the formula =AVERAGE(B5:H5) in cell 15 to calculate the mean number of sales. *There is more on averages in Unit 5*
- Enter the formula =MEDIAN(B5:H5) in cell J5 to calculate the median number of sales.

3 The data in the following table shows the number of goals scored, goals conceded and point totals for the 24 football clubs in Division 1 in the 1999/2000 season.

	A	B	C
1	Goals scored	Goals conceded	Points total
2	79	45	91
3	78	40	89
4	71	42	87
5	88	67	82
6	65	44	77
7	69	50	76
8	64	48	74
9	62	49	74
10	49	41	67
11	62	53	66
12	55	51	62
13	45	50	57
14	57	68	57
15	53	55	56
16	57	67	54
17	59	71	54
18	55	67	54
19	55	66	51
20	46	67	51
21	41	67	51
22	43	60	49
23	52	77	46
24	48	69	36
25	38	77	36

(a) Enter the frequency table headings and all the data into columns A, B and C of a new spreadsheet using rows 1 down to row 25.

(b) Enter the heading "Goal difference" in cell D1.

(c) Enter the formula =A2-B2 in cell D2 and copy it down to cell D25.

(d) Use the chart wizard to create the following 3 scatter graphs – remember to place each graph as a new sheet at the final stage of the wizard:

goals scored against points total

goals conceded against points total

goal difference against points total

(e) For each scatter graph describe the type of correlation

(f) On each graph click <u>C</u>hart on the menu bar and Add T<u>r</u>endline … [In Excel a line of best fit is trendline]

(g) Enter the formula =AVERAGE(A2:A25) in cell A26 and copy it *across* to cell C26 to calculate the mean for columns A, B and C.

(h) Enter the formula =MEDIAN(A2:A25) in cell A27 and copy it *across* to cell C27 to calculate the median for columns A, B and C.

(i) Enter the formula =MODE(A2:A25) in cell A28 and copy it across to cell C28 to calculate the mode for columns A, B and C.

Hold down the Ctrl key on your keyboard to highlight any columns not next to each other

18.5 Generating sequences

You can use a spreadsheet to generate the terms of a sequence if given the nth term of the sequence.

There is more on the nth term of a sequence on page 190.

Example 3

(a) Find the first 20 terms of a sequence with nth term equal to $5n$.

	A	B
1	Term number	Sequence
2	1	=5*A2
3	=A2+1	
4		

Drag these squares down to copy the formulae to row 21.

- Enter "Term number" in cell A1 and "Sequence" in cell B1.
- Enter the number 1 in cell A2.
- Enter the formula =A2+1 in cell A3 and drag it down to cell A21 to create the term numbers.
- Enter the formula =5*A2 in cell B2 and drag it down to cell B21 to create the sequence.

(b) Find the first 20 terms of a sequence with nth term equal to $6n - 5$.

	A	B
1	Term number	Sequence
2	1	=6*A2-5
3	=A2+1	
4		

$6n - 5$ with $n = 1$

- Enter "Term number" in cell A1 and "Sequence" in cell B1.
- Enter the number 1 in cell A2.
- Enter the formula =A2+1 in cell A3 and drag it down to cell A21 to create the term numbers.
- Enter the formula =6*A2-5 in cell B2 and drag it down to cell B21 to create the sequence.

Exercise 18E

1 Use a spreadsheet to calculate the first 20 terms of a sequence if the nth term is:

(a) $3n$ (b) $n + 5$

(c) $n - 8$ (d) $4n - 3$

(e) $n \div 2$ (f) $\frac{1}{10}n$

(g) n^2 (h) n^3

18.6 Using your powers key

You can calculate the value of numbers like 3^5 using the  key.

3^5 is shorthand for $3 \times 3 \times 3 \times 3 \times 3$

You say "3 to the power of 5"

$3^5 \longleftarrow 5$ is the power.

There is more about powers on page 68.

Example 4

Find   (a) 4^6 (b) $5^3 + 6^6$ (c) $9^3 \div 6^3$

(a) Press

Answer = 4096

(b) Press

Answer = 46 781

(c) Press

Answer = 3.375

Note:
Some calculators have a 'cubed' button:

Press

Exercise 18F

1 Calculate 9^4

2 Calculate 7^8

3 Calculate $11^6 + 11^3$

4 Calculate $6^8 \div 3^5$

5 Calculate and arrange in order of size, starting with the smallest
$$2^{30}, 3^{20}, 4^{14}, 9^9, 5^{12}$$

6 (a) Calculate $(2^3)^4$

(b) Calculate $(2^4)^3$

(c) Calculate $(4^3)^2$

7 (a) Write down the value of 100^1

(b) Calculate a^0, where a is any positive whole number.

8 (a) In the book *One Grain of Rice: A Mathematical Folktale* by *Demi* (Illustrator), a young woman called Rani outwitted the Raja to gain food for her starving people. Rani demanded that she be given 1 grain of rice on day 1 and each day after for a total of thirty days the number of grains of rice given should be doubled. Calculate the total number of grains of rice Rani obtained for her people.

The total number of grains of rice is $1 + 2 + 4 + 8 + 16 + \ldots$ or, in power notation, $2^0 + 2^1 + 2^2 + 2^3 + 2^4 + \ldots + 2^{29} + 2^{30}$

(b) A packet of rice contains approximately 17 000 grains. Approximately how many packets would be required to obtain the equivalent amount of rice in modern times?

9 What do you notice about the digits in the questions and answers if you calculate

(a) $3^3 + 4^4 + 3^3 + 5^5$ (b) $88^2 + 33^2$

(c) $4^4 + 3^3 + 8^8 + 5^5 + 7^7 + 9^9 + 0^0 + 8^8 + 8^8$

(d) 567^2 (e) 854^2

Entering 0^0 on your calculator may give an error. Enter 0 instead.

10 For $n = 1$ to 10, which of $2^n - 1$ are prime numbers?

There is more about Prime numbers on page 59.

Index